COMMON SENSE LIVING

It Just MAKES SENSE

IN AN EVERYDAY WORLD

7 PRINCIPLES for a JOYFUL and STRESS-FREE LIFE

Kym Coco, M.A. and Stephen Thompson

Imbue Press

NEW YORK

It Just MAKES SENSE
7 PRINCIPLES for a JOYFUL and STRESS-FREE LIFE

Kym Coco, M.A. and Stephen Thompson

ISBN 978-1-61448-022-8 Paperback
ISBN 978-1-61448-023-5 ePub

Library of Congress Control Number: 2011930383

Published by:
MORGAN JAMES PUBLISHING
The Entrepreneurial Publisher
5 Penn Plaza, 23rd Floor
New York City, New York 10001
(212) 655-5470 Office
(516) 908-4496 Fax
www.MorganJamesPublishing.com

Interior Design by:
Bonnie Bushman
bbushman@bresnan.net

In an effort to support local communities, raise awareness and funds, Morgan James Publishing donates one percent of all book sales for the life of each book to Habitat for Humanity.
Get involved today, visit
www.HelpHabitatForHumanity.org.

For our fathers,

Mark Jeffrey Coco

who inspired Kym's passion for writing

and

George A. "Corky" Thompson,

who taught Steve the importance of living

with a common sense approach

Table of Contents

Authors' Notes

Why we wrote this book

Hello, I'm Kym Coco.

And I'm Stephen Thompson.

Stephen: We welcome you to our new book, *It Just Makes Sense.*

The concepts that form this book have been stirring around in my brain for over a decade. After a serious motorcycle accident in 1990 severed my career as a successful interior designer, the course of my life needed a new direction. I underwent 28 reconstructive surgeries, endless physical therapy, and a whole paradigm shift in 6 years of recovery time.

I re-entered the working world as a new man. With strong values to support my direction, a clear, logical approach to re-form a business, and a passionate heart to heal the emotional body, I founded the Personal Search and Growth Center. My new focus became holistic healing for the mind, body and spirit.

This might seem like a 180-degree shift from my career in interior design, but it actually returned me to my post-collegiate career in sociology. Yet, my first placement in crisis management at the age of 22 left me feeling overwhelmed and frustrated. I felt unable to truly help people in need with the modalities I had learned in college.

Now with seasoned wisdom and time on my side, I have helped numerous clients increase self-esteem, boost prosperity, rebuild relationships, and enhance communication skills over the past 15 years. Despite societal chaos and a fast-paced lifestyle that challenges us all, I've been able to teach people how to take charge of their life and create a path to follow their dreams.

In this book, we teach many of the techniques and concepts that I've developed throughout my time as a healer, teacher, and mentor. Now, a blessed relationship with my wife, Kym Coco, has allowed my techniques to be put into written word. She has enriched this text with her unique perspectives and life experiences to fully make the sharing of this message possible.

Kym: For the past ten years, I've been working with college students in the realm of sports psychology. University life is a unique time where students are challenged with living on their own for the first time, creating a balanced schedule between work and play, and learning how to develop practical skills that will serve them for the rest of their lifetime.

While Stephen teaches many of our Common Sense Tools to adult populations across the country in workshop format, I teach these basic life skills in the classroom. I see many of my students stressed out, burned out, and burned up because they lack the ability to manage their emotions. In fact, many of them have never been taught anything about what it takes to keep their life energy high. They have not learned how to create their own well-being, develop meaningful relationships, or foster a career path that they'd enjoy.

Since my own stress-filled collegiate experience, I embarked on a personal journey into psychology, personal growth, and meditation. I am now happy to share my wisdom, sparked with a non-traditional flair, with the many students I encounter each year.

Stephen: We've noticed that people of all ages are bombarded daily with numerous distractions. There are 24-hour news outlets, ceaseless advertisements, and multiple avenues of entertainment. Cell phones keep us constantly connected to the internet and others. There is XM radio, electronic book readers, and cable television that offers at least 200 channels—and that doesn't even include the sports packages or movie channels. We are plugged in, logged on, or checked out at almost any given moment of the day.

While we receive many benefits from modern technology, there is a flipside to the opportunity coin they present. The forms of entertainment we seek, which are often deemed now as necessities, cause a distraction from our true selves. We are often too busy to take time for personal reflection, creativity, and enjoyment of ourselves as our own best friend.

It's our goal for you to make confident decisions—ones where you can say, *"It just makes sense"*. This is what we call Common Sense Living. It's where balance is established within you first. Then, that poise and wisdom can infiltrate all other areas of your life. By reducing internal stress, we live longer and healthier. By knowing our game plan, we proceed with ease and effectiveness. And by finding inner contentment, we worry less.

Kym: We designed this book to be a hands-on guide to create your own common-sense approach within your work environment, relationships, and creative passions. Common Sense Living encourages you to take a slower pace amidst the rapidly-increasing speed of things around you. As a result, you can increase your effectiveness, your joy, and your peace of mind.

This book is for you, so use it in a way that fits your unique personality and lifestyle. You might want to start at the beginning and read it cover-to-cover. Or perhaps you'd like to find an area of your life where you feel stress and begin reading there first.

Whatever approach you choose, there are two Common Sense Symbols to guide you through the journey.

Common Sense Tools indicate a concept or activity that can be used to enhance your learning.

Common Sense Tips are main ideas set apart for easy understanding.

Steve: Now, trying to master every Common Sense Tool goes against the very principles we're sharing. We recommend prioritizing the areas of your life that need the most support first. Then, focus on the related chapter and practice incorporating those Common Sense Tools into everyday life. Once you feel comfortable with your newly-acquired techniques, you can move on.

Above all, we suggest having fun with this process. Enjoy how common sense can allow you to see things more clearly, feel things more authentically, and recognize your beneficial and unique contribution to the world around you.

Introduction

What is Common Sense Living?

"Common sense is the knack of seeing things as they are,
and doing things as they ought to be done." —Josh Billings

Am I happy? Is this relationship worth pursuing? Am I ready to start over? Should I take this job? Is life meant to be this difficult? Why can't I get the things I want? Why am I always stressed? Is there an easier way for me to move through life? Why do I often feel overwhelmed? How can I simplify my life?

You might have asked yourself these questions during the course of your life. The answers inevitably change with the continual ebb and flow of circumstances. Relationships come and go. Jobs and careers transition over time. You also experience personal transformations throughout the years—births, deaths, and graduations, along with insights that result from such changes.

If you're anything like us, you feel like you have a good head on your shoulders. You are aware of your surroundings and ready to take planned, and inspired, action. Yet, you might not be able to figure out why you're still experiencing large amounts of stress in your life. For a long time, both of us recognized that chaos and confusion were an ongoing part of life. It wasn't until we learned, and created, practical solutions—many of which you'll learn in this book—that we began taking control of our lives.

Common Sense Tools are always available for you when assessing and directing your life through various experiences. That's what this book is about, knowing what's always available to you in your Common Sense Toolbox.

Regardless of your relationship status, geographic location, occupation, or life paradigm, Common Sense Living has the ability to:

- Enhance your self-esteem
- Offer direction and purpose on your life path
- Create clarity and confidence in your decision-making
- Reduce your stress levels
- Enhance communication skills
- Strengthen supportive relationships and redefine unsupportive ones
- Generate internal harmony and balance
- Increase overall energy levels

What is Common Sense?

Have you ever stopped to think about that? While you might think common sense is an innate quality in every human being, it's actually a skill. That's right. It's the developed trait of having good judgment that requires practice. Granted, some people naturally utilize clear thinking and prudence before they act, but how did they learn? Is it too late for you to implement some basic common-sense techniques into your life to help increase your energy levels and confidence in making decisions?

Common sense goes beyond simply being level-headed. It's the ability to take in all of the information bombarding you throughout the day and discern which of that information is necessary to make decisions. Your body's external senses, such as sight, smell, taste, touch, and hearing, can interpret and respond to over 40 million bits of information per second. That's a lot of data to sort through on an ongoing basis. Yet, through such senses, you're able to perceive the world around you. You're capable of viewing the commonalties and customs of your surroundings and creating meaningful connections with such information.

However, your sensory capability goes far beyond your physical surface. You have emotions which allow you to express feelings of sadness, anger, or joy, as well as discern deeper experiences of pleasure and pain. You have intuition, which appears as a hunch, gut response, or nagging feeling without factual evidence. This wise, internal wisdom works nonstop in conjunction with your emotional state to offer you direction. And, you have an invisible radar system. Just like an antenna has a corresponding field that collects data from its nearby field, you are an energetic being that can take in lots of information from your surroundings.

Common Sense Tip: Common sense is the capability of putting all of these innate gifts to use so that you can make confident decisions that support your goals.

Do you want to feel satisfied in your job? Do you yearn for time in your busy schedule where you can incorporate some fun? Do you desire to spend your life in a meaningful and intimate relationship? Regardless of your aspirations, common sense provides the insight and clarity to help make those visions a reality.

In order to understand what you want in your life, you often have to experience undesirable circumstances. These disenchanting encounters are accompanied by negative emotions in the body and many times a lack of common sense. So what does that look like in the everyday world? Perhaps it's hurtful gossip that was spread by a so-called friend. It could appear as complaining or dissatisfaction among co-workers at the office about a myriad of issues. It might even be the feeling of being let down based on expectations you had of another person that they were unable to fulfill.

The resulting confusion, mistrust, and stress from such circumstances can accumulate over time and create greater problems. Negative emotions are amplified. A sense of separation between you and others leaves you feeling isolated and alone. Miscommunication between lovers can build up and destroy the relationship entirely. Your physical body might develop an illness and your overall lifespan could be shortened. Whether the circumstances lacking common sense are individual or cumulative, chaos and poor decision making result.

Common Sense in Action: Debbie's Story

Consider Debbie, an office manager for three prominent surgeons. Her life's situation reflected imbalance. Her time was constantly in demand. The phones rang off the hook. Paperwork was endless and incoming requests often left important work unattended. It wasn't long before Debbie began to feel overloaded. The stress built slowly at first, but she silenced the signals beneath her primary need for financial security. This job supported her entire family.

Over a period of five years, Debbie's job stress became so intense that she could rarely make it home at the end of the day without vomiting first. Her personal life began to feel the strain. She was impatient with her kids and fell behind with the household chores. Her free time was often spent alone in order to recover, with little remaining energy to entertain or visit with friends. She was beginning to feel depressed.

Debbie realized that she needed to make some changes in her life. She learned some of the common-sense techniques shared in this book to enhance her communication and set some personal boundaries at the workplace. For one exercise, Debbie kept a "to do" list on her desk at the office. Each time a surgeon had an immediate request, they had to personally write it on her list. When the next doctor came through—also with an urgent task—the doctor had to cross off the other doctor's request and replace it with his own.

> Common Sense is the ability to combine information from your environment with emotions and sound judgment to create confident actions.

Within two weeks of implementing her newfound communication strategy— and an exercise that created awareness for her employers—the doctors realized that Debbie was severely overworked. They offered her a raise and hired two other part-time staff to ease her workload.

It didn't take long for Debbie to enjoy her job once again. Her mood at the office improved. Her husband and children noticed her extra energy at home each night. Debbie even saved money to take a vacation for herself and a friend at the end of the year. With a little direction and some common-sense tools, Debbie took charge of her own life. And she even placed a happy-faced doll atop her computer at the office to remind her daily of her success.

Creating Internal Balance

Just as Debbie returned to a state of joy and harmony, the **goal of Common Sense Living is to restore your personal balance.** It's what we call centeredness, which is the state in which you feel whole, connected, and in sync with all of life around you. It's that feeling of being in control of your energy and empowered with every decision that you make.

Imagine that you are on a boat in the middle of a lake and that watercraft symbolizes your life. The sun is out, the air is warm, and you can hear the peaceful sound of water lapping all around you. When you find a nice place to relax, you drop a line and anchor down to the lake's floor. That line represents your ability to be anchored, centered and balanced in the lake.

As the afternoon progresses, the wind might pick up. Gusts of air represent the various demands in your life, and the direction it comes from corresponds to those different challenges. As it blows from one direction, the breeze insists that you help others, agree with their point of view, and follow their lead. You might feel like you're going in different directions, out of balance.

If your line is too short, worn out or breaks, your anchor is not set firmly.

Without the ability to remain aligned with a calm, balanced self within, the demands of others can begin to blow your boat from the center of the lake into dangerous territory. The winds might blow so hard that you crash onto the lake's rocky shores. This results in disaster for your boat—or as in real life—your mind, body and spirit all suffer.

Or, while you're out in the center of the water, winds can blow from the other direction with instructions to put yourself first. While it's important to take time to care for yourself, an attitude of getting what you want, regardless of how it affects others, can be dangerous. Without a grounding line and anchor, you can become inflexible, resistant to change, and so self-centered that it results in a loss of friendships. This, at first, might just seem as though the wind has blown you towards shore. But, in extreme cases, can also cause you and your boat to wreck onto the shoreline of despair and isolation.

> "Everything you need you already have. You are complete right now—you are a whole, total person. Your completeness must be understood by you and experienced in all of your thoughts as your own personal reality." — Wayne Dyer

The purpose of creating a strong line, with the help of Common Sense Tools, will allow you and your boat remain anchored in a state of balance. You'll be able to keep your line firm, yet flexible, so that the demands of others and the lure of egocentric living simply appear as a breeze across the waters. You'll be able to recognize the imbalances that arise in your life, use Common Sense Tools to regain your stability, and remain clear-headed and purposeful as you float through life. And you'll be able to maximize your own energy to be used in the most joyful and productive ways possible.

Your Life Energy Bank Account

While the analogy of the boat helps us to understand the importance of remaining in personal balance, or centeredness, it's also necessary to manage the amount of life energy you have throughout each day to accomplish the numerous demands that you encounter. You know those everyday stressors of getting the kids ready for school, meetings with the boss, and unexpected road construction that makes you late for a lunch date with your best friend.

How are you able to cope with these events? How do you handle strained relationships or physical imbalances and still have enough zest to contribute to those aspects of life you truly enjoy? Are you able to come home at the end of the day without feeling entirely exhausted?

All of your daily life events, both those you dread and those you enjoy, require a certain amount of personal power. It's actually the amount of energy you have throughout the day that determines the amount of strength, control and poise you take with you in any given situation. **The overall goal is simply this: to enhance your life energy.** It's what the Chinese refer to as Chi or the Indians know as Prana. It's the amount of life force flowing through you that creates either a vibrant and expansive life or an exhausting and draining one. By managing that energy, you can choose which outcome you prefer.

What prevents you from achieving your greatest potential?

The answer is stress. It is life's pressures, strains, and traumas that knock you out of a natural rhythm. More importantly, it's the reaction to those stressors that directly affect your individual energy level. When responding to a challenge with common sense, life energy is enhanced. When acting in haste or chaos, personal power is diminished.

Let's use another illustration—a bank checking account—to create understanding of how energy affects you in the present moment and over the course of time. Instead of money, your currency is *life force energy*.

Obviously, there are certain common-sense realities about bank checking accounts. When you deposit a check into your account, the balance increases. When you write a check, it's considered a withdrawal and your balance drops. You want there to be a positive balance. You want there to be more money flowing into that account than coming out. You regularly want to check the account to make sure the transactions being recorded are accurate. Not to mention, you want to know exactly what's going on with your money so you can be prepared for an emergency and for the future.

The same principles apply to your own personal energy bank and every decision, whether big or small, affects the account's balance. On an even more subtle level, it's the emotions that accompany any experience that determine what happens to your energy levels.

While emotions for years have gotten a bad rap for being touchy-feely, ooey-gooey feelings, they're redefined here in a broader sense. Emotions include all experiences of courage, fear, anger and joy, as well as the most basic sensations. Pain and pleasure, as well as hunger and thirst, can trigger emotions. Even indefinable experiences, such as awe and bliss, are considered emotional states. According to the latest scientific research today, emotions can be linked with body chemicals that interact with the brain to produce beliefs *and* expectations—both of which affect your ability to make choices and take action.

So, how do you make a deposit into your energy account?

Common Sense Tip: Any choice or movement that you make which is backed by positive emotions increases your own personal energy.

This adds to your Energy Bank Account and creates a reserve to draw from throughout each day. An example of an energy deposit could be spending fun time with your kids. It might be completing a challenging project at work, finishing a Sudoku puzzle, or taking time to be in nature where you can feel entirely enveloped by the powerful aspects of the earth. This includes watching sunsets over the ocean or hiking in the Redwoods.

Conversely, **any action that you take involving a negative emotion creates a check written against your own personal Energy Bank Account.** What happens when you get angry and have a fight with your husband or wife, child or roommate? Not only do chemical indicators of anger last up to six hours in your body's system, but they negatively affect your ability to cope with the situations that immediately follow. You've probably experienced this before, where you had an argument and couldn't even focus clearly enough to drive away in your car. Perhaps you tried to work on your computer after an upset, but found yourself re-typing the same words because your mind was entirely distracted.

While strong negative emotions, such as hate, anger, fear or blame take away from your Energy Bank Account, a withdrawal can also be a bit more subtle. You might get irritated that the line is too long to get lunch at your favorite deli. You could also feel jealous that your friend bought the latest fashion before you did. Mild frustration might also arise when your favorite TV show is cancelled this week. Whether the situation is big or small, any negative emotion experienced throughout the day creates a deduction against your life Energy Bank Account.

Just like your checking account where you want to keep track of daily transactions, it's important to know your energy exchanges as well. This is where the first step of energy awareness comes in. By understanding the influence of emotions behind your actions, you can discover which events throughout your day are bringing you joy and which ones are increasing your stress. Begin to take notice of both kinds of emotions, strong and subtle, that are adding deposits to your energy account or those that are draining throughout your day.

Common Sense Tip: The purpose of Common Sense Living is to keep your energy account not only with a positive balance, but with as much of a reserve as possible.

The best way to do this is to recognize when you are writing a check on your account. By turning your attention to your emotions throughout your day, you can put a hold on any unwanted check writing. Just as an overdrawn bank account accumulates bank fees in addition to the overspending, negative emotions can spin your energy account into a downward spiral. It's as if you're writing checks against your own energy account that you know will bounce, but you're writing them anyway.

Take this example of a downward spiral of energy where one aggravating experience has already rolled over into other areas of your life. Let's say your teenager was upset that you couldn't give him a ride to the mall after school. After dropping him off for classes, you get a phone call that your two much-needed clients cancelled for the morning. To add to your upset, you smack your arm as you close the car door when you finally do make it in to the office.

How do you stop this downward spiral of negativity? How do you stop writing Energy Checks against an overdrawn account? The first step begins with awareness. When you notice the negative emotion, it provides the opportunity to make a new decision. You have the choice to keep making withdrawals or to stop the unwanted spending. Given the example above, you can stop energetic withdrawals by being okay with your son's feelings of frustration without taking it personally, using the extra time from your cancelled appointment to catch up on work, and laughing at your hurt elbow.

If you choose to end the energy drain, the next step is to find a way to bring your energy levels—and emotions—back to neutral. You can bring your energy back into balance quickly and easily in a way that works for you. Everyone does this differently. Perhaps it's taking a few deep breaths. It could be listening to your favorite song. It might be calling someone you love or looking at a beautiful picture. Consider these options to return to personal balance:

- Take a walk
- Watch funny or inspirational videos

- Call a trusted friend
- Look at pictures of loved ones
- Read an inspiring article or email
- Play with your pet
- Take a yoga class
- Watch the sunset

Once you've stopped withdrawing energy from your personal account, you can then use Common Sense Tools to add even more power to your reserve. The easy principles in this book provide numerous ways to add deposits immediately back into your energy account. You'll learn tools to enhance communication and be able to use your interactions with others to increase your energy. Creating a deeper understanding of your values and guiding principles will bolster your confidence and increase positive experiences in making decisions. Even transforming your perspective on life as a whole can multiply the amount of personal deposits you make daily.

This book will teach you how to comfortably and regularly check into your own Energy Bank Account. It will also offer numerous ways to make deposits. You can learn the skill of aligning your deepest attitudes and beliefs with your actions. You can use your body's emotions to maximize the quality of each life experience. You can even build your own energy reserve so high that no life challenge, expected or otherwise, can cause your entire account to crash.

The Three Spheres: Business, Personal, and Spiritual Balance

Taking care of your own Energy Bank Account is one of the best ways to enhance your personal power and restore a balanced life. Remember, the goal is to keep as much energy in your account as possible. This gives you the zest, passion, and resources to make the most out of each and every day. By bringing an observing eye to your energy account, you also discover where your unwanted withdrawals are taking place.

When unnecessary Energy Checks are being deducted from your account, life seems challenging or difficult. Whether you're a single mother with three children, a newly married couple in your twenties or a retired golf pro in your seventies, there are similar outlets where energy is exchanged every day. Regardless of financial status, title, or daily responsibilities, you can understand exactly where energy is being spent or saved throughout each 24-hour period.

Take a moment to think of all of the activities done in your daily cycle. Aside from the time asleep, where body healing and restoration occurs, what actions dominate your schedule? How much time is actually spent in each action?

Take a moment to reflect on your routine. Notice what happens from the time you wake up in the morning. Do you wake up naturally or do you battle the snooze setting on your alarm clock, fighting for just a few more minutes of shut-eye? How much time do you spend in the shower? How long does it take you to care for your personal hygiene needs? What amount of time is allocated for eating, commuting, working, resting, and socializing?

Since this is Common Sense Living, we're not going to ask you to sit down and calculate a minute-by-minute tally of your daily activities, but an estimate helps. You can get an idea of where your time demands exist throughout the day. Take a moment and jot down your ideas here:

_____

_____

_____

_____

_____

Common perception might indicate a direct correlation between the amount of time spent in an activity with the amount of energy from your Energy Bank Account used for that action. For example, if you spend eight hours of your day working, that requires more energy than an hour-long lunch with your mother-in-law.

However, **managing your Energy Bank Account in a common sense way moves beyond the linear world of a clock.** It tunes in to *how you feel* throughout each activity versus how much time is spent for it. Emotions become the guide through each experience and your feelings that follow a situation let you know whether the encounter was an Energy Deposit or Energy Withdrawal. Energy management also requires taking a look at the bigger picture to find out where you're making deposits in life and where you're making withdrawals. Are your activities creating health or are they creating more stress? Are you taking time to sit and enjoy a delicious meal or are you taking your food in on the run, stuffing it down quickly before you move on to your next activity or appointment?

The common-sense approach offers an easy way to keep track of how your energy is spent in the three most basic realms of your life—the Business, Personal and Spiritual Spheres.

These areas are like cogs working together. When personal energy levels are high in each area, your life runs smoothly. When energy is being wasted, one cog in your wheel of life gets jammed and creates stress, chaos, and imbalance in the rest. The overall goal is this: to maintain a high energy account that balances your business, personal, and spiritual aspects of life.

The Business Sphere

The business circle encompasses those everyday responsibilities required for your life to function. While the word 'business' often implies connection to a career, job, or workplace, it's used here to include everything that relates to the logistical aspects of daily tasks. It's putting in the hours at your job, grocery shopping for your family, paying bills and picking the kids up at school. It also includes any commitment that demands a prompt arrival or requires a specific time frame.

Events in the business realm can include:

- Current job or schooling
- Returning phone calls
- Organizing your planner
- Cleaning the house
- Washing the car

- Money management
- Checking emails and messages
- Automobile maintenance
- House maintenance
- Electronic updates
- Filling the car with fuel
- Washing the laundry
- Cleaning the dishes
- The relationship with your boss or employees

When the Business Sphere is balanced, everything else flows more smoothly. You have a sense of autonomy and control in your life. You are unaffected by the condition or your surroundings. You feel like you have enough time in the day to get the job done. When in balance in the business realm, you might have patience in rush-hour traffic or you could be calm amidst the crash of your entire computer system.

Spending too much time and energy in the Business Sphere can lead to a number of imbalances. Valuing money, success, dedication and hard work are not wrong or bad in and of themselves. The imbalance arises when spending too much time at the office or bringing work home with you on the weekends becomes a habit. Then, the single-minded focus in the business realm leads to the workaholic syndrome. More projects at work are undertaken. Time with family and friends is minimized. Using the business world as an escape from other aspects of living can become addictive and unhealthy.

Imbalance in the Business Sphere: Dale's Story

While it might seem beneficial to overly commit to the business realm, an underlying resentment often accompanies it. Dale, is a perfect example. He grew up in the Midwest fishing and hunting with his friends. They would love to get out on the stream early in the morning, with the water rushing at their feet, a thermos cup of coffee nearby, and not another soul in sight except him and his buddies.

Once in the business world, Dale poured himself into his company. He often missed the seasonal trips with his friends due to unfinished business at the office, but enjoyed hearing about the stories brought back each time. It was as though he was living vicariously through those that could afford to take the time away from work. His promise to himself was that when he retired, he would buy a small cabin on a river and fish to his heart's content. Dale kept his focus in the present moment on business, working over sixty hours a week, and allowed his dream of fishing later in life to keep him going.

When the time finally came for Dale to take leave from business at the age of 63, he had a stroke and lost control over his lower extremities. He was then limited to his wheelchair and his hopes of fishing daily were now physically out of reach. The hidden resentment that had built over the years, wishing he had taken time with his friends, created feelings of anger, frustration, disappointment and regret.

While learning Common Sense Tools to return his emotional state back to balance, it would have been an easier process if Dale had created balance in his Business Sphere in the first place. The goal is to prevent withdrawals in all three realms. By creating awareness of how energy is exchanged in your business circle—whether more deposits or withdrawals are taking place—you can prevent an extreme imbalance later on in life. You'll have more energy with your friends and the resources available to take good care of yourself.

While the business circle covers the broad spectrum of life duties, it can also be found in certain relationships. In chapter 6, you'll discover which relationships fit into the business realm and how communication in those relationships differs from those in the personal circle. You'll also learn how to manage the business aspects of life within a partnership, family, or friendship.

The Personal Sphere

The personal circle of your life revolves around the activities and relationships that offer joy, peace, and a sense of satisfaction. This sphere of life is a break from the business realm. Your energy could be used to join a volleyball league on Monday nights or spend a weekend at the cabin with the family. It might also include self-nurturing activities such as taking a bubble bath, turning on your favorite CD, or going out dancing. In fact, any activity that helps increase your sense of balance and internal harmony is included in the personal realm.

By taking time to invest in your Personal Sphere, you also enhance creativity. Studies show that middle-aged men who have ignored their creativity throughout life have a higher likelihood of developing prostate problems. Similarly, women who deny their imaginative abilities have similar reproductive problems later in life. This inventive side innate in all of us can manifest through taking a pottery class, building a project in the shed, problem-solving to rebuild a car, or making a collage.

When creativity is addressed in the Personal Sphere, the business circle benefits too. Google has a policy where 20 percent of their time on the job, employees can work on whatever they want. This offers autonomy, freedom and flexibility to tap into individual ingenuity. Not only do employees get a personal boost of creativity, the company benefits with new products, ideas, and inspiration. In fact, about half of Google's products have come from that 20% time.

When the Personal Sphere is balanced, you feel energized by your relationships. You can sit alone with a good friend and enjoy the silence or dance the night away with your best friend at the hottest club in town. You are inspired by the events and situations around you. Time becomes insignificant as you are able to focus on taking care of yourself, enjoying your company, or utilizing your innate creativity.

An imbalance in the Personal Sphere is like the ship at the mercy of a self-centered wind—crashing into the shore of selfishness or isolation. The desire to work diminishes and interactions with others suffer. It's as though you're creating a cocoon for yourself, where you are unaffected by the outside world, but also entirely tuned out from its workings, too. There is a healthy amount of time alone, focused on self-care, and an unhealthy extreme.

The Spiritual Sphere

While the Spiritual Sphere is most often overlooked throughout life, it is the most important of all three circles. This realm encompasses the values and guiding principles that are used to direct all of the choices made in daily living. It's the ability to gratefully approach each 24-hour period—a set of 1,440 minutes—as a one-time gift of opportunities. Meaningful rituals, covered in Chapter 7, often reflect this mentality—such as watching the sunset, celebrating birthdays, or sharing religious ceremonies with like-minded believers.

However, time spent in the spiritual circle to rejuvenate is different than those activities that nurture the self in the personal realm. Taking a bath to unwind or enjoying a glass of wine after a long day at the office are tools used to unwind from the business side of life. **Energy in the spiritual realm is unique. It is taking quiet space to listen to the Divine.** It's looking at the emotional aspects of yourself and discovering how you can best move forward in your life.

The other two spheres of life focus on the physical realm. The spiritual circle, on the other hand, turns your attention inward. This includes tapping into the power of the mind, through meditation or prayer. It embraces the divine nature within each individual and recognizes the unchanging aspects of love, power, and timelessness of the soul. **The Spiritual Sphere celebrates your uniqueness and sees the bigger picture of your purpose in life.** It also colors your existence with emotion, guidance, and inspiration.

When your Spiritual Sphere is in balance, you have direction in your life. There is a confidence in your decision-making and faith that everything will work out. It's not a blind faith, but a calculated series of experiments in the direction of your goals and dreams. The Spiritual Sphere is best used as a recharging agent to fuel the Personal and Business Spheres.

> "Information, when combined with experience, becomes knowledge. When this knowledge becomes the frequency upon which we base our thoughts, words, and deeds, then we are entering the resonance called wisdom."
> —Michael Brown

There are times throughout life when the Spiritual Sphere seems out of sync. You might notice the imbalance when it's difficult to make decisions. You might feel alone, confused, or doubtful. The demands of others might overwhelm you and shift you away from your true values. A spiritual disparity might also surface when your life appears to lack meaning or purpose and you find yourself asking what life legacy you are going to leave when you're gone.

Even putting a small, but meaningful, amount of time into the Spiritual Sphere has exponential affects on your energy levels. When you take a few minutes a day to care for your spirit, through prayer, meditation or any other emotional management techniques to purposefully direct your life, the Business and Personal realms flourish. Each small action creates an overflow of energy that you can use in the many other events and activities throughout your daily living.

The Business, Personal, and Spiritual Spheres are continually affecting one another and are fueled by your personal energy levels. When you are able to buoyantly move throughout your day, your spheres are in harmony. When you accomplish your business tasks, you can fully relax and enjoy your personal realm. Creativity boosts in the Personal Sphere inevitably enhance the productivity and ingenuity in the Business Sphere. Energy dedicated to the Spiritual Sphere provides the insight and meaning to the experiences of the other two.

Three Spheres Quiz

The goal of the Business, Personal, and Spiritual Spheres is to create an awareness of how your energy is utilized throughout each day. When your life energy is high, the various realms of your life can work in harmony. When energy is being wasted in one area, it negatively affects the other two realms. The goal is to manage your personal energy effectively in all three realms so that you can move buoyantly, joyfully, and purposefully through life.

Take this quiz and discover how your energy is being used in each of the three spheres. Determine which sphere is offering the most energy deposits and which realm is allowing energy withdrawals.

Directions: Read each sentence below and reflect on how it applies to the broader sense of your life. Go with your first instinct. If you consider the statement true for yourself, place a **+** in the space available on the left. If the phrase is false for you, place a **—** in the left column.

Business

_____ I am able to hold my boundaries with my boss, employees, or co-workers.
_____ I have all the time I need in the day to get my duties accomplished.
_____ I know others appreciate me for my work.
_____ I eat my food slowly without being rushed or distracted.
_____ I feel that I am in control over my responsibilities.
_____ I have the freedom to improve myself in my job.
_____ My financial needs are being met.
_____ My financial budget is in balance.
_____ I feel validated for the work I do.
_____ What I do and who I am makes a positive difference in this world.

Personal

_____ I have a regular bedtime routine.
_____ I have a good friend available to me at any given moment.
_____ I schedule time each day to be alone.
_____ I am involved in a creative activity during the week.
_____ I am able to speak truthfully to those around me.
_____ I look forward to time with family and friends.
_____ I surround myself with things and people that bring me pleasure.
_____ I appreciate and validate my friends and family.
_____ I am appreciated and validated by my friends and family.

Spiritual

_____ I have someone who provides spiritual guidance or counsel for me.
_____ I recognize that I am more than a physical body—with an expansive mind and timeless soul.
_____ I am confident making decisions from my values.
_____ I spend daily time in silence, either in prayer or meditation.

_____ I listen to and trust my emotions.

_____ I am always enhancing my spirituality.

_____ I focus on the good in my surroundings.

_____ I take responsibility for my decisions.

_____ I remain non-judgmental towards myself or others.

_____ Life is unfolding perfectly.

The Score: Go back to each section and total how many **+** and **−** you have in each section. Place those totals in the scorecard below.

Business: Deposits (+): _____ Withdrawals (-): _____

Personal: Deposits (+): _____ Withdrawals (-): _____

Spiritual: Deposits (+): _____ Withdrawals (-): _____

What it means: Each **+** represents a deposit you are making in your energy account each day. Each **−** indicates where you are taking an unnecessary energy withdrawal. Are any spheres of your life in balance—receiving very few, if any, withdrawals? Are there any that are out of balance? Which sphere of your life is receiving the most deposits? Which area is being depleted by negative emotions or limiting perspectives?

Observe where you had deposits to your Energy Bank Account. Celebrate those aspects of your life that are supporting you. Because you now notice that those areas of your life are increasing your energy, allow them to become bigger deposits simply by acknowledging them every time they occur. It could be as simple as a smile in the mirror or a self-pat on the back for a job well done.

Now, take a look at where you found any withdrawals. By looking at these areas, you know where to begin adding Common Sense Tools into your life to enhance your energy and personal power. Keep these areas in mind as you read this book.

The goal of Common Sense Living is to minimize all withdrawals and increase your energy reserves. Each principle and technique throughout this book will teach you how to stop unwanted energy drains. It will also help you bring balance back into the three areas of your life. When you have an abundance of energy to move throughout your day, your business, personal, and spiritual circles can have a better chance of working in harmony.

Putting it all Together

Common Sense Living encourages you to take a slower pace so that you can reflect on your environment and the options available to you right now. This book will teach you how to create a strong foundation of values that enhance your ease in everyday situations. It will reinforce your ability to make clear decisions that align with your goals. It will also direct you back to your internal compass—your wise, guiding principles—that allow you to fulfill the highest and greatest expression of you that is possible in this human form. From there, you'll be able to move forward towards your goals with purpose and passion.

New Common Sense Tools to Enhance Common Sense:

- **Energy Bank Account:** By increasing your awareness, you will notice which daily activities are adding energy deposits to your life and which ones are draining your account. It helps you maintain your personal power and internal balance.

- **The Three Spheres:** The Business, Personal, and Spiritual Spheres provide an overview of how and where your energy is utilized.

Chapter 1

I ONLY WISH HE'D CHOSEN A MORE PROACTIVE ROLE MODEL THAN GARFIELD.

Bolster your Values

"Honesty is the first chapter in the book of wisdom." —*Thomas Jefferson*

In this Chapter

- Define values
- Use values to create internal alignment
- Support yourself and your community with values
- Find role models that can lead the way

Values serve many purposes. They're the basis for what you think, say and do. They are your foundation—your psychological core—the very building blocks that the rest of your life rests upon. Values are what you believe to be important. They're the ideals you are willing to support or defend. They filter the way you process information and, in turn, color the rest of your thoughts. Values are the standards by which you are willing to uphold your relationships, business transactions, and community involvement.

If you value honesty, you will speak the truth to those around you. If you value acceptance, you'll be patient when you disagree with others and offer a chance to see their perspective. If you value time with your kids, you may modify your work schedule to pick them up after school. You might even plan a family vacation on the weekend to savor the extra time with those loved ones. If you value success, you may put in long hours at the office and glad-hand important community members.

Those values—the network of beliefs and attitudes you hold about life—infiltrate your every decision and action. Let's say that you walked into the local market for a fresh sandwich at lunchtime. When you decide to pay for your meal, you place a ten dollar bill on the counter. If, by mistake, the clerk hands you change for a twenty, what do you do? If you value integrity, then you might speak up, clarify the misunderstanding and return the overpayment. Yet, you might put yourself first, regardless of the situation. You could tell yourself that the clerk made the mistake and have no problem pocketing the cash. In the latter case, you devalue both yourself and the business that was negatively affected.

Whatever ethical guidelines you hold within are inevitably displayed in your choices and deeds. Your values are demonstrated in your everyday interactions and in the specific roles that you play. Essentially, your values provide a framework for your thoughts, words and actions. They determine whether you are pleasant with others or impatient. Values dictate your pace and tone in conversations. They help you decide whether to call a friend over for dinner or spend the evening alone. Your guiding principles reflect what's important to you, in habitual situations and those that require role-specific responses.

What is the Common Sense Value Triangle?

Let's look at the relationship between the core of your personality—your values, beliefs, attitudes, and ideals—and the decisions that you make. This connection can be best illustrated through the shape of an equilateral triangle, broken down into three parts.

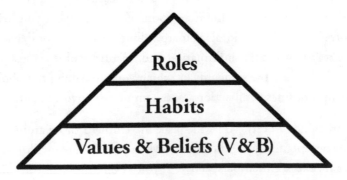

The base of your shape is occupied by your values, beliefs, and attitudes. Because values are at your foundation, your actions rest on top of such guiding principles. The second layer of the triangle is occupied by your habitual responses. It's the way you usually react to various components in your environment—traffic, running late, co-workers, family, or even winter months of severe weather. Finally, your role-specific behaviors which are based on your perception of the social situation, sit atop your triangle. In any given day, you might be a spouse, parent, employee, boss, coach, or friend.

Benefits of the Common Sense Value Triangle

Ideally, your core values are evident all the way from your foundation up through all roles you play in any given circumstance. By bolstering your values, and stabilizing your triangle, you make it much easier to become aware of how you respond to daily stressors. With an enhanced level of awareness, you can then utilize your power to make different choices instead of reacting habitually. A strong foundation of values will also keep congruence among your many roles, whether you are making a decision as a boss or working with a friend to clean up the neighborhood.

When you have a clear understanding of your values and beliefs, your personality triangle, and overall life experience, is stable.

The Common Sense Value Triangle in Action: Zack's Story

Zack strongly values awareness, family, and consideration of others. Those values serve as his guiding principles as he moves through his everyday routine. He changes his voicemail daily to keep clients informed of his activities. He shares inspiring stories about the community wherever he goes.

Zack's foundational principles also affect the roles he plays as husband, friend, and grandfather. His lunch schedule is set to accommodate his good friends and his weekends are often spent taking his grandkids to baseball games—which, on any other day, he would begrudge. Zack's firm foundation is built with social graces, thoughtfulness, connection, and activity. His triangle is balanced and secure, thus adding meaning to his everyday habits and purpose to his role-specific relationships.

The Effects of an Inverted Value Triangle

What happens if you're unclear about the values affecting your actions? What if you're just responding in defense of specific situations, often with added amounts of stress and internal chaos? It's as though you've taken that same triangle and turned it upside down.

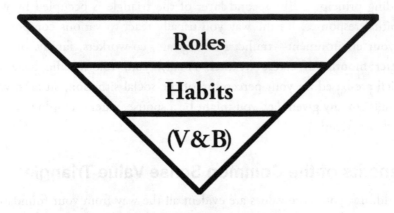

You're now in reaction mode, relying on your ability to counter momentary events and make spontaneous decisions to do what's right and still come out feeling like you're in charge. However, it's like being in the passenger seat of your personal vehicle. It's giving up your power to choose, be prepared, and offer direction for your own life.

Now, your triangle is teetering on its peak. It's unstable and very vulnerable to outside influences. If you're confronted with the stressors of life—perhaps an endless to-do list, urgent demands at your job, or unexpected road construction that will make you late for your child's dance recital—then you lose balance easily.

An Inverted Triangle in Action: Frank's Story

Frank's story begins back in middle school, which was a time in his life when he had low self-esteem and few values to support his decisions. When he was approached by classmates to join a local gang, Frank was easily swayed. The support of the gang made him feel connected. He had a role to fulfill and regular habits that could define his character.

As is often the case with gangs, Frank's life became destructive. His few values were continually challenged by the chaos that surrounded him. Frank lost many friends in fatal shootouts and his health deteriorated due to drug usage. The collapse of his inverted triangle occurred when he was incarcerated.

The Common Sense Value Triangle Back in Balance

The good news is that it's easier than you might think to come into balance again. By taking time to enhance your personal values, you can knock your triangle over to the right or the left. In fact, the exercises in this chapter will teach you to do just this. Without much effort, your triangle returns to a stable position with your foundation supporting your habits and responses.

Yet, if you teeter back and forth trying to remain upright, despite the onslaught of stress, the pressure can build quickly. When you're unable to make important decisions quickly or your anxiety increases beyond a point you can handle, your triangle collapses. Instead of falling to the left or right to regain balance with your values, you fall face-forward—tired, burned out, and requiring a whole lot more help to get back to a balanced state.

The way your values affect your decisions is similar to the boat scenario mentioned earlier. Your values help you find a centered state from which you're able to make decisions with confidence. When the winds blow too hard in one direction or the other, and you're not anchored in with guiding principles, you can drift—or eventually smash—into the shoreline. This causes all spheres of life to be negatively affected.

But, **when you have harmony within, you're stable, confident, and balanced**. Instead of wasting unnecessary energy on worrisome thoughts or unsure actions, you'll even have more personal power to use in all other areas of your life. You can leave doubt, confusion and

> "Success is keeping your priorities in order and your integrity intact while using your talents, abilities, and gifts to pursue the achievement of your dreams and goals." —Steve Rose

misunderstanding behind and put certainty and clarity in its place. You'll return to the captain's seat of your boat, the driver's seat of your car, and the leader of your own life instead of being a passenger along for the ride.

Are you ready to be in the driver's seat again?

Discover Your Values

By this point, you recognize that **values are the ideals, ethical guidelines, and moral principles by which you live your life.** You also understand that those values not only create the foundation of your personality, but they influence every decision made and each daily action. By first creating an awareness of values that are important to you, you'll be able to add clarity and purpose to your relationships, your business world, and your own personal growth.

The Common Sense Value Wheel

By the end of this exercise, you will:

- Identify which values are driving your actions and life
- Have a visual roadmap to see those values
- Gain a weekly tracking tool to help you get back in the driver's seat!

Values determine your internal balance. Just as your car needs to be kept in alignment to ensure it drives in a straight line, its tires wear evenly, and it can offer a smooth ride, your own personal alignment requires continual maintenance. Tuning into your values is the best way to maintain balance and we'll use those values to create wheels for your personal vehicle—your life.

There are four parts to this exercise, and we'll start by helping you build one wheel at a time.

Part 1: Identify your Values

Take a look at the list of value words below. While many of these words are common sense and common knowledge, read them over and make sure you know their meaning. If you don't, take a moment to look up the word's definition.

Notice which words seem really important to you—words that you believe make a difference in how you make your decisions. Mark those words with a star or check mark. For an extended list of words, see the Appendix.

Abundance	Leadership	Perseverance
Calmness	Harmony	Wisdom
Success	Mindfulness	Endurance
Honesty	Respect	Originality
Selflessness	Love	Resolution
Compassion	Beauty	Reliability
Diversity	Logic	Joy
Imagination	Grace	Faith

Part 2: Build your Wheel

With the words from **Part 1**, we're going to begin formulating your first value wheel. By placing each principle on a spoke, we're building strength and stability for the entire wheel and for the ride of your life.

Step 1: Find Six Meaningful Values

Place the top six most influential values on the spokes of a wheel below.

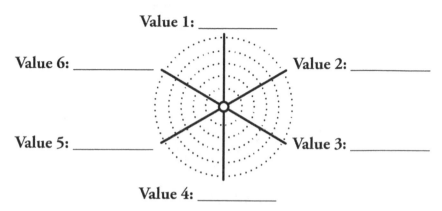

Value 1: _____

Value 6: _____   Value 2: _____

Value 5: _____   Value 3: _____

Value 4: _____

Once you have your six values on your wheel, calibrate how often you use each value in your daily life using Step 2.

Step 2: Rank your Top Six Values

Now that you have six values that are meaningful to you, we're going to look at how frequently those values are being used in your everyday life. Rank each value on a scale from 1 (you like the value, but rarely use it to make decisions) to 5 (you deeply understand and identify with the value as you make decisions).

Step 3: Mark the Spokes

Mark the spokes of each value—using a symbolic dot—according to the score you gave them. 1 is located on the hub of your tire and 5 is located on the outer edge of the wheel. This step provides a visual representation of the how frequently those values are used to make daily decisions.

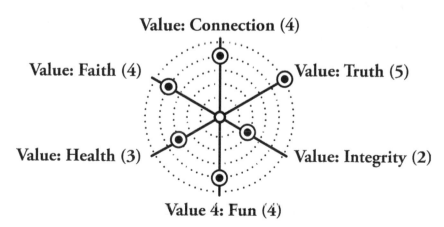

Value: Connection (4)

Value: Faith (4)   Value: Truth (5)

Value: Health (3)   Value: Integrity (2)

Value 4: Fun (4)

Step 4: Re-connect your Dots

Now that each value has a numerical value based on its everyday use, you can see the relationship of those values together. Re-connect your new dots to reveal the shape of your personal value wheel. This provides an idea of how efficiently values are providing a foundation, or wheel, for your life.

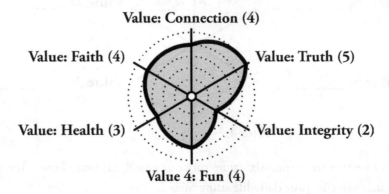

Value: Connection (4)

Value: Faith (4)   **Value: Truth (5)**

Value: Health (3)   **Value: Integrity (2)**

Value 4: Fun (4)

Part 3: Take Action

Perhaps, your tire looks more like the Flintstone's primitive rock wheel versus the modern round rubber ones used today. If so, there is room for improvement. If it's already fairly even-shaped, celebrate your success.

Regardless of what your wheel looks like, you've built the frame of your first tire. By drawing a circle around those spokes, you've created a wheel of values that have meaning and relevance to your life. It's time to take action and put your values into motion; for it's through the outward demonstration in your life that you know internal changes have taken place.

Step 1: Reflect on Value 1

Take a look at your first value and reflect on it for a moment. What does it mean to you? Perhaps you chose "connection", like the example above, and your time with family and friends is of utmost importance to you.

How can you strengthen that value today?

You might call your parents or you could send an email to a sibling. The power of choice is now in your hands and you can use it to have lunch with a co-worker, go to the gym with a buddy, or post an inspirational message to your friends on Facebook.

Step 2: Implement Daily Action with the Common Sense Weekly Value Tracker

The idea is to take one value at a time and begin to implement it in daily actions. For day two, choose another value from your personal wheel. Let's say this time you chose "truth". Again, take time throughout your day to place meaning and purpose on that word. Find new ways that you can incorporate the concept of speaking honestly and accurately to those you come into contact with, whether old friends, new acquaintances or business associates.

Common Sense Weekly Value Tracker

Mark your actions in the space below:

Day	Value Word	Action for the day
1		
2		
3		
4		
5		
6		

By generating one wheel of six values, you have a singular focus of enhancing your ethical foundation in fun, creative, and practical ways. You'll notice purpose in your decisions and meaning in your actions. You might even notice that you feel less stress or internal chaos. Using the value wheel, you uncover what's really important to you. You'll create a new understanding about yourself and offer new ways to create harmony in your relationships.

What to Expect After Your First Week

After your first week, re-calibrate your wheel. Hopefully your mindful action has increased the usage of each value in the decisions you've made over the last seven days. If some values are still low-scoring, you can focus on them again in the upcoming week.

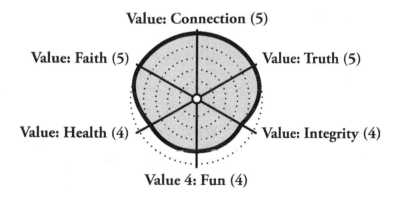

Value: Connection (5)

Value: Faith (5)

Value: Truth (5)

Value: Health (4)

Value: Integrity (4)

Value 4: Fun (4)

Continue to expand your first tire until all six values score a 5, meaning that you internally understand the meaning of the word and use it to guide your behaviors. Then, proceed to part 4.

Part 4: Create a Smooth Ride

Once you've completed the first wheel, and implemented actions based on your values, you can start on the next tire of your car. Follow the same guidelines, step-by-step. Choose five new values that are central to your ideals and attitudes.

> Purposefully putting your values into action can create internal alignment and provide a smoother ride through life.

Place those five principles on the spokes of your new wheel and then create easy ways to incorporate them into your world. By the time you're done with your four tires, you'll notice your personal life vehicle traveling smoothly, balanced, and directly moving towards the goals you want to achieve.

Additional Activities: Choose your Passengers

Creating four value wheels strengthens the foundation of values that directly influence daily habits and role-specific behaviors. When you have a clear purpose behind your decisions, others will notice. Why not invite others to share in this wonderful activity? Bring the value wheel activity into your office or home. Meet with your co-workers or family members to decide on what values are important for your shared space. These values can become a pact, or an agreement, for the decisions and actions within your close parameters. It can enhance trust, harmony, and communication among you all.

The Four-Way Test

The actions you take outwardly inevitably mirror those values held within. When moving from a place of purpose, both you and others begin to notice changes. People are able to feel more comfortable around you, relate to you with ease, and have a better idea of what makes you tick. Your internal balance becomes palpable and you can share that harmony with your relationships at home, work, and in the community as a whole.

One man who understood the power of this concept was Chicago Rotarian, Herbert Taylor. His goal was to unite the business members around him. He wanted a set of standards that could be followed to ensure integrity, fairness, and commitment between individuals. In order to create this ethical foundation, he formulated the four-way test back in 1932. He suggested four basic questions, all steeped in values, that would help people make wise decisions. Here are the four questions he thought each individual should ask themselves before taking action.

Question #1: Is it the truth?

Questions #2: Is it fair to all concerned?

Question #3: Will it build goodwill and better friendship?

Question #4: Will it be beneficial to all concerned?

Let's take a closer look at these questions.

Question #1: Is it the truth?

Yes, we understand that truth is relative and subjective. Each person has a different viewpoint on what is true based on their past experiences and beliefs. Yet, there are more similarities than differences between mankind as a whole, and there are certain commonalities shared by many that could make this question of truth applicable.

Just think for a moment about how you verify if the information you're receiving is accurate. Do you check out the sources online? Do you ask friends and colleagues for references or personal experience? The common-sense idea is that you do the research, come to your own conclusion, and then take action accordingly.

> "The Truth doesn't need you to believe it; the Truth simply is, and it survives whether you believe it or not."
> —Don Miguel Ruiz

There are numerous common truths that we share. Take, for example, the Green Bay Packers as the 2010-2011 Super Bowl champions. There are numerous videos on the internet, replaying incredible moments from the game. There are player interviews that reflect on meaningful and decisive moments on the field. There are millions of spectators around the country that would verify their own, emotionally-engaged experience of watching the event live or on TV. They would all agree that the Packers won the championship and took home the trophy. That's the shared truth.

But, how does this relate to values and relationships?

Questioning Truth in Action: Sarah's Story

Take the hypothetical example of a woman named Sarah. She's your friend who wants to start her own business in town and rent a small office in your building. Everything seems to work out smoothly in the beginning, but soon

Sarah is behind on her rent. This "once in a while" mistake becomes a habit, and she has created numerous excuses for why she's unable to come up with the money on time every month. Yet, to your amazement, she shows up the very next day in a brand new vehicle. Her deceit leaves you feeling disheartened and betrayed.

When talking to others, Sarah boasts of her success, confidence, and worth. The contradiction between her words and actions begins to bother you, so you start doing some research. When talking to a friend, you discover that Sarah has strained their relationship, too. She purchased some merchandise from this colleague months ago and has failed to pay back even half of what she owes. While blissfully oblivious to the consequences of her actions, Sarah is weaving a common thread in her associations. Many feel betrayed and used. Others frustrated and exhausted.

The point is this: Sarah's view of herself is very different from the one held of her by others. The shared truth around town is that Sarah is unreliable, fraudulent, and careless. She is rapidly becoming known for her dishonesty, yet Sarah still sees herself as a great friend and businesswomen.

So, whose version of truth do you listen to—Sarah's or everyone else's? The question really boils down to what's true for you. Your emotions and feelings, along with a dose of common sense, can help you clarify this. When you have valid input and sound research based in values, you can come up with your version of truth and move forward with actions that feel right for you. Inevitably, those core values that you hold about yourself and others do get exposed to the world around you.

Common Sense Tip: Find internal alignment first, and then support those values with your actions.

Ask yourself the following questions honestly:

1. How would you describe yourself?

2. What would others say about you?

3. Is there congruence in these beliefs?

4. Are you confident in the beliefs that you hold?

5. Are you able to communicate your ideas with clarity and openness?

6. Are you willing to hear the viewpoint of others, even if they disagree with you?

7. Who do you seek out for advice when deciding what's true?

8. What are the values and attributes of those people you admire?

9. Are you willing to decide what's true for you, or do you wait to be told what's right and wrong?

10. What actions do you take to verify truth?

Using your internal guidelines and values are the best ways to help you make choices that reflect truth. By tuning in to your emotions, and combining them with common-sense wisdom shared by others around you, there is the opportunity to take actions that are genuine, precise, and beneficial to all people involved.

Question #2: Is it fair to all concerned?

This question moves beyond individual truth and begins to take into account the effects of your decision making. Will the choice you are about to make reflect fairness to yourself and to the others that are also affected by such a decision? Is your action free from bias or injustice? This step is a simple check-in with your surroundings to make sure it's in the best and highest good for all concerned. It's designed to help you slow down and take numerous perspectives into consideration *before* taking action.

Let's say you're the meal preparer in your household, with a hungry husband and three growing teens. Let's say you decide to go on a health food kick and change all of the foods eaten by the family. Now the refrigerator and cupboards alike look entirely foreign to everyone in the house but you. Your husband gets upset and dislikes the new menu. The kids complain that they don't like their food. They even ask regularly to eat at their friends' houses for meals. You notice the discontent and are dismayed at the response.

You probably had good intentions of creating wellness for your family by upgrading the quality of food eaten at home. You want your kids to grow up strong and healthy. You want your husband's high blood pressure to be regulated and thought that a change in diet would probably help with the condition. You even thought it would help you lose some stubborn pounds that have crept up on you over the past few years. Yet, you might have to compromise some to honor your own desires for healthy foods and still acknowledge the needs of your family.

While the goal was to help your family, the idea backfired.

Why?

Because the family wasn't included in the transformation! They viewed the changes as unfair, perhaps even unnecessary. They felt out of control in the decision-making process. Yet, had they been included in the new plan for health, or if you had thought about their viewpoints before making such drastic changes, then everyone might have been willing, if not excited, for a new diet makeover.

Or, perhaps the question of fairness arises when you're given a monthly allowance by your employer for the frequent travel you do for the company. You might fudge the numbers here and there, padding your account and using the money elsewhere. While you might never get caught, deep inside you know that there is dishonesty at work. Your pocketbook smiles, but your internal guidance system—which affects all aspects of your life—will eventually expose the injustice.

Common Sense Tip: By taking the time to think about everyone involved in, or affected by, your decisions, you'll be able to slow down and see the bigger picture.

This offers you the insight about the repercussions of your actions before jumping in too soon. It also increases the harmony in your relationships by considering what's fair to all concerned in any given situation.

Question #3: Will it build goodwill and better friendship?

Although question number 2 focuses on possible effects your decision might have on others, this question focuses on the quality of the relationships *between* people. The goal of building goodwill is to make friends or improve your association with them. Something as simple as a smile still goes a long way. So do the words "please" and "thank you".

Enhancing Relationships in Action: Dorothy's Story

Dorothy was a seventy-two year old widow who was actively involved in her church. When she discovered a fellow worshiper was getting out of the hospital and needed some in-home assistance for three months, Dorothy wanted to help. It would offer her a chance to socialize as well as be of service.

Conveniently, a younger couple from the same church was looking for a temporary place to stay while their house was under construction. Dorothy, as usual, was thinking of others. She organized her own home and generously offered it to them while she would be away caretaking. Now Dorothy was able to enhance goodwill for her sick friend as well as for the temporarily homeless couple.

Common Sense Tip: While it's not necessary to dedicate several hours of your life to others—or to focus so much on others that your own Energy

Bank Account gets drained—there are some simple things that can be done to enhance goodwill and friendship.

The simple gift of a smile to those you come in contact with throughout the day can enhance goodwill. You might also take some time to genuinely listen to what others say and ask meaningful, pertinent questions that reflect your interest. Regardless of how you uplift those around you, the values of friendliness, trust, and helpfulness are at the core of your decisions and actions.

Question #4: Will it be beneficial to all concerned?

This question also addresses how others will be affected based on your decisions and actions. However, it suggests that you **look beyond your circle of influence**—those closest to you and who would be immediately affected in the given situation—and consider the affect on society as a whole. How will your neighbors be affected? Will it bring harmony or discord to your community? Does it affect the larger aspects of your state and country?

The goal here is to better mankind. It's like the familiar phrase—"do unto others as you would like done unto yourself". This question asks you to view all other humans as yourself.

Common Sense Tip: If you were put in someone else's shoes, no matter how far down the chain of events created by your decision, would there be any negative consequences?

If the answer is yes, perhaps reconsider. If not, then move forward knowing that you're doing the best you can, for yourself and for the rest of the world.

So, what's the overall purpose of the four-way test? **These four simple questions offer the opportunity to slow down the decision-making process and reflect on the values behind any movement.** They are a code of ethics that ask you to create a vision for yourself, your relationships, and your community as a whole. While there are no prescriptive answers to such questions, considering them enhances the values of honesty, justice, and helpfulness. The ultimate goal is to do the very best that you can in any given circumstance. You'll have clarity about your own beliefs and ideals. You'll even establish compassion and connection with those around you when taking their well-being into account. And you'll have the confidence to move forward in all aspects of your life.

Take Action Activity

While the four-way test was adopted by the Rotary Club in 1943, its benefits reach far beyond the confines of the business realm. Consider an important decision you're currently facing in any area of your life and reflect on the following questions:

- What are your thoughts about the challenge?

- What possible solutions come to mind?

- Who do you admire and what's their viewpoint on the situation?

- Who else is involved in this decision?

- Who could possibly be affected, either positively or negatively?

- Does it enhance your current relationships? If so, how? If not, why not?

- Will society as a whole benefit?

Look to your Leaders

Creating a value wheel and formulating your own code of ethics turn your attention back to the values that are driving your actions. But, what if you are unsure of what those values look like in action? That's where role models come into play. Numerous leaders around the world represent a strong foundation of values and serve as role models. You might have a sports star who exhibits dedication, physical prowess, and power. There are CEOs who demonstrate intelligence, hard work, and ingenuity. You also have stars that display generosity, audacity, and poise.

While it's common to observe public figures as role models, there are many people beyond the limelight who demonstrate strong values. You might have a father who taught you honesty and persistence. It could be a friend who has displayed faith and hope throughout their battle with cancer.

Take a moment to reflect on someone you admire. What do you like about that person? What values support their actions and behaviors? Do my own actions reflect those same values?

Look to your Leaders Activity

While we want you to be the one in control of your life, sometimes it does help to use the guidance of others to get you there.

Mentors are a great source of direction for your future.

While you may not be pursuing the profession of head coach for an NFL team or vying your way to a prime time network broadcasting position, take time to find mentors who reflect your own internal values can keep you motivated and excited on your own personal path.

Instead of just thinking of one person you admire, make a list of people you know personally and public figures that offer you inspiration. Describe what attributes about that person make them stand out in your mind.

If you know the person, ask to set up a time to meet with them. Perhaps take them to lunch or invite them to take a walk with you in the park. During that time together, request that they tell you their story. You can also ask the following questions:

- What was their childhood like?
- Who did they admire growing up and why?
- What challenges have they encountered along their path?
- What helped them overcome those challenges?
- What values guide their decisions?
- What advice do they have to give to you?

Use your creativity here and come up with questions that are meaningful to you. Utilize this time together to bolster your own values and encourage yourself on your journey.

If you chose someone in the public arena, many of them have books that talk about their story. Check out your local bookstore or the online market to see if they have a published work. There are numerous books on the market today that emphasize the importance of strong values. Tony Dungy, former head coach of the Baltimore Colts, discusses the process of building character, integrity, and courage out on the football field in his new release. Bill O'Reilly shares humorous personal stories that illustrate the values he learned through various life experiences. He also encourages his readers to embrace those values in their own lives through powerful and meaningful action. Oprah is another great example of someone who has lived the American dream and offers so much inspiration to millions of people around the world.

Find a book that interests you and that also supports adopting values.

It is also important to note that you can learn from those who actively embrace devaluing traits, such as lying, cheating, and stealing. You now recognize these as negative characteristics and move into more life-enhancing attributes.

Whether you met someone in person, or read a book about another's life story, make a value wheel for your chosen individual. How can you emulate these values in your life this week? Choose one a day and take determined action to boost your own Energy Bank Account through such activities.

Putting it all Together

Values, which are our principles and moral guidelines for living, create a foundation from which all of our daily choices are made. They also affect habitual responses and specific role-related behaviors that we undertake in various circumstances. By understanding which values have meaning for you, it's easier to set a direction for your life, remain centered along the journey, and successfully achieve your goals.

New Common Sense Tools to Bolster your Internal Values:

- **The Value Wheel:** This exercise compiles values to create awareness about your current level of balance and uses those values to enhance your well-being through practical daily actions.

- **The Four-Way Test:** Asking yourself specific questions, such as those posed in the Four-Way Test, slow down the decision-making process so that any action taken reflects your personal values and considers the community around you as a whole.

- **Look to your Leaders**: Role models can be found in all areas of life, from professional athletes, motivational speakers, and even those close relatives whom we encounter on a regular basis. Understanding the values of those you admire help you move forward with purpose and character in your own life. Also be aware of those who act from negative values and use them as lessons to contrast your uplifting values.

Chapter 2

Chapter 2

Create a Limitless Perspective

"When you change the way you look at things, the things you look at change."
—*Dr. Wayne Dyer*

In this Chapter

- Understand the self-conscious and the subconscious minds

- Discover beliefs that direct and define your experiences

- Use your hand to balance your human characteristics

- Create a limitless, positive perspective in an instant

- Enhance your creative ability

The color schemes on every aisle exceed the variations inside the loftiest of crayon boxes. Bicycles shimmer and shine vibrant shades of blue, green, pink, and yellow. Shelves the size of skyscrapers, stocked with games, gadgets, and gizmos, surround each child with effervescent splendor. Just when you think the eyes can't handle another shade of the rainbow shining from every direction, your ears perk up at the latest electronic sounds of a barking dog or fire truck. In addition, the myriad of colorful and noisy trinkets beg for your touch. They *feel* good—soft, cuddly, shiny, or sleek. They might even be an oddly-shaped rubber creation that peaks your tactile curiosity.

When was the last time you entered a children's toy store? Perhaps you visited one not too long ago with your own kids or recently perused the colorful aisles with your grandchildren. Or, maybe it's been years since you ventured into a treasure-filled wonderland. Regardless of the time frame in which your last toy store stopover occurred, consider how the interior captures the absolute attention of anyone in their formative years.

Consider that the toy store gurus are marketing to the attention of the up and coming generation. And, from a child's perspective, every one of their senses gets entirely engaged to produce a stimulating experience. Even when babies and toddlers are too young for words, their wide eyes are taking in all of the information about their environment without having to speak. This primitive point of view is easily enticed, since it operates from an incredibly influential standpoint.

What do you notice as an adult in such a space? Your mind now exceeds your senses, and you notice the cost of each item, the age-appropriate nature of the toy, and the quality of customer care provided by the clerks. Your point of view has changed. You are now influenced by your life experience. Your perspective may be jaded by your relationships, your feelings about yourself, and your understanding of your role in the world around you.

In essence, every belief you have about yourself and your environment affects your outlook on life.

These beliefs, whether spoken or unspoken, have been accumulating since you were born.

Common Sense Tip: When you are very young and impressionable, your senses—eyes, ears, tongue, nose, and skin—pick up important information from your environment.

There are things you are naturally drawn to, like bright lights, interesting sounds, and fascinating textures. You even have natural taste preferences, like enjoying carrots over peas. Perhaps even a cozy blanket became a childhood favorite.

Beyond the Five Senses

In addition to the traditional senses, each individual has the capability to pick up unspoken information. For example, consider that without understanding words, young children have the ability to derive meaning from vocal sounds and body language. They can understand when someone is in love, excited, content, insecure, afraid, or upset. Studies have shown that this also occurs in the womb, when even a fetus jerks in response to a mother's argument.

It is as though each child is a sponge in their formative years, taking in as much information as they can even before words are spoken. Through osmosis, they begin to understand their surroundings and develop a view of the world that will help them survive on their own.

Consider your upbringing for a moment. What were your parents like? Who were the important people who helped raise you? What was your neighborhood like? Were you raised in a religious environment? Did you have other siblings around? Reflect on all of the aspects of your childhood.

Thanks to your ability to pick up on sensory information, as well as unspoken cues, your mind began forming and storing beliefs, which became your perspective. If you had musically-inclined parents, perhaps you noticed that you enjoyed surrounding yourself with beautiful melodies. If your parents were struggling financially while you were young, you might have adopted their paradigm that accumulating and saving money is challenging. Even the beliefs that others held about food could be influencing the when, where, and how *you* eat.

Each experience, rich with sensations and their associated beliefs, have been stored in your subconscious mind. While this may have seemed like a daunting realm of the unknown, recent scientific research has opened the door to such mysteries. Light has been shed on how the mind works and how it acquires, stores, and recalls beliefs.

Common Sense Tip: Most importantly, you now have the power to change beliefs and set yourself free from any limiting perspectives you have adopted over the years.

Your Two Minds

While common sense acknowledges that you have a body and a mind, there is much about this latter component that helps clarify how and why your body undergoes certain behaviors. Let's revisit childhood once again and observe the first time you were taking steps.

It's possible that you don't remember the events specifically, but there might be pictures or video footage that recall this momentous occasion. You probably had your arms flailing out to the side in order to help you maintain balance. Perhaps you were holding someone's hand when you took your first steps, then realized you could continue on your own. Maybe you were a quick learner and jumped right to your feet to embark on the exploration of your environment. In any case, all of your internal and external senses were in a heightened state of awareness to make such first steps possible.

Because of the conscious mind—the first component of your non-physical mental capability—you were able to focus on the few events in front of you and make a choice to place one foot in front of the other.

Then, as you grew, not as much thought was necessary to take each step. Your body memorized the sensations of walking and you could carry on such a task without much effort at all. You could carry around a stuffed animal, walk towards your favorite toy, or take steps to keep up with the family dog. The part of the mind that stored the memory of how to walk was the second component of your intelligence—the subconscious mind.

The example of learning how to walk and then continuing with such an activity demonstrates how both the conscious and subconscious minds work together. When you are learning a new skill, such as riding a

> "We choose our joys and sorrows long before we experience them." —Kahlil Gibran

bike, driving a vehicle, or swimming, your conscious mind is highly engaged. It is responsible for processing one to three events at a time and allowing your short-term memory to store important information.

The Role of the Conscious Mind

The conscious mind, also known as the self-conscious mind, allows you to participate and to observe life at the same time, but it's not worried about self-image. When you passed through the volatile teen years (which might have been very concerned with looking good) and into adulthood, the pre-frontal cortex of the brain developed. This allowed you to not only assess the factors of your current environment, but also to reflect on the consequences of your actions.

According to cognitive neuroscientists, the self-conscious mind only accounts for 5% of all cognitive activity. Essentially, the other 95% of your decisions, actions, and behaviors result from the habitual subconscious.

The Role of the Subconscious Mind

For years, this part of the mind has been deemed the unconscious, mainly because of its primitive stimulus-response pattern. Yet, the subconscious is an amazing information processor that can respond to over 40 million nerve impulses per second. It takes in all sensory input in any given circumstance, records it, stores it, and plays it back when necessary. Once you have learned a particular behavior pattern, such as riding a bike or driving a vehicle, the subconscious takes over so that such complex actions can take place without such demanding concentration.

So, what does all of this mean?

Common Sense Tips:

- *The subconscious mind is a million times more powerful than the self-conscious mind.*

- *The subconscious controls every behavior that is not taken care of by the focused conscious mind.*

- *The majority of your actions are controlled by pre-recorded programs, each of which has been determined by your natural human instincts and your unique life experience.*

Two Minds in Action: Todd's Story

The following story about Todd is a perfect example of how both components of the mind work hand-in-hand to keep the body functioning at an optimal level. Now, Todd grew up on the California coast with parents who loved to sail, and they spent many weekends during his childhood navigating the Pacific Ocean. When he was old enough to sail by himself, his parents enrolled him in introductory classes, and then he continued to more advanced levels.

Over the course of many years, Todd sailed for hours on end. As an adult, he enjoyed the time alone out on the open seas, connecting with the tranquility and adventure the ocean offered.

On a particular solo trip from Indonesia to New Zealand, he encountered an unexpected storm. With waves towering to 50 feet, his tri-hull ship was tossed mercilessly through the rough water. His vessel didn't sink, but it was flipped upside down. Water began seeping into the cabin. He had to create a make-shift bed, survive on canned goods, and continually scan the horizon for help once the squall subsided.

One week passed by. No other ship was in sight.

A second week passed, with little hope for a rescue.

Todd checked for the possibility of other vessels every thirty minutes during his waking hours. He surely didn't want to miss any opportunity. Then finally, on the 17th day, he was saved.

Now, consider for a moment that it was Todd's natural survival instincts, combined with his creative ideas, which allowed him to stay alive in the face of adversity. He used his self-conscious mind to ration food, to sleep comfortably, and to reflect on the ever-changing situation. Yet, his years of sailing and the ability to remain calm also came into play. His subconscious beliefs that he would be okay, combined with his habitual experience on the water, helped him endure the life-threatening situation.

Common Sense Tip: While you may not be stranded in the middle of the South Pacific (in fact, we hope that's never your situation), both your subconscious and your self-conscious minds are constantly cooperating so that you can function at an optimal level.

While your subconscious is the powerhouse of the two minds, often controlling your actions from pre-recorded beliefs, the self-conscious mind does have the ability to observe and change those programs to create a more positive life experience for you in the future.

Two Types of Beliefs

As you recall, every childhood experience helps formulate a myriad of beliefs. Early conclusions drawn from parents, teachers, and immediate surroundings all have a strong impact on the mind. It tries to make sense of mental programs that are already stored as well as integrate new information from current life experiences.

Those subconscious beliefs, which determine nearly all behavioral responses, can be placed into two categories: beliefs that hold you back and beliefs that support you. We call these limited and limitless beliefs.

When you have limited attitudes, values, and ideas about the world, you are unable to reach your full potential. Life may seem difficult, hopeless, and depressing. You might even feel unable to impact your future. It's "the glass is half empty" perspective.

Oftentimes, limiting beliefs contribute to disappointing or unexpected circumstances. Because the self-conscious mind is focused elsewhere, the subconscious programming is running rampant.

Limited Beliefs in Action: The Elephant's Story

While not all limited thinking results in a victim mentality, there is often a form of suffering involved. Consider the concept of learned helplessness. You can tie one end of a strong rope to the hind leg of a baby elephant and the other to a nearby post. No matter how hard he pulls, he can't budge. Soon, the elephant perceives that the rope is an all-powerful force keeping him from roaming free. So, when he becomes an adult, with thousands of pounds added to its stature, he has already given up on running away. The belief that he is now limited by the reach of a small rope, despite his strength to uproot almost any post, is controlling the elephant's action to stay put.

Common Sense Tip: We, like the elephant, often impose constraints from our own minds.

Common Sense Top 8 Limiting Beliefs

In the developmental years of life, there are many limiting beliefs that can be adopted, which become the pre-recorded programs for your behaviors.

These beliefs include:

I am unsafe.

Security and safety are at the core of every female. If she holds the belief that she is unsafe or lacks security, it can negatively affect her ability to attain and maintain an intimate relationship. Whether male or female, if one's foundation of protection is challenged, this limiting belief could stimulate the need to lock every door, hide everything precious, or remain closed down out of fear.

Jerry's Story:

When Jerry was a young boy, he was bitten by a dog. Although he wasn't badly harmed at the time, it was a traumatic event. Now, when Jerry feels very unsafe around dogs despite his larger physical body, he believes he can't protect himself from them.

One evening Jerry stopped by the grocery store after work. The parking lot was full, so he had quite a walk on a cold night. As he passed a dark pick-up truck, a dog began barking loudly from within the camper shell. It made Jerry jump! His heart began to race, his skin began to sweat, and his entire body tensed up. He was so cautious on his way back out to his vehicle, that he walked two rows away from the animal just to avoid it.

I want to die.

Take for example an individual wanting to commit suicide. Based on their belief that they want to die, they'll orchestrate a plan to take their life. However, their survival instinct often kicks in, so when some pain is inflicted, they change their mind. Similarly, when elderly people feel the end of their life is near and want to die, the body and its natural instinct to survive often keeps them from making their transition.

In either case, internal chaos of the individual is present. Their conscious mind might want to end life, but it is powerless to the subconscious survival instinct which keeps the body functioning.

Let it be understood that a conscious belief can be repeated so often that it can become part of the subconscious programming, and thus allow the body to pass over.

Eddie's Story:

Eddie, a 46-year-old carpet layer, is the perfect example of the conscious mind rewiring the subconscious programming. Eddie had been in the carpet-laying business, which is a physically demanding line of work, for many years. At the end of every workday, Eddie would come into the shop saying, "This job is going to kill me. I'm so tired. I don't think I'll even make it to my 47th birthday."

Many thought that Eddie's brain aneurism the night before his 47th birthday seemed unfortunate and shocking. It might even seem coincidental now that you know his regular dialogue. Yet, those who understand the power of beliefs know that repeating the same mantra over and over can ultimately change the way our minds, and bodies, function. In the end, the subconscious can even surrender the physical body entirely.

> "We believe what we experience, but we often forget that we experience what we believe." —Stuart Grayson

My life is governed by chaos and chance.

While the universe may seem like a vast expanse beyond your immediate scope, this belief can be attributed to circumstances in your life that feel out of control. You may not see order in any event, almost feeling hopeless to direct your future because anything negative could happen by chance. This is a very self-defeating attitude.

George's Story:

George was the typical workaholic who owned and managed his own business. He took pride in being known as the problem solver, who could help employees with disgruntled issues, accounts payable with miscalculations, or collect from overdue customers.

But George was a risk taker. He often ordered inventory based on false projections. Then, when the market crashed and business slowed, he had to work three times harder to bring things back into balance. George felt his life was run by an unlucky turn of events and that the chaos of the current business climate caused his company to fail. George blamed outside circumstances instead of looking within for solutions to the problems at hand.

I hate myself.

This belief expresses the feeling of being unloved. While one might not readily admit such a strong negative belief, they often do feel responsible for their inability to receive love and for the numerous problems they experience as a result. Self-hate is a direct resistance to the beautiful uniqueness of each individual and a failure to recognize their divine nature.

Hate is the strongest, self-defeating word in our vocabulary that is often taken all-too-lightly in everyday conversations. You hear people say "I hate those flowers, or I hate the way that house looks." By using hate to describe the environment around you, or to portray yourself, you amplify a smaller negative emotion and give the subconscious a beating.

Betina's story:

Betina, a 53-year-old school teacher, embraced the idea of self hate. She had gained weight over the past twenty years which made it difficult for her to continue with activities she loved, such as dancing and tennis. At first, Betina was just disgusted with how her body looked. But soon, that idea of hate extended to her entire being.

She could no longer view her body as only one aspect of herself. She always talked down to herself and blamed herself for her difficulties. That hateful attitude further deteriorated her health, but also diminished her self-esteem and her ability to maintain friendships.

I can't.

With this belief, any task or situation becomes challenging. It could start at a young age when a child says "I can't read well" or "I can't play kickball." This belief can infiltrate all areas of life—from the ability to have a successful relationship, to getting a raise, or to buying a house. Think of all the times you tell yourself "I can't" in life. Based on your new awareness, you can implement tools in this chapter to change your perspective from limited thoughts of "I can't" to limitless ones of "I can".

Alicia's Story:

Alicia was a bright-eyed, enthusiastic college student. Her natural social grace was evident, just as was her common-sense logic, but when it came to test-taking, she felt out of control.

Her belief that she couldn't test well stemmed back to a 4th grade experience when she was scolded by her parents for a poor grade. Although she had really studied for that exam, the material was challenging. From that point on, Alicia felt that she could not test well. Her body would tremble and her breath would shorten each time she sat down for an assessment. Inevitably, the test results were lower than her knowledge due to her limiting belief.

I am separate from and unimportant to God.

This idea creates distance from the divine organizing nature of life. Whether you call this source God, Spirit, or Divinity, there is an all-knowing component that maintains order in the universe. When you feel cut off from this flow of well-being, life is perceived as challenging. You may even lose hope in your future because you feel unimportant and ineffective to make a positive difference.

Kym's Story:

When Kym was 13 years old, her father passed away from a malignant brain tumor. It was a time that greatly strained her spirituality. How could God cause such a horrible disease and take such a loving life? Was there any good left to come of her own?

Kym felt entirely alone. No other kids at school had lost a parent, and even if they had, they never talked about it. In her belief that she was disconnected from God, she lost sight of her youth and believed that life was simply destined to be difficult.

I deserve to be unhappy.

When you deserve something, you know that you are worthy to receive it. This belief plays against your idea that happiness is attainable because of who you are. You might believe that happiness can happen, but some hidden, or not-so-hidden ideas, keep that joy from making its way into your relationships, career, and personal growth.

Other people and forces control my life.

Just like the concept of learned helplessness, this belief defeats your ability to make an impact on your future. It is as though other people can make your decisions for you, or you may even let the behavior of others determine your emotional state. It could be people or environments that negatively affect you, but adhering to this program keeps you from feeling any sense of control in your life.

If these negative thoughts are programmed in the subconscious, take a moment to reflect on this question:

How many of my negative thoughts are affecting my life?

The Good News: Common Sense Top 8 *Limitless* Beliefs

The good news is that even those beliefs developed during the formative years of childhood can be rewired to create new outcomes for your life. Perceptions, which are shaped by memories and old programs in the subconscious, then become evident as actions by the self-conscious mind. Because your self-conscious is based on free will, you have the ability to mix perceptions with imaginative thoughts and form an unlimited number of supporting beliefs, and life-enhancing programs, to reshape the actions of your future.

These limitless beliefs, which support personal growth, spiritual expansion, and unbridled potential, are on the other end of the spectrum. It is the optimistic, glass-is-half-full viewpoint. The tools in this chapter will allow you to create this optimism in all aspects of your life.

You can transform your beliefs into ideas like:

I am safe.

You can truly know and understand that your security and safety are in line, no matter where you are. It is the unity within you that withstands any outside circumstance, and your personal power can never be taken away.

Heidi's Story:

Heidi is a single woman living alone in the low-income area of a large city. While many might express fear for her safety as she goes about getting groceries at night or coming home by herself, Heidi has an internal knowing that she is safe. When she locks the front door of her home, she feels secure. Heidi knows

she is going to be okay, regardless of any outside circumstance, and she trusts her
natural instincts will kick in when a need for protection arises.

I choose to live.

This life-supporting belief aligns with
your natural instincts to not just survive
the physical experience, but to thrive in
it. It's living with vibrancy and a sense of

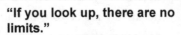

"If you look up, there are no
limits."
—Japanese proverb

aliveness. Joy, enthusiasm, and passion help carry this natural instinct of
living into a new paradigm of loving life to its fullest.

Life is supported by a Divine order.

This could tie into the butterfly affect, where all organisms are interrelated
and there is a Divine order. You can watch a caterpillar transform into a
butterfly or be amazed at the orderliness of a beehive or ant colony.

I love myself.

When you know who you are, and enjoy every aspect of yourself, you
are able to accomplish more than you ever thought possible. This does not
imply that you are perfect, but that your life has meaning and purpose. You
can learn powerful lessons from your mistakes and your weaknesses and view
them as aspects of your unique self with celebration. By understanding your
strengths, you can help others. And by recognizing your weaknesses, you can
allow the strength of others to help you.

Loving yourself is very different than the narcissistic focus of the ego.
This self-love is like looking in the mirror and seeing God's eyes looking back
at you. You recognize your own worth as an individual, you understand your
value, and you identify with the feelings of appreciation for yourself as you
make a difference in the world.

I can.

This belief embraces the idea that anything is possible, and with this
belief, any task or situation becomes easier. While there may be some
challenges in the given circumstance, you know that your creativity will pull
through and a solution will be found.

I am connected and important to God.

You may believe in God, a guiding spirit, or a divinity that underlies all aspects of life. This belief mirrors that divinity within yourself. You are able to co-create your future. You are able to tap into wisdom that is beyond your immediate scope by connecting with God or an almighty spirit. You can also utilize power and strength to move forward in any given situation with confidence.

Happiness is my natural state of being.

This belief supports the idea that happiness is not only an attainable attribute, but it is yours for the taking. You are worthy of having abundance, power, self-esteem, health, and freedom just by being you.

I am in charge of my life.

This belief enhances your personal power. There are no limitations here and while some temporary doors may seem to be closing on your path, you know that you have the inner resources to find a new direction to make your dreams come true. You are capable of taking positive action, and you have the supportive belief to enhance your natural abilities.

Whether your beliefs are supporting you or holding you back, they are the blueprint for your future. And, while they're stored in the subconscious mind, only sometimes are they brought to conscious awareness.

The objective is to quickly and easily recognize when your beliefs are out of alignment with your goals. By using the tools provided in this chapter, you will be able to create a limitless perspective. You can move from limiting, negative beliefs that stifle your potential into supportive, limitless ones that allow your dreams to be attainable.

The Common Sense Hand Model of Wellness

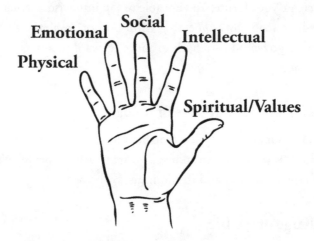

The first step to expanding your perspective from limited to limitless involves understanding the numerous aspects of yourself. Yes, you do have a body. Yes, you do have a mind. Yet, there are other non-physical facets of your being that contribute to an expanded way of living.

With a limitless perspective, you understand that you are an intricate individual. You are uniquely designed physiologically, with such intricacies as bone structure, height, eye color, and metabolism. You also have a distinct personality that creates special likes and dislikes, hobbies, interests, and friendships.

Beyond the individuality that is you, there are commonalities between you and all of the other individuals on this planet. Believe it or not, those similarities can be found on one of your hands—in what we call the Hand Model of Wellness.

How can your hand expand your perspective? Each of your five fingers describes an essential characteristic that contributes to your overall well-being, and when all aspects of your hand are in harmony, your body works smoothly, your stress levels diminish, and your ability to reach your potential is enhanced.

Your Physical Self: Pinky Finger

Let's start with your pinky finger. This digit represents your physical nature. You're a material being comprised of millions of cells that create the building blocks for your bones, organs, glands, tendons, ligaments, muscles, and every other part of your body. Each of those cells communicates constantly with one another to create an internal symphony. Your beating heart harmonizes with your breathing. Your bone structure corresponds with your musculature to allow steady and endless options for movement. And your nervous system cooperates with your blue, green, or brown eyes in order to relay important information to the rest of your body.

Check in with your current physical well-being and mark the frequency of each.

Physical	Rarely	Sometimes	Almost Always
I receive 6-8 hours of restful sleep each night.	O	O	O
My body is free of pain.	O	O	O
I sweat once a day doing physical activity.	O	O	O
I digest foods easily.	O	O	O
I have at least one bowel movement per day	O	O	O
I drink water regularly.	O	O	O
The foods I eat make me feel energized.	O	O	O
My body is able to deeply rest each day.	O	O	O
My muscles are able to relax and release tension.	O	O	O
I brush and floss daily.	O	O	O

The Emotional Self: Ring Finger

The ring finger represents your emotional aspects. While emotions often get a bad rap for being touchy-feely, ooey-gooey girly territory, emotions are actually all experiences of fear, joy, anger, and courage. Emotions also extend to the most basic sensations of pleasure and pain, hunger and thirst. And at the basic level, emotions are chemical messengers that network with the brain to create beliefs, expectations, and feelings.

If you think about it, as humans, we are the only species which is able to plan for the future or worry about the past. Because of our intellectual brains and the vast capabilities of our minds, we are able to live in time beyond the present moment. Emotions bring a sense of aliveness to those experiences.

Check in with your emotional side and mark the frequency of each statement.

Emotional	Rarely	Sometimes	Almost Always
I am excited to start my day each morning.	O	O	O
I have hopeful dreams for my future.	O	O	O
I feel good over the course of my day.	O	O	O
I am patient with others around me.	O	O	O
I enjoy my career or occupation.	O	O	O
People would describe me as flexible or easy-going.	O	O	O
I am able to let go of control when things are out of my hands.	O	O	O
I laugh often.	O	O	O
I can easily shift a negative mood to a positive one.	O	O	O
I am confident in my beliefs.	O	O	O

The Social Self: Middle Finger

Your middle finger appropriately corresponds to your social nature. Studies have shown that love and closeness offered by others is essential to the developmental nature of humans. For example, when children in orphanages received proper nutrition, but lacked affection and attention, they withdrew from life, sometimes to the point of autism.

Human interaction is essential to your wellness. Just reflect for a moment on how often you are involved with others. What were your surroundings like growing up? Do you have a family of your own today? Are you part of a book club, board of directors, sorority, fraternity, or community league? Do you join with other dedicated fans and support your local sports team?

Think of the people you spend the most time with daily. Are they demanding or supportive? Do they commonly experience positive or negative emotions? Would you consider others around you to be enjoying life or simply struggling to get through it?

The Importance of Balance

In order to expand your perspective, social balance is essential. Perhaps you are a busy mom—running kids to and from events, making family meals, and in charge of the school's parent-teacher association. Your life is full of social events. In order to bring your social elements into balance, scheduling daily time alone is important. Or, if you work in a solitary environment and live alone, joining a community club will add balance to your social life. Whatever the means, creating harmony in your social spheres contributes to your overall wellness.

How does your social self score with these statements?

Social	Rarely	Sometimes	Almost Always
I enjoy the company of others.	O	O	O
I take time daily for myself.	O	O	O
I have a positive network of supportive friends and/or family.	O	O	O
I like people.	O	O	O
People like me.	O	O	O
I am able to say no without feeling guilty.	O	O	O
My schedule is balanced between family, friends, and work.	O	O	O
I feel at ease going into a room full of strangers.	O	O	O
I am confident talking to others about myself.	O	O	O
I am comfortable listening to others talk about themselves.	O	O	O

The Intellectual Self: Pointer Finger

Your pointer finger symbolizes the intellectual self. You are an intelligent, creative being who enjoys using your imagination to generate the latest inventions, to organize your home, or to provide inspiration to others around you. Humans are innate thinkers. We are capable of transporting people and devices into outer space as well as tapping into the ethereal world of the internet, making global communication almost instantaneous. If you want to see innate creativity at work, just watch small children create a castle from a miscellaneous pile of Legos. Or observe children digging tunnels in the sand and organizing an underwater expedition from their newly-formed beach entrance.

When addressing the intellectual component of your being, the following questions offer insight into your creative health: How do I use my natural intelligence throughout the day? Do I give myself the freedom to create something new, such as painting, writing, or shooting photography? Remember, the goal for creating balance in your life is to open up your multi-faceted being. In relation to your intellectual self, how can you enhance your creativity today?

Intellectual	Rarely	Sometimes	Almost Always
I am a creative person.	O	O	O
I remember things easily.	O	O	O
I have a hobby I enjoy.	O	O	O
I am able to finish projects.	O	O	O
I do research before taking action.	O	O	O
I think for myself.	O	O	O
I am good at solving problems.	O	O	O
I read regularly.	O	O	O
My environment supports my creativity.	O	O	O
I am confident in my beliefs.	O	O	O

The Spiritual Self: The Thumb

Now, moving on to your remaining finger—your thumb—which signifies your spiritual self. While the word "spiritual" has various connotations, it is used here to identify your core values. These guiding principles, such as honesty, integrity or community, create your foundation and play a deciding role in every action you take.

Your thumb is very unique. It is an opposable digit, reaching out to touch the other four fingers on your hand.

Because of this, your thumb is the most important finger on your hand. It represents your free choice as an individual. You have the ability to choose activities and circumstances that support your other four areas of life—the physical, emotional, social, and intellectual areas—or you can make choices to hinder them. These decisions you make, at their core, ultimately reflect the values that you hold sacred.

For example, if you value physical health, you might choose to eat whole foods instead of processed ones. If you value social interaction, you might plan a summer BBQ with your friends to welcome in the warm weather. If you value creativity, you might take an art class or build model cars. If you value feelings of joy, you could plan activities in your daily routine that make you smile, like watching a sunset, playing with your kids, or renting a comedy.

The values that you hold determine the quality of your life and are an influential component of your overall perspective. If you want to boost your spiritual self, or your values, revisit the tools from chapter one.

Spiritual	Rarely	Sometimes	Almost Always
I have clear values and beliefs.	O	O	O
I recognize that I am more than just a physical body.	O	O	O
I am open to miracles.	O	O	O
I don't judge others.	O	O	O
I look at what I can learn from challenging situations.	O	O	O
I know what my values are.	O	O	O
I take responsibility for my actions.	O	O	O
I am able to remain centered and balanced in difficult times.	O	O	O
I trust that there is a Divine Guidance in the Universe.	O	O	O
I am connected to Divinity.	O	O	O

Your Hand Model of Wellness Score

There are ten statements from each aspect of yourself—physical, emotional, social, intellectual, and spiritual. If you have not filled out each segment, go back and mark the frequency each activity or pattern occurs in your life. To get your wellness score, use the following rubric:

Rarely = 0 points

Sometimes = 1 point

Almost always = 2 point

The highest possible score in each category is 20 points, making 100 points a perfect score if you're balanced in all aspects of your being. Total your score from each category below:

Physical: _____ /20 points

Emotional: _____ /20 points

Social: _____ /20 points

Intellectual: _____ /20 points

Spiritual: _____ /20 points

Notice which category had the highest score, indicating where you feel the most balanced. Observe which category had the lowest score, meaning you have room for improvement.

Common Sense Tip: Since you have this new awareness of yourself, you can take action to improve your overall well-being by bolstering weak areas first. Just like the cliché suggests, "we're only as strong as our weakest link."

Therefore, take time to transform any limitations into learning experiences to expand wellness in all areas of your life. It helps to create a limitless perspective of yourself!!

The Hand Model in Action Activity

Reflect on your score from the Hand Model of Wellness Quiz. Here are some practical ideas or activities to help you get started with personal transformation. The options for each category are endless, so we invite you to use your creativity and add to the list we've started here.

Various ways to enhance your well-being include, but are not limited to:

- **Physical Self:** take a walk, get a massage, do yoga, take a dance class, take a nutrition/cooking class, organize your bedroom so it promotes sleep, drink plenty of water, shop at a farmers' market, go to the gym

- **Emotional Self:** incorporate any activity from this book, watch funny movies, browse the humorous card section, send a thoughtful card or letter, practice deep breathing, play with a pet, watch children playing

- **Social Self:** schedule a date with a friend, schedule a date with yourself, help someone in need, donate time to a food kitchen, read to a senior citizen, hold a baby, get a bird feeder and watch the birds feed, join a fun organization, play games with friends

- **Intellectual Self:** draw, paint, listen to inspiring music, create a collage, play mind games like Suduko or crossword puzzles, play Scrabble, organize a flower arrangement, redecorate a room, take a cooking class, go to the theater, write poetry, sing in the shower, learn to play an instrument, find a creative hobby, read a thought-provoking book

- **Spiritual Self:** meditate, pray, take a yoga class, watch the sunset, read a spiritual or uplifting book, create a value wheel, talk with a mentor or spiritual teacher, practice deep breathing

10 Common Sense Ways to Change your Perspective Instantly

Your life experience is based on your focus. Where do you place your attention? What do you notice in the world around you? Do you view people embracing and sharing joyful interactions? Do you observe the deceit between others and end up questioning the honesty and integrity of others?

Common Sense Tip: Part of embracing a limitless perspective in life means changing the way you view your own current experience.

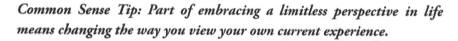

The best way to do this is by altering your level of awareness. Since the self-conscious mind works on a continuum from less aware to more aware, the goal is to enhance your attentiveness. This can easily be done through self-reflection.

The following questions are a powerful way to increase the level of alertness to the positive aspects of your life. By taking the time to think about these questions, it transfers your focus from what's going wrong in your life to what's going right. As you know, it is the positive emotions that give you energy and provide the power to take charge of your life. With feelings of control and purpose, you are able to positively impact the world around you.

These questions are designed to create more happiness, excitement, gratitude, joy, and pride as you move throughout each day. While we recommend that you take time each morning to reflect on these questions, you're not limited to that timeframe. In fact, any free time you have throughout the day can offer you a chance to instantly change your perspective. Any given moment offers the gift of the present, where you can change your perspective from limited to limitless.

The Power of "Could"

While each question holds power in itself, there may be some that are unanswerable. If you have difficulty responding, insert the word "could" into the sentence. For example, if the question asks "What am I most happy about in my life?" you can change it to read: "What in my life *could* I be most happy about?"

This gives the mind an opportunity to imagine. You can borrow from a past feeling, where happiness was a part of your life. No matter how long ago, reach back into your memories to discover what made you smile or what makes you feel proud. If you use your imaginative ability, the power of the subconscious mind stores the idea in the present moment for future recall. The subconscious lives only in the present moment, so imagining it to be true is just as powerful as currently recognizing it as true.

You might have days you wake up entirely void of motivation to get out of bed. Although there need not be another person standing in your way, limiting thoughts or perspectives can hold you back from experiencing positive emotion and feeling powerful to make the most out of each day. By taking a few minutes to think about these questions, you may notice an immediate change in perspective.

The Daily Support Questions

1. What makes me happy?

Consider what brings a smile to your face. It could be listening to great music, watching the stars, or spending time with loved ones. Whether it's a person, situation or experience that makes you happy, explore all of the positive body sensations that arise from your thoughts. Where do you *feel* that happiness in your body? What other emotions arise when thinking of this person, place, or thing?

You might also want to ask yourself, what do I enjoy? The word "enjoy" is broken down to simply "in joy". Life's about lightening up and having fun. So, what experiences create the expansion, sharing, and bliss? When do you notice yourself engulfed by positive emotions? What makes you laugh? In whose company do you find pleasure?

2. What do I appreciate right now?

Feelings of thankfulness and gratitude, which go hand-in-hand with appreciation, can be stirred by thinking of a pet that loves you unconditionally or a friend who is always by your side. When you focus your attention on what you appreciate, you increase your emotional power and invite your heart to work more efficiently.

3. Who do I love?

One of the most effective ways to experience love is by giving of yourself. In our relationships, we are offered the chance to make a difference in the lives of others. How are you helping someone else? How are you bringing joy to the lives of another? Who is on the receiving end of your positive emotions and ability to give?

This doesn't have to be a romantic, familial or deep friendship kind of love, although it often is. Take time to reflect on the deeper meaning of love. Accept someone just as they are and know that they are unique in their life experiences and beliefs.

Kym's story:

For example, Kym's experience of teaching yoga to senior women has allowed her to see that they have lived in different times, locations, and many of them have different world views than her own. Yet, Kym loves them and uses even a 30 minute class to experience connection, sharing, and acceptance.

Pets are often considered part of the family and qualify as someone, rather than something, to be loved.

The giving of love is just one side of the coin, however. The second side is represented by who loves you. Yes, we're all social beings and our wellness is determined by our ability to give *and* receive love. In many cases, it is much easier to give than receive. Just think of how many people you know, perhaps yourself included, who brush off compliments without accepting them. But, by not receiving, you are denying another a chance to give.

In what ways are you allowing yourself to wholeheartedly receive love, compassion, and caring from others? Are you denying another person an opportunity to share love with you? Even something as simple as responding to a compliment or gift from a friend with a genuine "thank you" can go a long way.

4. What in my life brings me spontaneous laughter?

It's a common phrase that "laughter is the best medicine". But why wait until you are sick, stressed, or drained of energy to bring in this powerful life changer? Laughter boosts the immune system, reduces blood pressure, and increases the level of endorphins in the body. So, consider what people, places and things make your mouth smile and your heart laugh? It might be watching a child skipping across the street or a clever and humorous commercial on TV.

Notice what experiences around you are causing unprompted, natural laughter in your life.

5.   What am I excited about right now?

Excitement is considered to be a state of arousal, when your mind and body are activated in conjunction with a positive emotion, such as enthusiasm or creativity. Is there an idea that makes you excited? Is it something already accomplished? Is it potential for the future? Is it connection with another person, perhaps a budding love or new friendship? Explain all aspects of your excitement and connect it to your physical body. Where do you feel your excitement?

6.   How am I demonstrating generosity?

Oftentimes the focus of many people is "What can I get from a situation or relationship?" This question focuses, instead, on how you give of your natural gifts, abilities, and charitable heart. How are you helpful to those you work with? How does your attitude rub off on those around you? Even a smile or genuine "How are you?" to the local clerk can be huge gift.

Steve's Story:

Steve had a meaningful experience of giving one evening after a particularly good day in the office. Since he knew he had to stop by the grocery store at 5 pm before going home, and that particular hour is usually full of frustrated and tired individuals, he made a conscious effort to smile and make eye contact with those he encountered in the busy aisles.

Just as he walked outside of the market, his gaze connected with a homeless girl waiting outside. She asked to speak with him for a minute. When he obliged, she went on to say she'd been feeling very depressed lately and even thought of committing suicide. In fact, she said he was the first person to have smiled at her in a long time.

Their momentary contact turned into a 30 minute conversation that left both feeling uplifted when they parted ways. The significant impact of heartfelt giving was a way that blessed both lives.

7.   What am I learning right now?

This question goes beyond learning a certain skill, such as playing the guitar or speaking a foreign language. While these actions can offer a boost to your Energy Bank Account, the goal here is to consider what larger life lessons you are currently learning. Days can often be filled with stressful encounters. We might get frustrated with other people, get angry too quickly, or say an impolite word in a reactionary moment.

Instead of brushing off such encounters, how can you learn from your own responses? How can you change your behavior next time? Can you look to your interactions and see where you could have done something different? Replay any situation in your mind with your new awareness and notice a difference in how you feel when rectifying the encounter. What did that situation teach you? What is your lesson in the experience?

8.   How am I investing in my future?

The choices we make and the actions we take today inevitably affect the outcomes we experience tomorrow. Oftentimes we view our current experiences as obligations, and use words like "I have to go here" or "I need to do this". These phrases reflect an emotion of limitation, leaving you no choice in the matter or with a sense of powerlessness.

In order to step back into your power, utilize the present moment as an opportunity to invest in your own future. This can be done by acknowledging your commitments via a new perspective. It involves taking responsibility for yourself and your actions. It reflects your ability to make a decision, have integrity behind your action, and follow through according to your word. By looking at a situation or relationship as an opportunity to be committed or dedicated, instead of feeling obligated to it, your perspective shifts.

By changing the way you look at a situation, a relationship or circumstance can move from an energy drain to an energy boost. It is just the way you perceive it. While you may think talking yourself into something is enough, you now understand that your mind has two parts. If your conscious mind is saying "I can keep this commitment" and your body is simultaneously tightening up, then you're actually experiencing internal chaos. It is as though your mouth says "yes" and your gut says "no". This leads to more stress.

Our goal for you is to reduce anxiety and unwanted tension. With the tools in this book, you can align your body with your mind and your gut with your mouth. Now, taking on your commitments with joyful responsibility versus dreaded obligation adds deposits to your life Energy Bank Account.

9.   Is there someone I need to forgive, including myself?

All of the great spiritual teachers throughout time have shared a similar message in that true healing is possible through forgiveness. By putting the past behind, and learning from the experience, you repair wounds so they can no longer hurt you.

Forgiveness also helps connect us to a higher power, knowing that all things happen for a reason. And, it is in that surrender, in that healing of the heart, all fear can be removed.

10. If I could improve on my life today, what would I do first?

There is always room for personal improvement and taking powerful steps to move into that growth demonstrates courage and strength. Yet, this also requires some simple, practical application of what you're capable of accomplishing today that will help you move towards your goals. Sometimes it is easier to look at the big picture and lose sight of what daily steps help you reach the end result. By confidently taking charge of your life with positive action, you are well on your way to achieving your dreams.

The Daily Support Questions Activity

Take time to answer these questions for yourself and reflect on the many positive aspects of your life that contribute to a limitless perspective.

Part of the fun is being as specific as possible. While it might be easier to say that "I appreciate my family" or "I am excited about a new project", try to be creative and detailed in your answers to the daily support questions. What aspect of your family are you grateful for? Do they provide a safe place to be open and honest? Perhaps you appreciate your daughter's thoughtfulness for drawing you a picture at school? If your new work project is providing new excitement, is it because you get to work with new people, or is your creative ingenuity able to be expressed in a new way? That project could even offer you the possibility to prove yourself at work, or it could even be a home hobby project that gives you much-needed time alone.

1. What makes me happy?
2. What do I appreciate right now?
3. Who do I love?
4. What in my life brings me spontaneous laughter?
5. What am I excited about right now?
6. How am I demonstrating generosity?
7. What am I learning right now?
8. How am I investing in my future?

9. Is there someone I need to forgive, including myself?

10. If I could improve on my life today, what would I do first?

I AM Able to Reach My Goals

Numerous studies have shown that by setting goals throughout life increase the chances of achieving your dreams. Whatever your goal may be—to lose weight, to find an intimate partner, or to move forward in your career—specifically outlining your destination can make the journey much more enjoyable and understandable along the way.

Think about how many times you go through your day deciphering likes and dislikes from the environment around you. For example, when driving down the road, you notice other cars you admire or when walking down the street, you observe clothing styles that peak your interest. You like the sunshine. You hate the rain. You enjoy the smell of fresh-roasting coffee. You loathe the taste of cream cheese. Sunflower yellow—yes. Olive green—no.

And, so it goes. The thoughts in your mind spark far more rapidly than your words, and without even speaking, you are categorizing your world into pros and cons, likes and dislikes.

While this may seem rather ordinary for daily life—and a beautiful aspect of your creative self—it often distracts the mind from what you really want. When living with a limited perspective, there is often confusion at the level of the subconscious. It could be as simple as deciphering between three tempting items on the local lunch menu or as complex as two conflicting beliefs about wanting to live or die.

In order to move into a limitless perspective where you have control and power to move forward into the life of your dreams, it is essential to clarify the goals you have for yourself. The following exercise will enhance your creative abilities by deepening your understanding of the creative process itself. And with that greater perception, you can then utilize this powerful practice to make your dreams a reality.

I AM: The Process of Creating

Look at the words "I AM" for just a moment. What comes to mind? You are, in fact, a multi-faceted being and the words "I AM" often describe your current status, emotional state, or character.

Make a list of your "I AMs" here:

Example: I am a mother.

Example: I am an artist, lover,…

_____

_____

_____

_____

_____

Many responses might naturally want to define your position: I am a teacher. I am a mom. I am an architect. I am a son. Perhaps your description covered your current mood: I am tired. I am enthusiastic. I am distracted. Or, you might have categorized your being on a broader level: I am compassionate. I am thoughtful.

While the subconscious mind stores these first-person statements as beliefs about the current environment, there are ways to use the "I AM" to broaden your perspective. Our "I AM" model is actually an acronym for:

I = Intention

A = Alignment

M = Manifestation

When you learn how to use these words and concepts to expand your state of being, you create a life with less stress, more passion, and clearer direction.

Intention

Many of you are familiar with the word "intention", which is synonymous for the word "goal". If it's an uncommon idea, then this portion of the "I AM" will offer you a valid introduction to the concept.

Intention is the organizing principle behind creativity. It is a trust that your desires will be fulfilled and that there are numerous forces around you working to support your goals. While the common misconception is that having intentions requires action on your part, they're actually created without any effort at all. Just like we said before, they might simply be thoughts about what you want and observations about what you like and dislike.

Essentially, those immediate thoughts send off messages to your body and your environment about how you would like things to be. Your thoughts, conscious or subconscious, are reflecting your ideals or desires and are broadcasting them to the world. It's what the spiritual teacher, Abraham-Hicks, calls "rockets of desire". Individual ideas are usually connected to other thoughts, and sometimes can send conflicting messages to the body. Thus, it's important to put focus and clarity to your thoughts—moving into a limitless space by concentrating on what you do want rather than what you prefer to avoid.

Intention is a natural force of the cosmos that helps align all of the messages being sent out into the universe daily. In fact, intention is a lot like the atmosphere—while you might not be able to see it, you know it is always there working on your behalf.

Common Sense Tip: In addition to intention as a natural part of life, it can also be used as a powerful tool to hone your focus, ideas, and desires to create a specific result.

When used as a technique for change, intention allows you to purposefully connect to the world around you. You can have the confidence to know that when you send a signal out into the world, it is the most influential and prevailing thought about the end goal you have in mind for yourself.

This directed intention is more than wishing on a shooting star. It is very specific. You have now aimed directly at an outcome, yet still have the flexibility and openness to receive that future gift in whatever way it comes into your life. The more specific you are the better, just as you used precision to draw forth a new perspective in the daily support questions.

What's your Frequency?

Without having purposeful or mindful intentions, it is like broadcasting a radio station with static. Even worse, it's like picking up on two frequencies or radio stations at once. Consider that you are holding a radio in your hands and you're picking up on conflicting frequencies. You notice the static and just want to get back to the music you were listening to before the interruption. The old methods of solving the problem would involve taking the radio with you to various parts of the room to get a clear signal.

Liken this to a goal you have to reduce your stress. You notice that the conflicting items on your daily agenda, which cause your heartbeat to race and your breath to become short, are diminishing your ability to concentrate. You try to "move" yourself around to stop the confusion. For example, you may try eating differently or cutting down on your assignments. You are looking for ways outside of yourself to solve the problem.

The good news is that there's an easier way to return back to the radio station. Instead of having to move yourself—trying all sorts of gadgets, devices, and 12-step programs—to make you feel sane again, you can now have the ability to tune the radio dial with your own level of focus. It's using your internal alignment to set your own station. You can harness the power of your intentions, creating clarity from within that is so strong that no other station, or distraction, can interfere with your forward progress.

But what about unexpected circumstances? Will everything work in my favor now without any challenges or setbacks?

While desire alludes to a sense of attachment to outcomes, intention lets go of the need to know what happens in the outcome. You might encounter some people or situations that seem to counter your overall goal. However, your heightened sense of awareness and purpose guides you from within. From that inner wisdom, you are able to perceive such a circumstance or individual in the bigger picture and learn from the experience to help you reach your goal.

By detaching yourself from a need to know how your goals will be accomplished, you open up to the freedom and surprising gifts that can accompany your initial idea as it unfolds. Intention has no clinginess whatsoever. Intention trusts the cosmic forces, like the atmosphere, which are constantly responding to the thought signals being sent out by your mind. Attaching to the outcome is limited, while trusting that the outcome will be even better than you pictured is unlimited.

Alignment

Alignment refers to a particular arrangement or configuration which can support a limited or unlimited viewpoint. For example, when your skeletal frame is in alignment, your bones stack purposefully atop one another to provide you with a strong, upright posture. Or, when your car tires are in alignment, the car runs smoothly, it gets better gas mileage, and the tires wear evenly.

Conversely, when one vertebrae of the spine is out of alignment, it can make moving difficult, your extremities might suffer or lose feeling, and your entire posture can deteriorate. This goes for the car tires as well. When they are not positioned correctly with the axle and car frame, the tires begin to wear unevenly; the car ride might become rough, and the gas mileage of the vehicle decreases.

Your mind—just like your body and your car's tires—is able to function at an optimal level when it's in alignment with your goals.

Alignment in Action: Betty's Story

Let's say Betty set a goal to retire in the next five years. She has her dream home picked out in a warmer climate. She and her spouse have invested wisely to take care of unexpected costs in their golden years. And she looks forward to dedicating more time to follow her hobbies, take more vacations, and volunteer in the community.

So, let's say it is your intention to retire. It is necessary to check in with what you believe—in your conscious and subconscious minds—and see if those ideas are in alignment with that goal. When your beliefs support that outcome, it will be much easier for you to effortlessly step into retirement. Yet, there could be beliefs that counter your dream. For example, you might worry about the unstable economy and fret about working more years to receive your pension. Perhaps you even vacillate on what you'll do with so much time on your hands.

When you hold limiting beliefs, it keeps you out of the position to receive your goals. Your intentions will keep springing forth, due to your naturally-creative self, but any perspectives that take away your personal power will make it much more challenging for those intentions to come to fruition. When your mind's programs are full of limitless beliefs, anything is possible.

More importantly, the power of your self-conscious mind can create specific ideas and actions that support your intention.

Let's go back to Betty and early retirement. Betty can line up her beliefs to match her goal, *and* she can use her daily attention to influence the outcome. If she has a particular place in mind where she'd like to move, she can cut out pictures of that location and place them on the refrigerator. She can talk with her husband about the finances and feel included in their investment decisions. Betty could even look up local community service organizations and churches she might want to be a part of when she relocates.

It's not only alignment of the beliefs, but the joyful and inspired attention.

By taking time to check in with what you believe, learning how to align your beliefs to match your goals, and creating a laser-focused attention on what you desire, you can achieve success in a graceful and purposeful way.

Manifestation

Manifestation is a fancy way of explaining the receiving part of the creating process. It's as though you've given your ideas and attention to God or the Universe, which takes care of the "I" and "A" part of the creating process. Now, through manifestation, you're ready to receive the results in a physical form.

Think of the last time someone gave you a gift. Did you thank them upon receiving it? When were you last paid a compliment by a co-worker, friend, or stranger? How did you respond? Did you shrug it off or did you genuinely take it to heart?

Your responses to these questions reflect on your attitude towards receiving. It's in your best interest to be a poised and authentic recipient. Therefore, you want to cultivate the same attitude towards receiving, and achieving, your life goals and dreams.

Manifestation is the materialization of your dreams. It is seeing your intentions become a reality. It's an expression from the Universe that it has heard your request and was pleased to respond.

Common Sense Tip: While your dreams might not show up like Publisher's Clearing House, with a larger-than-life check on your doorstep, they are often actualized in far better ways than you expected

Remember, that by setting an intention, you happily let go of the need to know how your goals come about. You can align your beliefs and focus your attention on your dreams; trusting the process of how and when it arrives.

The exciting part of the manifestation component of the "I AM" process is that you are able to celebrate! The subconscious mind loves reinforcement. It is as though you're giving yourself a pat on the back for a job well done. When you use your self-conscious ability to reflect on the process and journey toward your destination, you can fully appreciate the power and value of the present moment.

The "I AM" Activity

For the I AM—Intention, Alignment, and Manifestation—process of creating to be effective, it is essential to keep your intention at the forefront of your thoughts. This is why joyful attention is so important. When you know you are going to receive what you intended in the first place, good feelings help carry you through the process to completion.

Yet, if those beliefs—the ones that initiated your intention in the first place—get stored in an under-utilized region of the subconscious, they are less of a priority to come forth into manifestation. One of the best ways to keep your focused, positive attention on your goals is to have a group of people hold your vision with you. It is creating your own support team. Because every person has unique strengths, you're going to utilize the talents and wisdom of others to help you when you feel weak or simply need some encouragement.

Directions:

The goal of this activity is to create three categories of people who can stand by your intention and keep you moving forward with unlimited potential.

Step 1: Discover who you know.

- **Who do I know that is analytical?**

  The purpose of finding people with intellectual strengths is to utilize their capability to look at situations logically. They can offer sage advice based on sound judgment and can offer solutions to your ideas based on common sense. Note that someone who is analytical is not necessarily critical. However, they do offer a realistic viewpoint that can help clarify and modify your goal as you move forward.

- **Who do I know that is emotionally balanced?**

  A person with emotional strength is very considerate of your feelings and knows how to give you advice from a heart-centered perspective. They can offer solutions based on how they have felt in past situations and how they have had successes of their own in a similar realm.

- **Who do I know that is value driven?**

  The value-driven individual is someone who has a strong moral compass. They are not overly emotional or overly analytical. Because they are sound in what principles guide their life, and also know your most important values, they will be able to check your future goals and actions with your time-tested character.

Step 2: Before you put your support team together, it is important to establish your primary goal. Ask yourself the following questions:

- What do I want?
- What will I see when I get there?
- What people are around me when I accomplish this goal?
- How do I look and feel?
- When do I want this to happen?

Step 3: Now, let's take action and have you find three people, one in each category, who are willing to help you reach that specific goal.

Remember that you might have different intentions that could require guidance from different people. For example, if your goal is to strengthen and tone your body, your support team might include a nutritionist (analytical), a life coach (emotional), and your best friend (value driven). Or, if you are trying to start a new business, your team could be comprised of another local business owner (analytical), a trusted friend (emotional), and your pastor (value driven).

Write the names of those who come to mind in each category.

- Find someone analytical: _____
- Find someone emotional: _____
- Find someone value driven: _____

You can narrow down your options, and then contact them with your purpose, goal, and plan of action to move forward. Ask for their input or request that they be available when you need guidance along your journey.

Putting it all Together

Beliefs are powerful. They have been formulated since your early childhood years, but are flexible to be changed throughout your entire life. These beliefs fall into two main categories—limited and limitless. Feelings of powerlessness, negativity, and stress are associated with limited beliefs and feelings of confidence, enthusiasm, and potential accompany limitless ones.

New Common Sense Tools to Create a Limitless Perspective:

- **The Hand Model of Wellness:** This Common Sense Tool is designed to expand your perspective about your own wellbeing by looking at your physical, emotional, social, intellectual, and spiritual characteristics. The goal is to remain in balance. By keeping track of your wellbeing, you can discover and alleviate imbalances in your life.

- **The Daily Support Questions:** These powerful questions help you focus on the positive aspects of your life through the act of reflection. Generate more love, joy, pride, and excitement through this great exercise.

- **"I AM" Support Team:** The "I AM", which stands for Intention, Alignment, and Manifestation, is a tool to help you reach your goals. This specific activity involves creating a support team of analytical, emotional, and value-driven people to make the journey towards your goals more enjoyable and successful.

Chapter 3

Chapter **3**

Honor Your Voice

"Be who you are and say what you feel because those who mind don't matter and those who matter don't mind." —*Dr. Seuss*

In this Chapter

- Become an assertive communicator
- Learn to re-write negative self-talk
- Utilize the Common Sense Quadrants of Communication
- Generate direct, positive dialogue
- Incorporate the senses into speech

When surveying individuals over the past six months, those who are single and those in a committed relationship, we found the majority of people wanted to know how to communicate kindly, honestly, and effectively with others. The ability to speak in your authentic and unique voice is truly a common-sense skill, not an inborn trait, which we will discuss in this chapter.

We call it becoming an assertive communicator.

The word "assertive" has many meanings, including confident, self-assured, and forward. But it can also describe those who are pushy and aggressive. We are using the term "assertive communication" to define the delicate balance between being too passive with others, where you feel unheard, and the other end of the spectrum when you're acting aggressively to get your point across. With self-responsibility, which is at the foundation of communicating with yourself and others, we can have you move through your speech with clarity, poise, and meaning. When you become assertive in your communication, self-esteem increases. You'll also be able to remain aligned with your values, on track with your goals, and add deposits to your personal Energy Bank Account.

Before we dive into the concepts of being, or becoming, an assertive communicator, take the following quiz to see how you score at this moment.

Common Sense Assertive Communication Quiz

Directions: Read the following statements. Mark the appropriate frequency each statement occurs for you on a regular basis.

Intellectual	Rarely	Sometimes	Almost Always
I recognize my rights and stand up for them in conversations.	O	O	O
I accept challenges with an open mind.	O	O	O
I learn from my mistakes and use them as opportunities for growth.	O	O	O
I take responsibility for my own thoughts, feelings, and actions.	O	O	O
I am free to change my mind.	O	O	O
It is easy to change my attitude and behavior.	O	O	O
It is easy for me to admit that I don't know something.	O	O	O
I am able to say "I don't agree" in a conversation.	O	O	O
I am able to receive and offer respect.	O	O	O
I use openness and honesty as a way to respect others.	O	O	O
I accept when I am tired just as easily as when I'm energized.	O	O	O
I am able to say "no" without feeling guilty.	O	O	O
I deserve to be listened to and taken seriously.	O	O	O

Others do listen to me and take me seriously.	O	O	O
I am able to ask for what I want.	O	O	O
I understand when others refuse my request.	O	O	O
I have a high self-esteem.	O	O	O
I carry myself with poise.	O	O	O
I take responsibility for my feelings.	O	O	O
I am able to receive constructive criticism without becoming defensive.	O	O	O

Getting your Score: Notice how many times each answer was marked and attribute the appropriate point value to each response.

Rarely = 0 points

Sometimes = 1 point

Almost always = 2 point

Now total your score below:

Total Score: _____

The Results:

0-15: Change is knocking at your door. While you may spend many hours a day communicating with others, you're often writing checks against your own energy account. In this chapter, you'll learn how to enhance your body language, speaking skills, and transform your internal dialogue._Learn to boost your confidence and balance your energy account by utilizing the tools provided here.

16-29: Room for improvement. You're doing well so far. For the most part, you communicate your ideas with clarity and hold yourself with confidence. Now, it's time to shore up any weaknesses in sharing openly and honestly with others via the valuable communication techniques taught in this section.

30-40: Keep up the good work. Congratulations! Your skills as an assertive communicator help you successfully get your point across most of the time. By speaking kindly and clearly, you receive an energy boost when you interact with others. Continue on the path of effective communication and allow any of the suggested tools in this chapter to further enhance your skill set.

So, how'd you do on the quiz? Was your score what you anticipated? Did you have any new insights or ideas about yourself based on how you answered the questions?

If you were honest with yourself, and we hope you were, you now have a basic assessment for how often you honor your voice. It is essential to understand where you are right now, so that you can verify where any weaknesses or breakdowns may occur in your communication. You will also be able to know exactly how, and with whom, to utilize some of the great techniques shared in this chapter.

Over the next several pages, we will discuss ten components of assertive communication. You'll learn how to:

- Understand the process of communication
- Express yourself with honesty
- Take self-responsibility for your messages
- Articulate your point directly and positively
- Enhance the relationship with yourself and others
- Respect the rights of others
- Convey verbal content of your message with clarity
- Transmit composed non-verbal messages
- Create situation and person-specific dialogue
- Utilize your senses in the communication process

While communication is a necessary part of life, it's also an easily overlooked component when assessing your current stress levels. You may notice the arguments that take place with a loved one or the times it's challenging for you to say "no". When was the last time you actually broke down the process of communication to increase your understanding? When did you last notice what component of your interactions were actually collapsing? By looking at the following diagram, and understanding where you currently stand in your assertive communication skills, you'll know exactly how to move forward with common sense.

The Common Sense Communication Process

1) The Speaker decides to send a message.

2) The Speaker encodes the message.

3) The Speaker decides *how* to send the message.

4) The Listener eternalizes the message.

5) The Listener chooses if/how to respond.

We'll approach the process of communication from your point of view.

1.   The speaker decides to send a message.

In any given situation, you have a foundation of beliefs, attitudes, and values that are determining the quality of your thoughts. You might be feeling free and joyful about something, in which case you have an unlimited perspective. Or perhaps you are stressed and angry, where limited ideas have blocked your ability to move forward with clarity.

In either case, you have made the decision to send a message about something. Oftentimes, these messages just remain in the space of your own mind. It is what's known as interpersonal communication. You have the ongoing stream of thoughts that tell you what to do, how to be, reflect on your past behavior, or categorize the vast amount of stimuli coming your direction every second. At other times, the decision is made to share that information with someone else.

2.   The speaker encodes the message.

You draw from your massive subconscious file cabinet of ideas and beliefs to formulate a meaningful way to get your point across. This part of encoding also includes how you perceive the receiver of the message, as well as the situation as a whole.

3.   The speaker decides how to send the message.

This component is actually two-fold. Some aspects of sending the message include body language, tonal inflections, and actual spoken words. Another aspect of sending the message refers to the vehicle of the message itself. For example, you could choose to share your ideas in person with another or you could call them on the phone. Often a letter, email, or text is necessary. The ways to send messages are endless with the highly-effective technology we have today. However, the channel you use to communicate your idea is very important.

4.   The listener internalizes the message.

Their subconscious mind is busy assessing their own memory bank for what information is relevant to your message. They are processing your use of grammar, phonetics, and the meaning of the words themselves. In addition, their subconscious is framing your message in context and making inferences about what is being said. In essence, they are filtering your information through their own beliefs, ideas and attitudes, based on their own past experiences. And their world view, whether limited or unlimited, will drastically affect how they decide to act upon your message.

5.   The listener chooses if/how to respond.

Common Sense Tools to help in responsible listening and responding are covered in Chapter 4.

Becoming an assertive communicator involves the first half of the communication process. By now, you have begun to look at what beliefs and values you hold about the world around you. And it is through your heightened awareness of yourself and your perspectives that can help you enhance your skills as an effective communicator.

Mastering the skills of listening, and managing emotions in response to others, involves the latter half of the process. Those skills will be covered in Chapter 4.

The Most Important Relationship— the One with Yourself

Effective communication begins with the most important relationship you have—that's the one with yourself. By your wonderful nature as a creative and evolving being, you are constantly taking in information from your environment and organizing it in a way that makes sense—hopefully, common sense. Essentially, you are either matching your incoming stimuli with your pre-recorded beliefs or noticing a chasm between them.

In almost a reflexive nature, you notice that those subconscious beliefs rise to the surface of your mind and become self-conscious thoughts.

Common Sense Tip: One of the best ways to become an assertive communicator is to do so with you first.

Before you send messages to others, you're continually sharing messages with yourself. And, those thoughts can either support a limited perspective on life or an unlimited, free viewpoint.

When your thoughts are peppered with words such as should, need, must and want, then you're actually holding yourself back. We call this regret language. You might even recognize some of these phrases that replay in your mind:

- I shouldn't worry so much.

- I must get this project in before the deadline.

- I hope my back pain doesn't flare up again.

- I have to invite (fill in the blank) to our party.

- I need to take a vacation now!

- I could have done better.

When the language of your internal dialogue uses words such as *wish, must, have, should* and *could have*, your subconscious mind views them as restrictive. These thoughts give your power to the past, which cannot be changed. Or, these thoughts put limitations on your future. It takes your power away from the present moment and puts it into the past or the future.

In either case, your subconscious mind believes that what you desire is not yours and is therefore unattainable. It creates an internal resistance before you even begin to take action towards your

> "Make yourself so happy, that by looking at you, other people become happy."
> —Yogi Bhajan

goals. This is when your two minds begin to battle—your self-conscious mind goes into willpower to get the job done and your subconscious mind has the pre-recorded belief that you cannot succeed.

If you recall, the subconscious mind is a million times more powerful than the self-conscious. So, you know which one runs the show.

Rewrite your Internal Dialogue

In order to change your regrets into a language that supports your goals, it is essential to re-write your self-talk in a way that your subconscious mind understands. While regrets place your power in the past or future, statements phrased in first-person, present tense bring your power back to the present moment. And, that's the overall goal—to place the strength and control in your hands so that you can choose the next step for yourself.

Since words precede actions, it is essential to have your thoughts—or internal dialogue—enhance your power, boost your confidence, and increase your level of self-trust.

The easiest way to do this is to rewrite your own messages. This is the first step in transforming your perspective from limited to limitless. In the process, it aligns your beliefs with your intentions. If you recall, that's an intricate part of turning your dreams into realities.

So, what phrases does the subconscious mind understand?

Use the following guidelines to create new supportive self-talk:

1. Speak in First Person

Simply put, speaking in the first person directly refers to the speaker himself, using words such as I, me, and mine. It is very common in everyday language to shift focus away from ourselves. When we do this, we subconsciously give our power away to outside forces.

Some examples of first-person, present tense sentences are:

I am doing the best I can.

Choices *I* make today support *my* goals.

I have all the tools I need to relax right now.

2. Use Present Tense

Now you might wince, thinking we're going to have an English lesson. Technically, the tenses we're talking about apply to the way verbs are conjugated. When we speak in past tense or speculate about the future, we allow those times to have more influence over our lives.

However, the past is like a cancelled check and the future is a promissory note. Therefore, we want to speak in the present moment. Using present-tense verbs return your focus to right now.

Instead of "I will take action, which is future tense, you say "I take action with confidence **now**."

Instead of "I should have done better", which focuses on your past, switch your actions to the moment of now by saying, "**Right now**, I am doing the best I can."

3. State Things Positively

This keeps your focus on what you do want rather than what you want to avoid. This aspect of rewriting your internal dialogue centers around the most positive aspect of what you are creating.

Change the phrase "I am good at creating." to "I am a great and powerful creator."

4. Be Succinct

The goal is to be brief and concise with your ideas. The subconscious is fundamental, understanding basic concepts and clear ideas.

Often, our regular dialogue is full of complex, intertwined thoughts. This activity asks you to simplify those thoughts into exact phrases. Instead of a run-on sentence that contains numerous ideas, separate them into smaller, succinct ones. Take your newly-formed positive thoughts and simplify them.

For example, "I have all the tools I need to relax and calm down and be able to think clearly as I make decisions." Instead, you can split this idea into two sentences. "I have the tools to relax and calm down." and "I make decisions with clarity."

5. Fill your Statements with Meaning

The goal is to fill your statements with as much energy and passion as possible. While it's easy to say that "I am ready to start my day." it has more power to say that "I am excited and ready to start my day."

By adding positive emotions to your statements, you're inviting meaning and purpose to infuse your words. Naturally, all parts of your body, including every cell, also benefit from the enhanced energy in the well-formed belief.

The Common Sense 21-Day Plan Activity

While it might be easy to change your internal dialogue on paper, it's putting these beliefs into action that makes all of the difference. That's why we created the 21-day plan to guide you through simple steps to construct new ways of talking to yourself.

Step 1: Write down energy-draining statements or feelings

In the morning or evening, preferably in a quiet place, write down three negative statements you notice in your internal dialogue. They can be regrets, problems, or complaints. Write one concise sentence for each issue and be as honest as possible. For example, we'll use some of the sentences mentioned previously.

- I am so tired.

- I must get this project done by the deadline.

- I need to take a vacation now.

Step 2: Cross out the negative words and replace them with positive ones

Now, the goal is to return the verbs to the present tense, so that your subconscious can relate. We also want to take out any negative parts of the sentence and replace them with positive counterparts.

- "I am so (tired)" becomes "I am so exhilarated"

- "I (must) get this project done by the deadline" changes to "I am able to get this project done by the deadline"

- "I (need) to take a vacation now" transforms to "I have a vacation in mind right now"

While you might not believe these new statements, they serve as the ideal beliefs to hold in the mind that can create actions to support your dreams.

Following steps one and two have increased your awareness about your internal dialogue. When a thought crosses your mind, in the form of a regret, it will stand out to you. Based on your newly-formed insight, you have the choice to take action or not. Either way is okay. However, if you decide to take action, you know how to transform your dialogue into positive self-talk.

Steps 1 and 2 are very effective ways of creating awareness about your internal dialogue. It helps you notice negative thoughts and change them to positive ones. Just taking these steps will begin to change your perspective from limited to limitless.

Yet, if you want to go a step further and incorporate the new belief at the level of the subconscious mind, move on to step 3.

Step 3: Rewrite your new belief into the subconscious mind

Choose one of your newly-formed positive statements. Sit in a brain integration posture (shown in the figure above), which is a position that creates a whole-brain state. The whole-brain state, which is discussed in detail in Chapter 4, increases your self-programming flexibility. By using the brain integration posture, you are allowing both hemispheres of the brain to be activated. In this state, they are open to receive new information as well.

By combining a supportive belief statement with this body position, you program the new belief into your subconscious mind, creating a balance for that statement in both brain hemispheres. This creates a strong foundation of supporting beliefs for your mind, which will impact your actions and habits of the body.

Once in this position, close your eyes, and repeat the new sentence to yourself until you feel a shift in the resistance to the statement. This usually takes only two to five minutes.

Once you are tired of saying the phrase to yourself, open your eyes and uncross your limbs. This can be repeated with all of the statements you have written.

Step 4: Create a plan of action

As we explained earlier, beliefs held in the subconscious mind are the programs that often dictate your actions. With your new awareness, and freshly rewritten statements, it is beneficial to make the choice to put those ideas into motion. This step is how the self-conscious mind reinforces the subconscious. You are powerful and your thoughts in the present moment provide the back-up support you need to move forward.

Reflect on your statements and think of something simple and joyful that you could incorporate into your daily routine that would reflect your new insights.

For example, if the statement is "I am so exhilarated," then you could take a few deep breaths at your office that could boost your energy.

If your sentence was "I am able to get this project done by the deadline," then you could choose one aspect of the project to tackle at the moment. It might be that you create a list of priorities necessary to accomplish for the project, and you can choose one of the easiest to tackle first. You could also look at the requirements for the project and decide which component would be most effective to work with in the timeframe available to you at the moment.

***Common Sense Tip:** The whole purpose of creating an action plan around your newly-acquired perspective, or beliefs, is to allow your self-conscious mind to reinforce the subconscious one.*

The best way to do this is through celebration! When you change your perspective around the project, you might be able to experience some enjoyment instead of resentment. Yes, work deadlines are necessary. But they can be done with less stress along the way.

If you chose the third sentence, "I have a vacation in mind right now," it's what we often call a "staycation". You can find relaxation by looking at travel logs or pictures of beautiful beaches. Invoking your imagination, such as picturing yourself drinking hot chocolate at a ski resort after a long day on the mountain, can brighten your spirits. Even recalling pleasant memories from your past can have many of the same physiological effects as actually experiencing the sensations firsthand.

Your own daily routine could also be looked upon with vacationing eyes. You know, the kind of eyes that sense excitement in each small and unique event that fills your day. Maybe you take a walk around your block and notice the birds singing, the clouds moving across the sky, or the leaves changing colors with the season. Just like when you spend time in a new location, you have senses that appreciate the newness at your fingertips. You can do the same thing in your current schedule. It is just changing the perspective…from limited to unlimited.

Now, what does the 21 days have to do with it?

Consider what could happen if you talked nicer to yourself for the next three weeks. Not only are you creating a new habit with a new level of awareness that supports you, but you're also laying the foundation of new neural networks in the brain. You are using the power of your subconscious mind to support your goals and aligning your internal beliefs with the daily actions you choose to take. By transforming your internal dialogue into positive self-talk, you become an assertive communicator from the inside out. You enhance your relationship with yourself, which can then support the relationships you have with others.

The Four Common Sense Quadrants of Communication

While the 21-Day Plan teaches you how to speak with straightforward and supportive dialogue internally, the four quadrants of communication demonstrate how to move into direct, positive communication with others. In addition, this model offers a guide map on how to decipher what kind of language is being used by others in conversations. When you are able to assess how others speak, you will be more prepared to use terminology they understand and move the conversation into a direction that is best for all concerned. **This chapter focuses on how to speak with direct positive communication and Chapter 4 addresses how to listen using the four quadrants.**

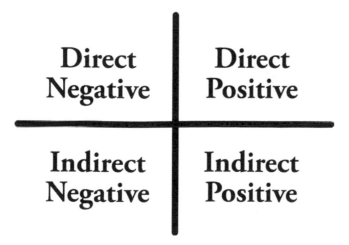

Before we explore the direct positive quadrant of communication, which is the goal for an assertive speaker, let's take a look at what kinds of dialogue reside in the other three sections.

Indirect Negative: This lower left quadrant is defined by language that is unenthusiastic, unhelpful, and often pessimistic. While the words may be downbeat, they are often structured in a way that is unclear. Phrases such as "I think," "like," or "maybe" can be confusing. Similarly, generalized statements can leave the listener feeling unsure about the meaning behind the speaker's words. Thanks to other hints, such as tone and vocal inflections, it can often be very clear that there's a negative spin on the message.

A great example of an indirect communicator is a mother who tries to make everyone else feel guilty when things don't go her way. She blames her husband for her inability to take action, or she complains about how her life is miserable without her kids here for holiday meals. While she goes on and on about the wrongdoings done to her by her absent children, she is draining her own Energy Bank Account with her agitation, and she sets a tone when those listening to her often take a defensive position.

If a friend was listening to her, she might view her as negative or unloving. Acquaintances might choose not to be around her, as they notice her cup is always half empty rather than half full. Because most of us have an aversion to people, places, and things that make us uncomfortable, the subconscious sets up a block to move away from those types of individuals.

When using negative language, it drains the energy of the speaker and can potentially drain that of the listener if they are unable to maintain a neutral position.

Consider the following indirect negative comments:

- I am so stressed out and overwhelmed.
- Everything I seem to do always turns out wrong.
- I just don't know why I can't get anything right.
- I hate it when people are always trying to get me to buy something.

Direct Negative: The upper left square is similar to the indirect negative quadrant in the fact that it's harmful and off-putting speech. Yet, instead of speaking around the point, the message is clear and straightforward, and these messages can be directed towards any person, place, or thing.

When you direct negative language toward a person, it causes the listener to take a defensive or protective posture. This often leads to an argument or a fight. And, because these types of phrases can be so hurtful, they can destroy a longstanding friendship.

Each of these statements is an example of direct negative communication:

- I hate you.
- You're not a good writer.
- You are a poor manager of money.
- This rain is making me depressed.
- You drive me crazy when you tap your fingers on the desk.

Indirect Positive: When speaking in indirect positive language, words are constructive, upbeat, and encouraging. However, they can be spoken in an unclear and roundabout fashion. The meaning behind the dialogue is often supportive, but it can leave the listener unsure about the content or purpose of the message. It might also make you unsure if the speaker is making a specific request of you that requires action.

- Maybe we could go to the movies.
- I am hungry for dinner.
- I sure would like someone to go on this trip with me.
- Wow, I'm feeling great! Isn't this day wonderful?

Direct Positive: This is the most effective quadrant of communication. The speaker is clear and concise while maintaining an awareness of all individuals concerned. Dialogue in this quadrant is straightforward and specific. There are often times when you need to set or keep your own boundaries with direct, firm dialogue. However, the intention behind communication in this quadrant is compassion and consideration.

- Some common direct positive statements include:
- I love you.
- That blue sweater makes your eyes look great.
- I'm so glad you came to visit today. You tell the best jokes and fill my afternoons with laughter.
- Great job on the project!

The main idea here is that each of us spends time in all four quadrants. Recognize that we all take turns in each one. The goal is to be aware of the quadrant in which you are speaking as well as the quadrants others use with their words. When you understand where you and others are, then you can politely guide the conversation to direct positive dialogue. It is best to get there as soon as possible.

Common Sense Tip: Once you have the awareness of which quadrant you are using in your speech, then you can switch to clear and specific language.

It does take practice to speak in the direct positive quadrant. However, with awareness, time, and application of direct positive principles, it becomes automatic, like driving a car or brushing your teeth or writing your signature. You will learn to respond more easily and confidently once you have integrated the concepts of this exercise.

Some people are naturally either more direct or indirect. Yet, there is still room to improve and move into direct positive language through some very simple steps. We'll show you how.

Transform your Dialogue to Direct Positive

Let's look at how each of the previous statements from each quadrant can be transformed into direct positive communication. Sometimes, it just takes small changes to the words used or the tonal inflection behind them to let the listener know that you are open for clear dialogue.

Indirect Negative Comments can become…	Direct Positive Communication
I am so stressed out and overwhelmed.	I am feeling very stressed out by _____ (fill in the specific blank—my workload at the office, the need to clean my house, etc)
Everything I seem to do always turns out wrong.	I tried (fill in the blank) and it didn't work out. I tried to plant new varieties in my garden and since they didn't survive, I'm going to try new ones next week.
I just don't know why I can't get anything right.	I am having trouble getting this computer to do what I need.
I hate it when people are always trying to get me to buy something.	The pushy salesman on the car lot deflated my desire to get a new vehicle.

Direct negative Comments can become...	Direct Positive Communication
I hate you.	I am upset by your disrespectful attitude. *Or* I am angry about how you took care of my pet while I was away.
You're a horrible writer.	I can see that you are challenged with the skill of writing. I know of a great book, full of creative writing exercises, if you're interested.
You're never able to save any money.	I notice that you are often having trouble with managing money. Is there anything I can do to help?
The rain is making me depressed.	When the weather turns cold, I notice it's easier for me to feel less motivated to start my day.
You drive me crazy when you tap your fingers on the desk.	I am feeling irritated by your finger tapping. Would you be willing to stop while we finish our project?
Indirect Positive Comments can become...	**Direct Positive Communication**
Maybe we could go to the movies.	I would like to take you to the movies. *Or* Are you able to go to the movies with me this afternoon?
I am hungry for dinner.	re you hungry? I am. Can we have sushi for dinner?
I sure would like someone to go on this trip with me.	I am going on a road trip up the west coast next month. Would you like to go with me?
Wow, I'm feeling great. Isn't this day wonderful?	I just finished a yoga class and my body feels great. The beautiful sunshine outside adds to this wonderful day.

6 Habits to Generate Direct Positive Communication

Here are a few ideas that can help you communicate directly and assertively. By following these simple guidelines, you increase rapport with others. Rapport is a bond, a mutual harmony between people. Rapport is the way to establish a safe and supportive environment in which an open exchange of ideas can take place. Generate direct positive communication habits by practicing these actions as an assertive speaker:

1.   Stay focused on the subject at hand

In order to be specific in your dialogue, it helps to have clear thoughts that precede your words. When you have an idea of what you want to say and what you want to accomplish in your conversations, you will have a greater likelihood of keeping your listener engaged. If you are trying to resolve a conflict, you may express what has gone wrong and how you hope to rectify the situation. Perhaps your goal is to share new information with others. Understanding your audience and the perception of your listener will help you target your speech to meet their needs. In any case, it helps to stay on the topic at hand.

You may know people who start to talk about their upcoming travel, but end up sharing problems their sister is having at home, the complications of the political

> "Words are, of course, the most powerful drug used by mankind." —Rudyard Kipling

scene, and the rash on the bottom of their foot. While all may be interesting topics, they are entirely unrelated to their trip to Thailand.

2.   Use short, descriptive sentences—speak in bullet points

Consider the effectiveness of bullet points when you're reading a book or manual. They give you the main points in a clear, concise manner. The concepts are also easy enough to understand in a sentence or two. Just as if you were going to write out your dialogue, it helps to organize your thoughts into main ideas.

Now, just because you have short and specific concepts you'd like to share with your listener, it doesn't mean you have to be dry and boring. In fact, quite the opposite is true. Using descriptive sentences and adding flare to your words helps keep others' attention.

- Thailand is such an exotic country. I'm excited for my trip there next month.

- I have heard that the people of Thailand are very warm and friendly.

- With the reasonable airfare and exchange rate, the trip fits nicely into my budget.

- This will be an adventure, yet a nice, relaxing time with my wife.

3. Acknowledge the other person's thoughts, feelings, and ideas

One aspect of taking responsibility for yourself in a conversation includes acknowledging the other person's thoughts, feelings, and ideas. Everyone wants to know that they have been heard. And while you may not agree with another's viewpoint, there are ways to validate their perspective. Then, you can gracefully and respectfully disagree, if necessary.

For example, it could be someone who has a different idea for a project at work. Your team of experts has been brought together for a big account on a short deadline. Now, when another offers their input, you have the option to respond assertively.

- That's an interesting concept you have there.

- Wow! I'd never thought about [fill in the blank] that way before.

- Thank you for sharing your viewpoint.

- Let me have some time to think about that for a while. I'd like to take the rest of the day to come up with some ideas of my own, and I'll get back to you in the morning.

- I hear what you're saying, and I'm not sure I agree with it. I respect your opinion, and I know you respect mine. Perhaps we can just agree to disagree on this subject.

4. Take your time

Common sense is often missing in everyday communication due to the fast-paced lifestyles we all live. Starting at a younger age, children are scheduled with school, tutors, after school sports, play dates, and music lessons. This busy-ness is often continued regardless of age. Even seniors, who live in retirement communities, are offered bridge groups, exercise classes, trips to the market, doctor appointments, and scheduled meals.

To further enhance direct positive communication, slowing down your verbal pace can help. Now, your daily planner might have just as many activities as it did last week, but there are simple ways to take your time in conversations with others.

You can take a deep breath, focusing on the exhale, which aids in the relaxation of your entire body. Conversely, when you talk quickly, you often take in more air on the inhale and mildly hyperventilate.

Taking your Time in Action: Steve's Story

During his wedding rehearsal dinner, Steve began telling a funny story to the entire table. His speech was getting faster and faster as he approached the punch line. While his breath shortened to match his quick speaking pace, a small piece of meat became lodged in his esophagus. He then couldn't breathe and ten people around the table looked at him with wide-eyed horror.

Thankfully, Steve gained his composure, and breath, quickly. He did have to excuse himself from the table for a few minutes, but he learned a valuable lesson about talking, laughing, and chewing—the lesson being that all three activities shouldn't be done at the same time. In fact, it's best to slow down altogether and take your time

In addition to taking slower and deeper breaths to help communicate clearly, you could also genuinely compliment your spouse, co-worker, or friend on their presence today. By taking your time to clarify your thoughts, such as taking a few notes before interacting with others, you'll be able to connect more effectively in each encounter.

5.   Say what you mean and mean what you say

The goal of direct positive communication is to have your mouth and your gut respond the same way in a conversation. How often do you say "yes" with your mouth when every cell of your body is screaming "no!"? By aligning your intentions of an interaction, and being clear of the outcome you would like from it, you can speak more freely with those around you.

This often includes using self-expressive words such as "I" or "me" to demonstrate that what you are saying is strictly a reflection of your viewpoint or feelings.

The thought that comes to mind here is when dating couples are ready to end their relationship. Now, it's a common joke that people say "It's me, not you. I need more time. I am unable to commit."

But what if there was a way that you could speak honestly and be upfront, knowing that you are doing the best you can and still respecting the feelings of others? Like, "I have really enjoyed spending time with you, however I don't see this relationship going any further. I wish you nothing but the best as you go on with your life." More relationship-specific information will be discussed in chapter 5, so stay tuned.

Common Sense Tip: The goal is to be able to walk away from a conversation, knowing that your energy bank has either remained the same or has added a deposit.

When our words contradict our internal desires, then we actually take a withdrawal.

Are you able to say "no" when asked to a party you'd rather not attend?

Are you able to ask for a well-deserved raise?

Are you able to honestly tell someone how that dress, shirt, or outfit looks on them?

Are you able to say, "I don't know" when you really have no idea how to answer?

Or, more deeply, are you able to openly share your feelings about a given subject or person without offending the listener?

6. Develop rapport with your listener or listeners

Rapport is the state of harmony and understanding between both the speaker and the listener. While there are many ways to enhance this connection, we are going to focus on practical, verbal methods that fit into the direct positive quadrant.

First, you can begin to match the pace of your listener. Perhaps you talk really slowly and you are accustomed to people always finishing your sentences. Or, you might be a fast talker and notice how easily annoyed you become when someone can't keep up. While you may even speak with a more common tempo, it can change, depending on your mood.

By becoming flexible with your tone and talking speed in a conversation, you will make the listener more at ease. You might have to speed things up to get a word in edgewise. Or you might have to slow it down in order for the other person to be willing to hear what you have to say.

Yet, instead of mimicking the slow speaker, which could frustrate or infuriate them, just casually reducing your own verbal pace might suffice. When you have a fast talker, and you're unable to keep up with them, it is entirely acceptable to ask them to slow down a bit. Remember, rapport works like a two-way street. While you may be doing your best to match their verbal pace, you have just as much right to request that they speak at a speed that makes you comfortable.

You can also observe their body language. Cues that let you know the person is interested in your words include consistent eye contact, nodding their head, smiling, or turning their body towards yours with openness.

There are also indicators that they would prefer to break rapport. When others are looking at their watches, crossing their arms, looking away, or shortening their breath, oftentimes it is better to respect the listener by commenting on their behavior. You might ask them something like:

- "Perhaps this isn't the best time to continue this discussion. Can I call you later? Or would you like to set up another time to talk?"

- "I can tell we're unclear in our communication. Is there anything I can say to clarify this information? Would there be a better time to talk about this?"

While there are many ways body language can enhance or break rapport, it benefits an assertive speaker to take all aspects of the conversation into account before proceeding. This heightened level of awareness is often noticed by your counterparts and increases the levels of trust, confidence, and harmony in any given conversation.

The Common Sense Responsibility Spectrum

Responsibility is known as the ability to respond in any given situation. When you take self-responsibility in communication, your words are backed by your values. People trust you and depend on your honor. You are also accountable for your messages, knowing that you have done the best you can in each circumstance.

Under-Responsible   Self-Responsible   Over-Responsible

While speaking for yourself is the goal in communication, it only represents a small portion of the responsibility spectrum. On one end of the continuum you have under-responsibility, where people have a challenge acknowledging their own ideas and often give up their own personal power by allowing others to make decisions for them. On the other end of the scale, you have over-responsibility. People in this range are often mistaken for assertive communicators, because they use their force to speak for others.

Self-responsibility is the delicate balance between the two. Take a look at the chart below, which describes the attributes of a self-responsible speaker in between those with less or more authority using their voice.

Which column best describes your communication in regular conversations? **Be honest with yourself here.**

Under-Responsibility	Self-Responsibility	Over-Responsibility
Allows others to choose	Chooses for oneself	Chooses for others
Denies own rights	Respects personal rights and the rights of others	Denies the rights of others
Conceals differences to maintain peace	Encourages the disclosure of differences	Coerces agreement to avoid differences
Uses vague terminology	Uses terms like "I" or "me"	Uses terms like "you" or "we"
Asks permission to make decisions	Makes decisions and takes responsibility for actions	Makes decisions without regard for others
Avoids or joins with others	Respects others	Dominates others
Self-denying	Self-enhancing	Self-enhancing at the expense of others
Has difficulty accepting compliments	Can accept or give a compliment	Has difficulty giving compliments
Suffers silently	Expresses needs and wants	Orders, blames, demands, and manipulates
Over-apologizes	Apologizes sincerely	Never apologizes
Does not achieve goals	May achieve goals	May achieve goals, but at the expense of others

Utilize your Senses

Neuro-Linguistic Programming (NLP) research has discovered that the senses play a major role in how you not only acquire and store information, but also how you share that information with others. While there are five main senses—seeing, hearing, tasting, smelling, and feeling—three of those senses take precedence over the other two. The visual, auditory, and kinesthetic senses, when utilized by an assertive speaker, can effectively create clear communication with others.

Take a moment to consider the benefits that your eyes, ears, and skin offer to your entire being. Your eyes interpret colors in your environment. They also process depth of objects in space, relative to your position, and allow you to recognize your own body parts in relation to one another.

Your ears not only hear incoming sounds, they also help you establish a sense of balance and equilibrium for your whole body. They let you know when you're upright in space, or when you've been turned upside down, horizontal, or any combination of the above. The vibrational sound molecules that enter your ear are then transmitted as auditory signals to the brain's temporal lobe and processed for understanding.

Finally, your skin, which is the largest body organ, is responsible for your tactile sense. The numerous nerve endings throughout your epidermis help alert your brain of new physical feelings and help regulate your body temperature. In addition, the skin comprehends subtle information that passes across its surface.

However, the visual, auditory, and kinesthetic senses expand beyond how you simply communicate within your own being. Senses also play a large role in how you communicate your ideas with others.

And you can utilize the senses to develop rapport.

This is founded on the idea that each individual has their own sensory preferences that work in conjunction with their unique world view. Information from each person's environment is collected, organized, processed through the senses and stored in the subconscious mind. Certain senses are preferred over others due to past experiences, relationships, and encounters.

While you are capable of using all of your senses equally, you often prefer certain senses over others based on your past experiences. What if you had parents who scolded you frequently for not listening to their commands? Or what if you weren't held very much growing up and rarely experienced physical contact? Perhaps you were taught to take everything literally and rarely used the visualization ability of imagination?

All of your experiences throughout life, especially those as a child, greatly affect the senses you use to process information and communicate with others. In this next section, we'd like to show you how to bolster all of your senses in the communication process. By maximizing your potential to see, hear, and feel with words, you have a greater likelihood of creating harmony with more individuals, regardless of their sensory preferences.

In order to have rapport through the senses, we want to match the sensory picture of the person we're communicating with. It means that we are going to attempt to see the world through their eyes, hear it through their ears, and feel it from their position.

Common Sense Tip: *The more accurately we can meet our counterparts from their perspective, the more we can share our message and create harmony in conversations.*

Now, the English language is full of sensory words and phrases. We can match the sensory language of others by paying attention to what words they're using and we can expand our dialogue to include all of the senses to match our audience.

Let's take a look at some of the sensory language preferences.

Visual: People who are visual see vivid internal images or have a vibrant imagination. To these individuals, a picture is worth a thousand words. They often have the ability to read something and remember where on the page they saw it. They learn with visual aids. When finding directions, visual communicators can easily find their way based on landmarks or particularly colorful signs. When remembering a situation, they utilize the eyes to scan the situation.

Visual speakers use words, or phrases, like:

- Let me paint you a picture of what this will be like.
- That's picture perfect!
- Did you witness that event?
- Keep your eye on the ball.
- Take a peek at what's to come.
- Looks like clear sailing to me.
- I'll put this into perspective.
- I see what you mean.
- Did you catch a glimpse of that?
- What a bright future!

Auditory: People who are auditorily sensitive, or prefer hearing as a way to understand the world, generally pay attention to word choices that people use in conversations, the tone, inflection used, and the meaning of those words in context. They often like to talk things through until they make sense. Noisy rooms can often be too stimulating, depending on the severity of their sensitivity.

Those with an auditory strength often pick up subtleties that many others miss. And, they can be heard using phrases like:

- I'm speechless.
- I'm tongue-tied.
- Let me voice my opinion.
- Did you hear that rumor?
- Describe what you heard?
- Please enunciate.
- It's loud and shrill!
- He/she is such a blabbermouth.
- That is clear as a bell.
- I hear what you're saying.

Kinesthetic: Kinesthetically dominant individuals pay attention to how they feel over what they hear or what they see. They often dress for comfort, versus appearance. They are in tune with their emotions. They are also aware of body sensations, such as stiffening when sitting too long or fidgeting when in an uncomfortable chair.

While the overall feeling of their bodies is their greatest reference point for communication, they use their words to reflect such a viewpoint. Common phrases for a kinesthetic communicator include:

- I've come to grips with that situation.
- I just fell apart.
- She's so hard-headed.
- They really got my goat.
- He's sharp as a tack.
- I held on for dear life.
- Things fell to pieces.

- I was beside myself.

- When push comes to shove, I'll take action.

- They're all washed up.

Incorporate the Senses into Speech

The goal as an affective communicator is to be able to use all three representational systems in your dialogue with others. You want to be proficient across the board—including visual, auditory, and kinesthetic phrases.

Awareness and attention are components of successful communication, both speaking and listening. When in conversations with others, be aware of which representational system others are using and choose words that match their sensory preference.

If you have someone who is describing all of the sounds they heard that day at the zoo, you can create rapport by matching their preference and say, "Wow! That sounds amazing!"

Perhaps you are telling someone about your trip. You might include what you saw, new sounds you heard, and the way you felt on the trip. That way, you cover your bases and make listening easier for the other person because they will have something in their representational system that matches how you are describing the situation.

This is often why classrooms are using multi-faced means of providing information. Videos are shown, the teacher presents a lecture, and then a tactile activity is applied so that everyone can comprehend the new material.

This creates a win-win situation for an assertive communicator.

Putting it all Together

Our voice is one of the best means of self-expression. When we deny ourselves the right to speak, our confidence, purpose, and energy bank are challenged. By becoming an assertive communicator, using self-responsibility and clarity in our conversations, we can stay connected to our values while moving forward towards our goals.

New Common Sense Tools to Honor your Voice:

- **The 21-Day Plan:** Power as a communicator begins with your internal dialogue. The 21-Day Plan rewrites negative self-talk into supporting personal beliefs at the subconscious level.

- **Four Quadrants of Communication:** The Four Quadrants of Communication teach you how to speak directly and positively in order to get your point across or set personal boundaries. Discover where you currently communicate and utilize the various suggestions to speak in the direct positive quadrant with ease.

- **Utilize Your Senses:** By utilizing all three systems—visual, auditory and kinesthetic—you can engage with others in a more harmonious and productive way. This Common Sense Tool helps you understand which sense you prefer when speaking, as well as understand the preferences of your listener. As a result, you can create harmony in your conversations with the use of the senses.

Chapter 4

BUT I THOUGHT YOU'D LIKE
A BEDTIME STORY

Chapter 4

Master the Art of Listening

"Deep listening is miraculous for both listener and speaker. When someone receives us with open-hearted, non-judging, intensely interested listening, our spirits expand." —Sue Patton Thoele

In this Chapter

- Discover the skill-set of a master listener
- Become proficient in asking questions
- Create a 2:1 listening-to-talking ratio in conversations
- Transform old listening habits into new ones
- Learn when to keep (and when to break) rapport

While the previous chapter focused on speaking with your authentic voice, that's only half of the communication equation. Taking responsibility as a listener is just as important as communicating your ideas clearly to others. Being a good listener means that you are willing to ask questions and really hear the messages others are sharing with you. Thus, the skill of speaking assertively and the art of listening go hand in hand to allow information to be exchanged via communication.

Becoming a skilled listener has many benefits. It lets others know that you are interested in them as a person. It is a sign of respect for those you are with and it conveys a non-judgmental attitude. By taking the time to slow down in conversations, you are able to show you are interested in what the other has to say. And, by actively engaging in listening, you confirm the value of your relationship with the other person.

Now, as you recall, the first half of the process of communication focuses on honoring your voice as you share messages with others. As a listener, you are constantly encoding the information being sent your way.

However, listening is quite different from the simple act of hearing. It is true that our brain recognizes sound as it enters the ears and hearing, in and of itself, is nonselective. The short-term memory, which is controlled by the conscious mind, then holds the incoming signals. Based on the limited capacity of the self-conscious, the short-term memory is easily disrupted and the information you hear is easily forgotten.

But, it's our perception that decides which information to select out of the various noises.

Listening, then, becomes a choice. It's a purposeful and determined action. We listen because:

- The message is important.
- The message is interesting.
- It evokes emotion.
- The information has been heard in the past.
- We like or respect the person speaking.

The subconscious mind, which is full of pre-recorded programs, selects the sounds that fulfill certain needs or personal interests. It's why we can say people have selective hearing and only listen to what they want to hear. We choose what we want to listen to, based on our past choices and experiences. And then, that information we select can be moved from short-term memory into long-term memory storage.

Your subconscious mind is also processing the verbal content, the non-verbal expressions, and the context in which the message is being sent. You're filtering all new dialogue through your past experiences, your beliefs, and your perspectives of the world.

Common Sense Tip: How you filter what others are saying through your beliefs—and combine them with your skills as a listener—creates the opportunity to internalize the message and respond.

Now, experts understand that the unique upbringing and life experiences of each individual directly affect one's varying ability to utilize auditory skills. Perhaps, you were rarely heard as a child, or you were continually scolded for not paying attention. In which case, auditory sensory input gets diminished, or discouraged over time. However, you have the power to choose in the present moment what you would like to do for the future. By understanding your current strengths, and weaknesses, you can decide where to make improvements to become a more effective listener in your relationships.

In order to master the art of listening, it is important to learn from positive and negative behaviors that are demonstrated on a regular basis. Take the following quiz to assess your own current habits when listening to others.

Common Sense Quiz: Are you a skillful listener? Part 1

The following characteristics are found in those who have mastered the art of listening. The goal of this quiz is to clarify where you already have strengths in communicating with others as a listener. Simultaneously, you also notice areas for improvement.

Directions: On a scale of 1-5, with 5 being the most frequent occurrence of the skill, fill in the degree to which you already practice supportive listening behaviors. **The first time you go through the list, consider your actions when with a person you enjoy.** Then, go through this list a second time reflecting on your listening ability with someone you find frustrating, irritating, boring, or bothersome.

	Enjoyable Conversation (Rate 1-5)	Challenging Conversation (Rate 1-5)
1. I make regular eye contact with the speaker.	_____	_____
2. I ask questions for clarification.	_____	_____
3. I show concern for others by acknowledging their feelings.	_____	_____

4. I restate or paraphrase to make sure
    I understand what is being said.   _____   _____

5. My primary goal is to comprehend
    what is being said. My secondary
    goal is to have the other person
    understand me.   _____   _____

6. I am poised and emotionally
    controlled.   _____   _____

7. My non-verbal responses are
    appropriate to the conversation (a
    smile, nod, frown, etc.)   _____   _____

8. My mind rarely wanders.   _____   _____

9. I respond with conscientious actions.   _____   _____

10. I warn the speaker before changing
    the subject.   _____   _____

What's your Score for Part 1?

Score for an enjoyable conversation: _____ (out of 50 points possible)

Score for a challenging conversation: _____ (out of 50 points possible)

The highest score possible in each column is 50 and the higher the number in each column, the more effective you are as a listener already.

Was there a difference in your scores between someone you enjoy listening to and others you find challenging? If so, where did you lose points? If you noticed your emotions get out of hand, you now have an idea of where to start strengthening your skill set. If you rarely restate information or ask questions for clarity, some of the tools in this chapter will increase your ability to comprehend messages, regardless of the listener.

Common Sense Quiz: Are you a skillful listener? Part 2

The following habits are the most destructive in effective communication. The second part of this quiz focuses on what listening behaviors are still present when you converse with others.

Directions: Mark the frequency of each habit as it appears in your conversations on a scale of 1-5. 1 means that action seldom occurs and 5 indicates that action frequently occurs. Fill in the degree to which you already practice supportive listening behaviors. The first time you go through the list, consider your actions when with a person you enjoy. Then, go through this list a second time reflecting on your listening ability with someone you find frustrating, irritating, boring, or bothersome.

	Enjoyable Conversation (Rate 1-5)	Challenging Conversation (Rate 1-5)
1. I interrupt their words often.	_____	_____
2. I jump to conclusions.	_____	_____
3. It's easy for me to finish their sentences and I do so often.	_____	_____
4. My responses are often advice-driven, or parental.	_____	_____
5. My mind is made up before I have all of the information.	_____	_____
6. I am a compulsive note taker.	_____	_____
7. I rarely give a non-verbal response.	_____	_____
8. I am often impatient.	_____	_____
9. It's easy for me to lose my temper when I disagree.	_____	_____
10. My replies are formulated while the other person is speaking.	_____	_____

What's your Score for Part 2?

Score for an enjoyable conversation: _____ (out of 50 points possible)

Score for a challenging conversation: _____ (out of 50 points possible)

The highest score possible in each column is 50. The larger the number in each column indicates that there is more room for improvement in the listening realm.

Was there a difference in your scores between someone you enjoy listening to and others you find challenging? What habits scored the highest in each type of conversation? If poor listening behaviors occurred in both columns as a high number, then you now have an idea of where to make improvements first.

If you noticed you often feel impatient with others and finish their sentences, than the skills in this chapter will guide you to transform those negative emotions into ones that support the relationship. If you observed your habit to always act like mom or dad and give advice to others, perhaps just enhancing your ability to listen without responding will be beneficial. In fact, you might learn how to ask appropriate questions so that you can create harmony with others without parenting them.

The Common Sense Four Quadrants of Communication Revisited

The purpose of the four quadrants of communication is two-fold. First, this model indicates how to speak to others in a direct, positive voice in order to get your message across in the most effective manner. The second reason for the four quadrants is to help the listener discover which type of language is being used and then decide how to most effectively respond.

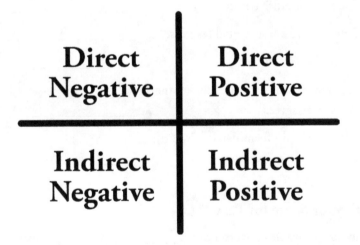

Let's first review what each quadrant represents. The indirect negative quadrant contains words or phrases that are unclear, downbeat, sometimes unrelated to the topic at hand. Direct negative language is characterized by specific, derogatory language. It's easy to understand what people mean by their words and their body language. The indirect positive quadrant consists of non-specific words, even though they may be shared with an enthusiastic or optimistic flare. Even if their words cannot convey their upbeat message, their non-verbal cues fill in the missing links. And, those speaking in the direct positive quadrant are precise, detailed, and assertive with their verbal and non-verbal messages.

Common Sense Tip: *Just as an assertive speaker wants to communicate in the direct positive quadrant most of the time, it's best for the listener to guide all conversations in the same direction.*

While not all talkers use clear and supportive language, becoming a skillful listener will allow you to take any type of dialogue and create a better understanding between parties.

Question Everything

The best way to guide conversations into the direct positive quadrant is to ask questions for clarification.

Consider the following comments that reside in the other three quadrants. By formulating a thoughtful and precise question, you can draw the speaker into more direct dialogue. Even if the speaker responds to your questions with indirect negative, direct negative, or indirect positive phrases, you can keep asking questions until they come around to a specific answer.

Indirect Negative Comment	Direct Positive Questions
I am so stressed out and overwhelmed.	What in your life is making you feel anxious?
My job is lousy.	What would you like to do instead?
Direct negative Comments	**Direct Positive Responses**
I hate you.	I'm sorry you feel this way. Why do you hate me?
The rain is making me depressed.	Is there anything I can do to make you feel better?
Indirect Positive Comments	**Direct Positive Questions**
This day is great.	What is making you feel so happy today?
Everyone seems happy.	What do you notice that makes you say that?
Direct Positive Comments	**Direct Positive Questions**
I really like this dessert.	I agree. What do you like most about it?
I appreciate all of your hard work.	Thank you. Is there anything more I can do to help?

While asking questions is an effective tool to use as a listener, it's the quality of the question that matters most.

Common Sense Questioning in Action: Sally's Story

Let's look at Sally, who is a stay-at-home mom. She had a rough time getting the kids off to school. A phone call from one child, who forgot his lunch, interrupted her morning cleaning. Now, her own lunch meeting would have to be rescheduled due to her unexpected trip back to school. And, to top things off, the washing machine just broke, leaving water to leak into three adjoining rooms.

As soon as her husband, Ted, gets home, she begins complaining about how stressed she feels. Sally explains how she's overwhelmed by her daily responsibilities and that she's unable to rely on anybody else for support. Sally might as well do everything herself, but that further increases her stress.

Can you decide which quadrant Sally is using to communicate her frustration with her husband?

If you guessed indirect negative, give yourself a pat on the back. Yet, Sally is using non-specific words such as "stressed," "overwhelmed," and "isolated" to describe her day.

While these are all very valid feelings, Ted has no idea why she feels so upset. He can only guess the cause of her negativity. And, because he doesn't know the root of the issue, he is unable to help solve any problems or know what to do with the information being presented by Sally.

Ted has the opportunity to respond in a number of ways.

The **direct negative retort** could be:

"Well, what the hell do you want me to do about it? I just got home from a long day of work myself and I'm exhausted, too."

This would further escalate the negativity being experienced.

The **indirect** reply could come with a change in tone: reply,

"Wow, it sounds to me like you've had a really rough day."

That's an in-direct response, but it validates the emotions that she's experiencing at the current moment.

"Yes, I have." Sally replies. The 'yes' that Sally provides is a direct positive answer. However, she can immediately follow with more indirect language by not further explaining what exactly went wrong at home.

The **direct positive question** Ted could ask is:

"Is there something I can do to make your day better?"

If Sally says, "Yes, there is something you can do. Would you be willing to take care of dinner tonight while I take an hour by myself to unwind?" Then we have established rapport in the direct positive quadrant for speaker and listener alike.

With her response, Sally specifically tells Ted how to provide her with the opportunity to reduce stress and return to balance. There is an open line of communication that has been established. Once Sally comes back into a more centered space, then perhaps she and Ted could talk about the items around the house that now need fixing, such as the washing machine. They could also sit down with their kids, if necessary, and brainstorm ways to help mom out before and after school.

However, if Sally responded to Ted's question about what can make her day better by saying, "Well, I don't even know. I am so exhausted." She is still in **indirect negative**, unspecific and focusing on what's going wrong.

Ted could then proceed with a **direct positive question**, "Is there anything you could suggest that would make you feel better?

If she is still hesitant and unclear, Ted as the listener could offer ideas such as, "Well, honey, why don't you let me take care of dinner tonight while you go upstairs and take a soak. Does that sound good to you?"

His use of direct positive language gives her a simple yes or no option, which makes it much easier for the speaker to use specific responses. Even if the speaker continues in other quadrants, it can just take a little longer for the listener to guide the conversation back to the direct positive quadrant.

By continually asking questions and opening up the door for direct positive dialogue, it creates the opportunity for understanding and harmony between everyone involved.

This scenario of Ted and Sally demonstrates the numerous options a listener has to respond to a speaker. While assertive dialogue from the message sender is optimal, it is rarely the case. Thus, it is the job of the listener to clarify the message and gently steer the conversation to direct positive language.

Common Sense Tip: Remember that all of these suggestions become easier with awareness and practice. Focus on your improvements, not your failures.

The Three R's

While the four quadrants of communication paint the broader picture of communication between speaker and listener, it's the three R's that teach the listener to communicate most effectively within them. This tool builds on the foundation of asking questions described earlier and directs the listener into a 2-to-1 listening to talking ratio. This ratio is recognized by experts to be a very effective tool in clear communication. The three R's stand for:

Request

Repeat the request

Respond

Request: This is when a speaker, whether using assertive language or not, decides to make a request to the listener. This message can be sent via any of the Four Quadrants of Communication.

Repeat the Request: This second step is where the listener repeats, or rephrases, the content of the message they just received. Neuro-linguistic programming refers to this as backtracking, and it gives the speaker a chance to verify if what the listener heard was correct.

Respond: Again, this is the role of the speaker. If what the listener repeated in step two is correct, then the speaker has a chance to confirm that the message was properly understood. But, if the listener was mistaken in any way, they have a chance to clarify the errors.

The three R's may slow down a conversation, but they also offer the listener and the speaker a chance to create a mutual understanding of the message.

When the three R's are not used, there can be a lot of confusion in conversations. When misunderstandings take place, it can lead to small arguments, larger disagreements, and even uncommon disasters. When communication breaks down, there is often a domino effect of unwanted events.

The Three R's in Action: Steve and Kym's Story

The perfect example takes place years ago when Steve and Kym had just started dating. It was the beginning of the summer season and he wanted to show her his beloved boat. Now, his vessel was a 1972 vintage Bay Liner that had been passed down through the family and refreshed many of his fond childhood memories. The boat had also been recently restored with hours of his precious labor and time.

While Steve knew that Kym was an avid water-skier and wake boarder, he didn't quite realize that her time on the water was spent in pristine sport-specific crafts.

But she humored him, nonetheless, and they coordinated a trip for the following Saturday.

When the boating day arrived, the thought of being in the cool water was a refreshing option on such a swelteringly hot afternoon. With the gear packed and the trailer set, they pointed their truck west towards the Black Butte Reservoir.

After the 45-minute drive, they arrived at the quiet launching area. This already desolate area was further deserted due to the strong wind that had already picked up in the Sacramento valley. But, Steve and Kym weren't hindered by the weather. In fact, they were quite determined to take the boat out for its seasonal maiden voyage.

As they prepared to launch the boat in the water, Steve and Kym were busy taking care of the details. Kym loaded up the ice chest, towels, and gear into the boat while Steve untied the rear straps and paid the parking fee.

Kym called out to Steve, "Did you get the boat plug?"

All she heard in response was, "Yes."

What Steve heard her say was, "I've got the boat plug."

So, Steve backed the truck and trailer down the launch ramp. With the lake already low for this early in the season, the ramp was over 50 feet long. When the boat entered the water, Steve vacated the driver's seat and hopped into the boat. Because the Bay Liner was an outboard motor and Kym was only familiar with inboard ones, Steve wanted to pull the boat out onto the water.

Without even hesitating, Kym finished the task of parking the truck in the lot at the top of the ramp.

But, as she walked back towards the water, she was slightly confused. The boat engine wasn't running, despite the battery pre-test on shore. She noticed that the stern of the boat was much lower in the water than the bow. Then, like a blinding flash of the obvious, she saw Steve standing in the middle of the boat, waving his hands and something else vigorously in the air—the boat plug.

Now, the afternoon wind had progressed over the last hour. Steve was now too far from the dock to tie the boat safely near shore, and he was continually being pushed further out into the middle of the lake.

Kym ran back up the ramp and attempted to back the trailer back down the launch ramp. However, her skill and good judgment were clouded by her heightened stress levels. Thankfully, a fellow boater arrived and offered to assist in the rescue mission.

Simultaneously, Steve had jumped ship and was trying to tow the boat back to the dock with his manly strength. However, he could not compete with the wind. More water continued to fill the Bay Liner as it moved further away from help.

Kym felt entirely helpless on shore. But, thanks to an incoming vessel that helped tow the boat to safety, and the kind man who helped load the boat onto the trailer, both Steve and the precious Bay Liner survived.

When the trailer was pulled back up to the parking lot, it took over an hour and a half to drain the water from the boat. The battery was waterlogged and the boat failed to start.

The playful plans for a day on the water had been foiled by a simple miscommunication.

Using the Three R's in the Boat Plug Story

Steve and Kym could have easily avoided such calamities on their trip to Black Butte Reservoir had they utilized the three R's when preparing the boat for the launch.

> "I know that you believe you understand what you think I said, but I'm not sure you realize that what you heard is not what I meant." —Robert McCloskey

When Kym asked Steve, "Did you get the boat plug?" Steve could have repeated her request by saying, "Kym, do you want *me* to get the boat plug?"

After Steve confirmed that he heard the message being sent by Kym, she could then respond with an affirmative, "Yes. I would like you to put the drain plug in the back of the boat."

While this may seem to move the conversation at a snail's pace, slowing down the conversation actually enhances clarity between Steve and Kym. When they are both able to communicate specifically and positively, there is little or no room for misunderstandings.

Then, with the boat plug in place, they could have enjoyed an afternoon on the water.

The Three R's in Daily Conversations

Take some time this week to notice when your conversations feel out of sync. When you hear a request from another, see if you can slow down your pace and repeat the request back to the speaker. By opening the door for clarity in your dialogue, you might also notice more harmony in your relationships, ease in your conversations, and receptiveness of your ideas by others.

See if you can take one day this week and challenge yourself to incorporate the three R's into your conversations. In three separate conversations throughout the day, try to repeat someone's request.

Reflect on the conversation by asking yourself the following questions:

- Did repeating the request feel natural or awkward?
- Did it enhance the quality of the conversation?
- Was there a clearer level of understanding by using the three R's?
- Did others notice what you were doing?
- If so, did they seem to appreciate your consideration to understand their message?

There is always room for improvement. With practice, this becomes more natural and you'll know when to best use this technique to bring clarity to your communication. By starting small and incorporating the three R's into your daily conversations, you will enhance your listening skills and create harmony in your relationships.

Non-verbal Listening

While asking questions can help you come into verbal rapport with individuals, there are many non-verbal cues that dictate the quality of your response. The following body language positions can be used to match your words and create a harmonious reply.

Some examples of non-verbal cues that enhance communication include, but are not limited to:

- Nodding your head
- Smiling, or appropriate laughter
- Eye contact
- Suitable hand motions
- Even, rhythmic breathing

Beginning Steps to Mastering the Art of Listening

Refer back to the "Are you a skillful listener, part 2" quiz, which asked you to take personal inventory of habits that are possibly hindering your communication. Perhaps you notice that you are impatient and want to interrupt others. Maybe you take things personally and become overly emotional in conversations.

If you scored perfectly, without any self-defeating habits, congratulations! Pat yourself on the back and celebrate your successful listening skills. The following tools will simply be a reminder of what you're doing well.

For the rest of us who continually have room for improvement, use the following guidelines to enhance your listening skills.

Catch Yourself in the Act

Awareness and personal recognition of poor listening skills is the first step in making changes. Not only does the quiz enhance the skill of self-observation, but it also gives you an idea of where you want to create new listening habits. And, because of your increased awareness, you can easily recognize destructive habits and catch them in the act.

How many times have you left a conversation thinking, "I wish I would have done this" or "I should have done that"? Besides taking an emotional hit with those regretful phrases, you have to wait until the next opportunity to make changes.

Instead of putting your insights on hold, take charge of the present moment by noticing where you slipped into undesirable behavior. Admit your observation immediately.

If you notice:	You could say:
You just interrupted the speaker	"I'm sorry I just interrupted you. Please continue with what you were saying."
You just finished their sentence	"I apologize for finishing your sentence. What were you going to say?"
That you respond to the speaker with advice	"What I probably said sounds like advice. It's really just my opinion. What thoughts do you have about the situation?"
That you're mind's already made up before they finish speaking	"I notice that I am having a bias to your thoughts. Can you please tell me more about this?
You rarely give non-verbal responses	"I (see, hear, or understand) what you're saying."
You are feeling impatient	"I am feeling a bit short with my time, or temperament, right now. Please don't take it personally. Could we finish this conversation another time?"
You are becoming upset or are about to lose your temper	"I can tell I am highly emotional right now. Can I have some time to cool off before we continue this discussion?"
You are formulating responses in your head before the speaker finishes	"My mind just wandered to another thought. Can you please repeat that?"

Notice how each of these responses tie in various elements of being a skilled listener. They reflect a sense of self-responsibility by acknowledging their behaviors and feelings. Often, the phrases end with a question, which facilitates direct positive communication. They also validate the speaker for what they are saying with respect and courtesy.

Acknowledge your Success

Every individual wants reward, recognition, and response for their ideas or behaviors. Acknowledging your own success is no different than honoring those accomplishments of others. Celebrate! Celebrate! Celebrate!

Even the smallest changes in your listening ability are to be congratulated. Give yourself a pat on the back when you notice that you're using your best listening skills. Smile when you catch yourself in the act and notify the speaker accordingly. Put five dollars in a vacation fund when you notice immediate steps have been taken to change your listening habits.

You can also include others with your ongoing list of successful moments. Find a close friend or family member and tell them about the listening skills you are trying to improve. When they notice a successful encounter, ask them to praise you. It can be as simple as the comment, "Nice job," or as lavish as a treat to the finest restaurant in town.

Just think of how you encourage children to tally their good behaviors. In second grade, Kym had a teacher who kept track of positive behavior with a star chart. Perhaps you had teachers with similar tricks to encourage values and cooperation through your developmental years. In any case, each time a student was observed helping out another individual, they received a star. When their desk was clean at the end of the day and their chair was pushed in, another star was added to the board. Every little action that supported the individual and the community as a whole was rewarded.

Who's to say that you can't do that for your newly-discovered listening skills? Develop a way to track your own success and have a prize waiting for you at the end. Just like the students who collected one hundred stars received a toy from the treasure chest, you, too, can reap the rewards of your training. Treat yourself to the latest tool on the market, a new book or CD, or a day at the spa. Even time alone with yourself can be a desirable incentive.

> "We have two ears and one mouth so that we can listen twice as much as we speak."
> —Epictetus

The goal is to have fun in the process. Celebrate your small successes and enjoy the larger gifts they bring to your more harmonious relationships.

Transform Old Habits into New Ones

There are several ways you have learned thus far to transform old habits into new ones. You have discovered how to make a value wheel to infuse your new actions with meaning. In chapter 2, you learned how to take your perspective from limited to limitless by responding to morning and evening power questions. You also learned how to alter negative internal dialogue to positive self-talk via the 21-Day Plan.

Any and all of the activities can be used to powerfully become a master in the art of listening.

Create a value wheel as a skillful listener

List five values that you feel are the most important when listening to others. Is it respect? Is it companionship? Visit Appendix A for a complete list of value words. Then, list those value words on a sheet of paper and keep them in your wallet, on your desk, or on your refrigerator. Have the guiding principles behind your desire to become a skillful listener easily accessible throughout the day. Then, when you realize that you are slipping into old behavior patterns, you can switch your focus in an instant, back to the values behind your goals for change.

Modify the Daily Support Questions for listening

The following questions can be taken into the specific realm of a skillful listener. Take some time in the morning to set the intention for your day. This helps keep your focus on the goal to pay attention closely when others are speaking.

What/who am I happy about listening to right now?

What/who am I excited about listening to right now?

What part of listening am I grateful for right now?

What/who have I listened to that makes me proud?

What/who do I enjoy listening to right now?

What/who am I committed to listen to in my life right now?

Who do I love to listen to/who loves to listen to me?

With these questions, you can turn your attention to the positive aspects of the communication process and shift your perspective into the positive realm regarding listening. Again, have fun with this process and acknowledge your successes along the way!

Give your self-talk a makeover

Think of the things you tell yourself when you notice you've slipped into old listening habits again. While these thoughts can be subconscious programming appearing to your self-conscious mind for awareness, you also have the power to change those programs through the 21-Day Plan.

First, list the things that are self-sabotaging, like:

I am not a good listener.

I screwed up again and almost ruined a friendship.

I shouldn't have lost my temper.

Then, rewrite your internal dialogue with phrases that support your goal of enhancing your listening skills. The above three sentences could be changed to:

I choose to listen attentively to others.

I forgive myself for my mistakes and use my relationships as a learning experience.

I am able to remain composed while listening.

You can follow the steps on page 87 for in-depth instructions for the 21-Day Plan.

The process of replacing old habits with new ones is designed to be easy and pleasurable. Find a technique that you enjoy in this book and apply it to your skills as a listener. The possibilities for such changes are unlimited!!

Be Patient with Yourself

Often times we are much more tolerant with others than we are with ourselves. Take a deep breath and cut yourself some slack! The process of change, regardless of what attribute or behavior you're trying to improve, takes some time.

Reasons to Master the Art of Listening

There are several reasons to master the art of listening that we have discussed thus far. In addition to creating harmony in relationships and preventing miscommunication in conversations, here are some other reasons to strengthen your listening skills:

- To learn something
- To be entertained
- To understand a situation
- To get information
- To be courteous
- To be responsible
- To prevent accidents
- To be a team player
- To ask intelligent questions
- To improve confidence

- To find out people's needs
- To protect freedom
- To negotiate effectively
- To be valued and trusted
- To use money wisely
- To evaluate accurately
- To make comparisons
- To share in the lives of others
- To analyze the speaker's purpose
- To be liked by others

- To get the best value
- To improve self-discipline
- To build relationships
- To satisfy curiosity
- To be a supportive friend
- To make intelligent decisions
- To give an appropriate response
- To create win-win situations
- To settle disagreements
- To maintain a flexible attitude
- To share the gift of hearing

Use your Whole Brain

Just as Chapter 3 focused on using all of your senses in communication, it helps to utilize all components of your brain in any given moment.

This is what researchers call a whole brain state.

In a perfect world, the right and left hemispheres of your brain would work congruently as you face life's circumstances. Yet, just like your senses can be blocked by certain negative life experiences, so can portions of your brain.

Consider the processing capability of your left hemisphere. It allows you to understand detailed information. Thoughts can be logically ordered and large concepts can be broken down into smaller parts for comprehension.

The right hemisphere helps to balance out the left by placing incoming information into pictorial form. It allows incoming data to be placed into context of a larger whole and it comprehends emotions.

The whole brain state maximizes the potential of both hemispheres simultaneously.

Common Sense Tip: When communication between the right and left hemispheres is fluid and continuous, it's easier for you to learn new things, recall stored information quicker, and make appropriate decisions clearly.

In addition, you have a heightened sense of awareness and creativity. This whole brain state also increases your ability to re-program any pre-recorded thought patterns that may not be supporting a limitless perspective. It's no wonder that using your whole brain has been deemed a super learning state!

And while limiting past experiences may temporarily hinder access to usage of one hemisphere of the brain, simple techniques can restore a whole brain state effortlessly.

Hold Your Boundaries

The question remains, how do you remain in this neutral state while around difficult people?

A perfect example of this is a family member who upsets you, yet you have to see them at regular family gatherings.

The following expanding balloon activity is an easy, effective Common Sense Tool that can help you remain emotionally neutral around a stressful person. Remember, if you can remain in a centered, whole-brain state, you can think clearly, respond appropriately, and remain energetically neutral.

When you are unable to hold your boundaries, it's easy to become upset, agitated or even aggressive. Thus, the expanding balloon exercise teaches you how to stay in control of your emotions and energy.

While stressful people and situations may be unavoidable, this exercise prevents that individual or circumstance from overpowering or controlling you.

There are a few simple techniques that can allow you to listen to others speaking without taking an energetic withdrawal.

The Common Sense Expanding Balloon Activity

When you are in a conversation and notice yourself starting to feel stressed, and you're unable to break rapport, use this activity to neutralize any negative energy coming your way.

Directions:

Step 1: Imagine your favorite colored balloon floating between you and the negative person you're with (spouse, boyfriend/girlfriend, co-worker, boss, anyone that causes you stress).

Step 2: With the balloon as a buffer floating between you and the other person, picture their negative language or actions going directly into the balloon. Imagine each of their stressful or negative words blowing up the balloon more and more, even to the point where it would pop.

If the conversation is ongoing, you might need to let the balloon of negativity pop entirely. This way, you are unaffected by the energy as it floats off harmlessly and formlessly away from you. Then, quickly place another balloon in its place. Continue to envision any tension from the other person filling up your favorite color balloon.

This activity can be done over the phone lines as well. With the mobility that cellular phones offer, we can talk to others from any place on the globe. Any time you observe internal stress as a result of the conversation you're having, then visualize a balloon between you and the other person absorbing their negativity.

If you feel that you're unable to hold the vision of the balloon between you and the challenging person, then their energy is overpowering you. At this point, you know you always have a way out.

It's called breaking rapport.

There are numerous tools and phrases throughout this chapter that remind you to take a break, step away from the situation, and reconvene at a time when you can keep yourself composed.

Breaking Rapport

However, there are times when no matter how many questions you ask to clarify your understanding, the other person will not make it into the direct positive quadrant. When you have tried your best to remain neutral and it fails, there is another solution.

At this point, you realize that you have done your best to create harmony in a given situation.

But, when you're unable to retain control of your own energy, like when the speaker is so direct negative it's upsetting you, or the other person is clueless to your uncomfortable state, it's best for you to break rapport and end the conversation.

> It's always in your best interest to bolster your listening skills. It is, however, very important to establish personal boundaries so that you don't accumulate unwanted stress. Remember, no one has a right to write a check against your Energy Bank Account.

Remember, it takes two to be in rapport.

When you are associating with people who push your buttons, making you feel angry, frustrated, or upset in any way, your body is responsible for processing those negative emotions. And what happens to your energy bank when you're feeling any emotion in the negative spectrum?

The answer: A withdrawal of your own life energy is taken when you remain in the presence of such people.

Common Sense Tip: When others choose not to come halfway, then it's best for you to keep your energy reserves high and step out of the dialogue before you become energetically drained.

Yes, there are times where you are confronted with difficult or challenging individuals. However, there are ways to keep your Energy Bank Account neutral.

We'll show you practical tools to use when placed in uncomfortable communication settings, as well as show you how to step out of a situation where you notice you've already taken a negative emotional hit.

The goal is to keep your levels of awareness high and your emotions on the positive end of the spectrum. In both cases, you create energy reserves in your Energy Bank Account as often and as long as possible.

Three Common Sense Ways to Break Rapport

There are many natural ways we break rapport when listening to someone else, such as ceasing to make eye contact with the speaker, looking repeatedly at our watch or nearby clock to indicate we're out of time, or even turn our body away from the one who's talking. Each of these non-verbal cues sends the message that we are ready to end the discussion.

Some speakers will notice your body posture and begin to end the conversation. Yet, others are entirely unaware of your subtle cues. We call these individuals "cling-ons". In these cases, it's necessary to become an assertive speaker and take charge of your own energy.

Imagine that you are stopping by the store and you run into an old friend who you haven't seen in a while. She just returned from a month-long trip to Europe and can't wait to tell you all about it.

However, you're on your way home to meet some other friends for dinner.

Because you don't want to be late for your engagement, and you want to break rapport with your current counterpart, there are simple and easy ways to end the conversation.

Option 1: Reschedule

You can say, "Wow. It sounds like your trip was amazing. Can we get together at another time to talk more about it?"

If you really want to hear about her adventures, then it's best to set a timeline for your next meeting. You might schedule a date for later in the week or any time you have available, even scheduling a time to talk on the phone to decide on a time to meet, keeps harmony between both you and your friend, even if you have to leave at the moment.

Option 2: Take Control of the Conversation

If you want to break rapport, but don't want to see this individual at another time, it's still essential to take control of the conversation by saying, "Wow! It sounds like your trip was amazing. I am on my way to another engagement at this time and it's not a good time for me to talk. Welcome home. It was great to see you."

Option 3: Interrupt an Oblivious Speaker

If the speaker is oblivious to your subtle ways of breaking rapport through your body language, you might have to interrupt her dialogue and say, "I'm sorry to interrupt. This is just not a good time for me."

At this point, you can decide whether to set another time to meet or just leave the conversation graciously.

Whatever option you choose, the goal is to keep your energy levels high.

How to Break Rapport When Faced With Negative Tones

Now, what if the person you're talking to is taking on a negative tone and you need to break rapport?

The same rules of using direct positive questions to respond to your counterpart apply here. If the other person sounds upset, you can say, "I sense a difference in your tone. Is there something you would like to share with me? What's going on behind your words so that I can better understand the situation?"

After listening to their response, you have the choice to stay in the conversation with them, or say that you need to think about their request and talk another time.

Now, if a person is just being negative in their dialogue and you notice your own Energy Bank Account being drained, you ask the speaker directly:

- "Well, how would you like it to be instead?" (This shifts their focus to the direct positive quadrant.)

- "If you could make things turn out differently, what would you like to see happen? (This gets the person to begin thinking about solutions instead of the problem.)

- "Is there something you would like me to do about it?" (This removes the responsibility from your shoulders to take action. Most of the time, the speaker just needs a listening ear. If they do request that you take action, you can accept or decline based on your own energy levels. If you can remain neutral throughout this process, then you can stay in this conversation. If you feel drained, it's best to break rapport.)

Regardless of the way another person is talking to you in a conversation, it's how you respond to that information that matters most. The goal is for you to stay whole-brained, balanced, and positive. When you notice you are feeling stressed as a listener, it's best to break rapport.

This can be done by asking yourself, "What is the simplest way to handle this situation?"

With practice posing direct questions to your speaker, it gets easier and easier to maintain control, poise, and confidence in any situation.

Putting it all Together

Listening is the flipside of assertive speaking on the coin of communication. As a skilled listener, others feel respected, validated, and valued in their relationship with you, even if for a brief moment.

New Common Sense Tools to Master the Art of Listening:

- **The 3 R's:** By hearing a request, repeating that request, and then responding, you slow down a conversation and create an understanding between both parties before moving forward.

- **Ask Questions:** Using the Four-Quadrants of Communication from Chapter 3, listeners are able to understand which language a speaker is using and move the conversation into direct, positive dialogue.

- **Expanding Balloon Exercise:** When challenging people are encountered, it's not always easy to remain balanced while listening. The visualization of a balloon can help you set non-verbal boundaries and remain unaffected by potentially negative speech.

Chapter 5

WELL IF YOU'D ONLY AGREE WITH ME WE WOULDN'T HAVE TO ARGUE ALL THE TIME!

Chapter 5

Generate Harmony in your Relationships

"Rejoice in all your relationships, the ones that are easy and the ones that are not. They are bringing you exactly what you need to know for your soul's awakening and evolution."—Mary Manin Morrissey

In this Chapter

- Use compassion in relationships
- Understand the different needs of men and women
- Make your intimate relationship last
- Hold your boundaries with love
- Clearly and directly ask for hugs
- Easily resolve conflicts

Relationships exist all around you. Based on your natural instincts as a social being, you interact with numerous people around you daily. Relationships occur in your home, your workplace, the schoolyard, your immediate community, and with the world at large.

Your beliefs, and life perspective, directly affect how you create, maintain, and dissolve relationships.

Yet, communication is the common denominator in all human interactions. There are times when you're the speaker and times when you're the listener. The goal of those relationships is to have successful communication.

For relationships to have success, several components must be present. First, there must be a desire for both people to share openly and honestly, where communication between all parties serve as the vehicle for both to feel heard and validated. Second, it's important to maintain an understanding that a relationship is not just about you. This includes keeping others' feelings in mind. And third, successful relationships look to find solutions that allow everyone to win. When this happens, everyone involved can feel like a deposit was made in their life force Energy Bank Account.

Emotional Energy in Relationships

While the basics of communication refer to the speaking and listening that occurs between individuals, there is an emotional undercurrent below each action.

All actions are energetic and so are the emotions behind them. Just like a magnet, we have the ability to attract or repel others. And it's the quality of our emotions that affect our life Energy Bank Account—you either add a deposit or experience a withdrawal based on your interactions with others.

Consider the simplistic idea that there are two kinds of people you interact with on a daily basis—positive people and negative people. Positive individuals have a high life Energy Bank Account balance. They radiate any range of positive emotions, from contentment and peacefulness to joy and love. When in their presence, or in any type of conversation with them, their positive emotions are contagious.

The other kind of people you see daily are the negative individuals who display emotions such as frustration, apathy, anger, or fear. Their own negativity continually takes energy from their bank account, which can often cause them more irritation, illness, and discontent.

So, what happens in relationships when these kinds of people interact?

The energetic principles of relationships are very simple.

Common Sense Tip: When positive energy (people) meets positive energy (people), the positive energy swells.

Thus, when you have two excited people, the excitement grows. Think of the last time you went to the concert of your favorite musician. You might have a room, stadium, or amphitheater full of others just like you who love that artist. When your favorite songs are played, thousands of others share the same passion, and the enthusiasm of the crowd expands.

When positive energy meets positive energy, relationships are formed and fostered.

Negative energy follows a similar pattern when it meets any other form of negativity. When negative energy (people) meets negative energy (people), the negative energy gets larger. Notice what happens when you have someone complaining about life. If they meet another individual who also feels disgruntled or upset, the combined negativity of both people creates a stronger sense of negativity.

If two people forget about the positive reasons they've stayed together, relationships can end when the negative energy gets too strong on both ends.

The question now arises, what happens when positive energy (people) meets negative energy (people)?

The answer: Whichever energy is stronger prevails 100% of the time.

Let us explain. Consider you are feeling a negative emotion. If you run into a friend who is full of laughter, their good feelings can bring you around to feeling better, as if you borrowed their energy to support your own. They can help take you from an energetic withdrawal to an energetic deposit.

The goal, when aware of any negative emotion, is to stop the drain on your Energy Bank Account. You can then use your awareness to make a conscious choice to move into more positive energy.

Now, when you are experiencing a positive emotion and you run into someone who's having a difficult day, there are two things that can happen.

First, if your positive energy is strong enough, you can overpower their negativity. This can help bring them around to a pleasant attitude. However, if their negative energy is stronger than your good feelings, they can pull you out of a centered state and begin to write checks against your own Energy Bank Account. This can happen when one person is upset in a relationship and they try to bring their unhappiness to the attention of their partner, friend, or coworker.

Emotional Energy Exchange in Action: Trevor's Story

Trevor is a self-motivated, focused individual. When left alone, he worked at a rapid pace. But when someone else walked in to share their problems, Trevor would listen to show respect. Oftentimes, he would get sucked into their negative energy spiral and find it difficult to re-focus after they finally left his space. His thoughts were scattered. His body was tense and he was irritable. Trevor would have to take a short walk before he could even reconnect with his previous activity.

In a broader sense, when you notice differences within groups of people, or between yourself and others, you might create negative energy. Remember, all wars are fought over differences. On the contrary, positive energy is created when similarities between people are recognized. In fact, we share more commonalities with people than differences in the broader perspective of life.

It's our goal to help you maintain a positive Energy Bank Account and eliminate unwanted withdrawals of your life energy. There are numerous Common Sense Tools in this chapter that will teach you to either maintain your positive energy or break rapport when you can't stay positive. Learning to use these specific communication skills can then return a relationship back to the positive realm as quickly and easily as possible.

The Top Three Emotions in Communication: Sympathy, Empathy, and Compassion

Three very common and often misunderstood emotions in communication are sympathy, empathy, and compassion. While there are many definitions for these words, we're going to reference them in the context of relationships. And, in fact, each emotion has an energetic equivalent when dealing with others.

It boils down to positive and negative energy continually interacting. Your own energetic reserve and skill level in communication will determine whether you respond to another with sympathy, empathy, or compassion.

> The emotions of sympathy, empathy and compassion can be used in many arenas. Our goal is to understand their role in relationships and communication.

The goal is to recognize the attributes of each emotion when it arises in your relationships and become aware of the consequences each might present. The emotions of sympathy and empathy often cause you to leave an interaction feeling drained, guilty, or upset. These negative emotions can drain your life Energy Bank Account.

Conversely, the positive emotion of compassion keeps you feeling neutral, at worst, and uplifted with energetic deposits, at best. The goal is to feel comfortable expressing yourself honestly to others with your emotions, keeping yourself and the other person in the most positive position possible.

First, let's look at what each emotion represents.

Sympathy

Sympathy is when you buy into another's problem and you pick up the same residual energy or negative effect from their issue.

Sympathy in Action: Jessica's Story

Jessica is having a miserable day at work with another migraine headache. When her coworker, John, walks into her office, he says, "Wow, Jessica. It's too bad you have another brain buster! My head hurts, too, from all of the number-crunching I've been doing this morning. If I have to look at my computer screen another second, I'm pretty sure my head's going to explode."

In this case, both Jessica and John are validating the other's condition. They commiserate together and not only confirm the negative experience, but get sucked into a larger vortex of unsupportive emotions. You have negative energy meeting negative energy and that feeling grows larger.

As John listened to Jessica's story, he amplified the negative energy by sharing his own painful problems. John engaged in sympathy. When this happens, the listener gets pulled into the sympathetic response unknowingly. Sometimes people tell the negative stories with others out of habit. Other times, you start sharing unintentionally.

In either case, both individuals end up in a negative space. John initially intended to enter Jessica's office to see if she had the payroll ready for the month, and unexpectedly walked away with a stronger headache that when he began his conversation with her.

The sympathetic emotion can amplify and further cause a domino effect. For example, Jessica's pain at the office was magnified by John's. Then he had a conversation with another co-worker, who engaged in sympathy, and also enlarged the problem. Soon enough, everyone in the office had a headache. All of this started by the sharing of a negative experience.

Sympathy is often experienced by easily-worried individuals, like some mothers, for example. Let's say a pre-school mom hears word about the compromised safety of the school district. Now, instead of dealing with the stress herself, and her limited perspective clouded by fear, she decides to tell every other mother she knows about the lack of safety for their kids at school.

Now, the other moms who buy into the same fear have taken the sympathetic route. It's now created a domino effect of worry.

So, when anyone engages in sympathy, both people can experience an energetic withdrawal from their life Energy Bank Account because nothing is done to resolve the issue. John didn't help Jessica with her headache and the mothers didn't improve the school system's safety.

Empathy

Empathy is when the listener hears what is being said by the speaker and remains fairly neutral. It's as though you're listening to what's going on, but you're not entirely engaged in what the other is saying.

Empathy in Action: Erin's Story

Erin's friend, Katie, constantly complained about her son's problems as a freshman in college. She listened politely to Katie's stories, often responding with simple phrases such as "That's too bad. I know the first year away from home can be challenging for many kids". Yet, Erin didn't intend to get emotionally involved in Katie's problems. She knew she was already juggling way too many of her own. Instead, Erin was simply listening to show respect for her good friend.

Empathy might also have a disingenuous component.

Empathy in Action: Evelyn's Story

Evelyn, the grandmother on the popular Two and a Half Men television series, perfectly demonstrates insincere empathetic responses. She verbally expresses that she wants more time with her sons, Charlie and Alan. Yet, when she actually takes the time to see them, she's more concerned with her latest social catastrophe or surgical procedure. She feigns interest in her sons momentarily, but quickly returns back to her own concerns.

When a listener carries an empathetic tone or posture, it's as though they are often in a defensive position. While they appear to be hearing the speaker, they really don't want to engage in an emotional connection with what the speaker is sharing. And they definitely don't want to commit to help out with the problem. It's as though they know what the frustration, depression, or discomfort is like and they avoid sympathy to bypass sharing those emotions.

Empathy in Action: Mark's Story

This happened when Mark worked with Lee at the same school. In fact, they shared the same classroom, day in and day out. Lee always talked about his problems with women and Mark was forced to listen to them in their small shared space, often when he had other important things he needed to do. Mark found that he was giving up his own energy to Lee and could not offer any solutions.

When Mark could not hold his own boundaries, he became defensive. He didn't want to drain his own energy, but didn't know how to help his friend, either. Mark could only respond by saying, "You've got to be kidding" or "That sounds horrible", all the while trying to get away from the situation and break rapport. Over a period of time, a strain on the relationship occurred.

Just as in the example above, listeners can have their own boundaries crossed when internally confused about how to effectively handle the situation. On one hand they want to remain neutral. But on the other hand, they've set themselves up with a protective buffer to the negativity of the speaker. In any case, they are unable to maintain a neutral or positive life Energy Bank Account or offer any real help or support to their counterpart.

Compassion

Compassion entails genuinely listening to the speaker, finding out what you can do to help, and offering some kind of assistance. By showing compassion, you know that if you do the best you can, and your advice isn't heeded by someone else, you don't take it personally.

However, if you offer advice and feel offended by the other person's lack of action, then you're really in judgment. Your negative emotions really reflect an internal belief that your ideas or solutions to the problem are right and any other

> "If you want others to be happy, practice compassion. If you want to be happy, practice compassion." —Dalai Lama

action would be wrong. In addition, you step into an over-responsible role. When you take responsibility for another individual and their actions, you drain your own Energy Bank Account when they don't take action as you suggest.

When using compassion, you realize it's not about you. You understand that the other person is ultimately the one responsible for their actions and you know you've done your best. This genuine giving of yourself, without expectation, keeps your energy reserves high, regardless of another's behavior. Then when you experience and share compassion, you are able to remain centered, balanced, and honest with everyone involved. This creates the most positive outcome for all concerned and utilizes direct positive communication skills.

Compassion in Action: A Lost Pet

Let's say your neighbor loses his pet. When he comes frantically to your door, you share your time and energy to help him out. Instead of talking about how painful it is when this happens or keeping your distance while sharing empathy, you are led to a heartfelt response to help make the situation better for everyone. This can be printing flyers on your computer for your neighbor, or taking the time to put those flyers up, or even walking the nearby streets yourself looking for the pet.

Your Turn: Is it Sympathy, Empathy, or Compassion?

To re-emphasize the difference between sympathy, empathy, and compassion, imagine that you're on a ship at sea when another passenger goes overboard. The recent storm has created rough waters and large waves. While you immediately think of ways to save your drowning counterpart, there are a few options that come to mind.

Your first choice is to secure one end of a safety line around your waist and the other around the ship's mast. You make sure to wear a life vest, so you don't drown in the rescue process, and you're ready to jump right into tumultuous waters. However, when you feel the water splash against your face before you leave the ship, you think, "Wow, that water's cold!"

Instead of taking the plunge, you yell out to your friend, "You're in such a tough position with those crashing waves and freezing water temperatures! You must be having a rough time out there. But, I'm here for you. I feel your fear."

Is this sympathy, empathy, or compassion?

While you offer your support to the person in need, you are still safe on the ship and you don't really take any action to alleviate the situation. This is empathy.

The second alternative is to jump into the ocean and try to bring the struggling individual back onboard the ship.

Is this sympathy, empathy, or compassion?

If you make this decision, both you and the other person are now in trouble. You're now much worse off than a few minutes ago. This would represent sympathy.

The third option is you take a nearby life buoy, throw it out to your friend, and help bring him or her back safely on board. You also wrap them in a blanket, give them some warm tea, and remind them that they're going to be okay.

Is this sympathy, empathy, or compassion?

By doing this, you get yourself into a safe place on the ship and utilize your clear thoughts to make the most out of the situation. If you guessed compassion, congratulations!

Moving into Compassion

Like many of the previous common sense tools in this book, the first step to making any changes begins with a heightened sense of awareness. You might have new insights about yourself that result from a new situation or perhaps think about the world differently based on new ideas presented in recent research. This increased awareness provides a fresh perspective from which you can make confident decisions about how to move forward.

The same principles of awareness apply when deciding whether to respond with sympathy, empathy or compassion in a relationship. When dealing with others, or perhaps someone who's challenging, the goal is to experience and share compassion. This increases your own Energy Bank Account and offers the other a change to uplift theirs. If, in the process, you're unable to maintain your own positive energy, you can break rapport respectfully. This section teaches you how to move into compassion and the following one provides tools to break rapport.

The expressions of sympathy and empathy arise from individual vulnerability. When you recognize your own weaknesses, you can shore them up and then move into compassion.

Compassion in Action: Dealing with a Negative Co-Worker

Let's say you have a consistently negative co-worker. Even if you don't know someone like this at the office, you probably recognize people in your life who view the world with "the glass is half empty" perspective. Anyway, when this person speaks, you'd rather be anywhere else but caught in the web of downward spiraling dialogue.

If you break rapport and lash out at them because you are tired of listening to their downbeat stories, then your reaction comes from a defensive position. You're trying to remain neutral, but your outburst creates animosity between you two. If the speaker took your words personally, it could destroy any chance for harmony in the relationship.

Instead of coming from the mindset that "they're too negative," you could respond to their language by saying, "I've noticed that you've been more negative lately. Do you just need someone to listen so you can get things off your chest? Or "is there something else I can do to help?"

Using the power of questions to turn the dialogue into the direct positive quadrant of communication shows compassion.

Feel, Felt, Found

If you have a friend who is struggling, and it's hard for you to be around them, compassion acknowledges their situation and offers some ways to improve it. The "feel, felt, found rule," commonly found in the business world, is an easy way to let the speaker know you recognize their feelings. You also create a bond with them by giving an example of when you may have felt that way in the past.

If the situation is something you've never experienced personally, it's more effective to liken the situation to one of a friend or something similar of your own. Remaining honest is essential for rapport. Finally, you can offer some guidance or direction from your own experiences. This helps move the conversation from a limited, unsolvable issue to an unlimited, solution-focused mentality.

Compassion in Action: Break-Up Blues

The conversation could hypothetically go as follows:

Person 1: "I just had the worst break-up of my life. Now, I've wasted the last five years of my life on a relationship that went nowhere. The worst part is, I feel so empty inside. Will I ever find someone who is right for me?"

Person 2: "I'm so sorry that happened. I know how you **feel**. I've **felt** that way when I was going through my divorce. I **found** that allowing myself to feel all of my emotions was very healthy. I also **found** that spending some time with close friends helped boost my spirits. Would you like to join me and my friends in our weekly book club?"

The Feel, Felt, Found Template

Here is an example of how the Feel, Felt, Found Tool can be used to create harmonious relationships:

Person 1: This is usually the initial speaker in the conversation, or at least is at this point in a given conversation. They are hurt, frustrated, angry, or experiencing some form of a negative emotion.

Person 2: This is the listener at this point in the dialogue. Repeat the speaker's emotional hurts, thus acknowledging their feelings. This can be as simple as saying, "I know how you **feel**." You can also be more specific and say, "I know how overwhelming anger can be" or "I know how depression can seem debilitating".

Then, share some specific, personal, and honest example of when you had a similar experience. "I have felt that

Allow some time for **Person 1** to respond.

Then, you can use compassion to move into a more positive direction. Think of what helped you solve the problem in the past. What techniques, tools, people, or circumstances allowed you to resolve the issue? You can add, "I have found that _____ or by doing _____, this _____ occurred."

Taking it a Step Further: Ask a Question

If you want to go above and beyond the "feel, felt, found rule," you can add a question to bring them into the direct positive quadrant of communication. "Would you like me to refer you to someone or give you some more ideas or just be here to listen?" Closing with the phrase, "Does this make sense?" is often useful is showing the other person respect.

Asking specific questions will help them give you a more direct response. Then, instead of guessing or turning defensive, you know exactly how to move forward to make the situation beneficial for everyone.

The WAWAHs

This acronym stands for **Who Asks Who And How**.

In addition to verbally showing compassion through the "feel, felt, found method," giving a hug can be one of the best ways to demonstrate compassion non-verbally.

Scientific research supports the theory that physical touch is necessary for physical, social, and emotional well-being. Touch can make us feel better about ourselves and help relieve pain. Hugging, which is a special form of contact, has many benefits. In addition to showing compassion for another person, hugging:

- Feels good
- Dispels loneliness
- Overcomes fears
- Enhances self-esteem
- Spreads happiness
- Reverses the aging process
- Alleviates tension
- Expands joy
- And keeps shoulder and arm muscles firm

In addition to being portable and heat-building, hugs are an easy way to share kindness with others.

We created the WAWAHs to help you decide **when hugs are appropriate** and **what kind should be shared** based on the situation. Just as an assertive speaker takes responsibility for their spoken words, sharing compassion with a hug requires thoughtful and respectful action.

The first part of the WAWAH, the "who asks who component," reflects on the permission aspect of hugging. Most times your close friend or lover will welcome a hug. However, there are times when respect for another's space or privacy is needed.

Sometimes you receive non-verbal messages that a hug is permissible and you respond with a warm embrace. There are even other times when you announce your desire to share contact by saying, "I'd like to give you a hug. Is that okay?"

The importance of WAWAHs is to understand who asks who for a hug. Many times you recognize that the other person is in need of some compassion, in which case you might ask, "Can I give you a hug?"

Other times, you're feeling down and want some compassion from a friend or partner. In this case, you become an assertive speaker and directly request for a hug. This can simply be stated, "I could really use a hug right now. Would you give me one?"

> "Love yourself enough to surround yourself with friends who listen, cherish, honor, esteem, and support your worth."
> –Scott Peck

You might even say, "How about a hug before I leave for [work or my interview or match or wherever you're heading]?"

Common Sense Tip: If you want more hugs, fewer hugs, longer hugs or shorter hugs, it's your responsibility to speak your mind. Because we don't always get what we want, it's important to compromise when another is not willing to share.

The second part of the WAWAH, which refers to the how of hugging, teaches you which type of hug is appropriate in any given situation. A compassionate, friendship hug is obviously much different than a lover's embrace.

There are heart-to-heart hugs, ten-second hugs, two-minute hugs, and sideways embraces. You can hug playfully. You can hug supportively. You can even hug affectionately or tenderly.

Knowing which type of hug to share is just as important as knowing when to ask or give a hug.

The WAWAH Activity

Practice asking for a hug until you become comfortable with it. Practice giving hugs until you feel comfortable with it. Use hugs in daily relationships. Kym does this with those in her senior yoga classes. Oftentimes they are too shy to ask for a hug, but Kym knows that they receive less physical interactions now that they are in a specific senior home. By offering to give a hug to those she encounters, the seniors can accept or decline without any feelings getting hurt. The hugs are friendly and compassionate.

Take one day this week and see if you can use the WAWAH. Ask if you can give four hugs to different people and ask to receive four hugs from various people. If four sounds daunting, start with asking to give one hug and asking to receive one hug.

The goal is to increase physical contact with love, compassion, and awareness. Are you ready to give and receive hugs?

Similar and Complementary Relationships

While moving into compassion is the goal in any given relationship, there are those intimate connections that require some specific attention and understanding in order to create harmony.

Intimate relationships, like friendships, often form because of shared interests or other commonalities. It's the same principle of positive energy meeting positive energy to create an even more positive experience.

Now the formation of an intimate relationship stems from similar interests or complementary characteristics. These two ways of coming together form what we call Similar Relationships or Complementary Relationships. In either case, these bonds are created based on the unique personalities, interests, and goals of each individual.

When two people come together with many shared interests, they form a Similar Relationship. It's when two people have numerous "matching pictures."

He says, "I like tennis."

She says, "Me, too. In fact, my regular Wednesday league is fantastic, and we all go out to our favorite restaurant, Yum-Yum Diner, for food and drinks afterwards."

He replies, "Wow, Yum-Yum Diner makes the best burger in town. I love going there!"

You get the idea. When two people match pictures, they find commonalities in their routines, behaviors, likes, dislikes, sense of humor, and styles. With numerous compatible traits, Similar Relationships have the highest success rate for lasting happiness. In fact, this is what the whole online dating scene is based upon—creating matching pictures with the hopes of creating sustainable relationships.

Complementary Relationships, on the other hand, are when two people come together because of strengths they see in their romantic counterpart. It's like the yin and the yang uniting to create perfect balance. One partner has something the other wants or desires, and vice versa.

For example, you have one individual who's an artist, with a fluid sense of creativity, freedom, and spontaneity. The other partner is an attorney—very logical, focused, and realistic. One can decorate a beautiful house and the other can balance the checkbook. They help each other out in numerous ways.

While each individual brings certain strengths to the relationship, their weaknesses are balanced out by the capabilities of the other. Complementary Relationships do have some similar attributes, but the differences far outweigh the commonalities.

Complementary Relationships are the most exciting, but often are the most challenging to keep together over a long period of time.

4 Types of Intimate Relationships

Whether a couple is complementary or similar in nature, the two people end up creating one of four relationship types—dependent, co-dependent, interdependent, or soul mates. Based on habitual patterns of behavior, each person ends up taking on familiar roles over the long term. These roles can either support or undermine the success of a relationship.

Relationship Type 1: Dependent

Dependent

Dependent relationships are generated when one person is reliable, consistent, and steady and the other person leans on them for support. Person 1 is strong and the other relies on them for strength. And, this type of relationship can be female-dominated—matriarchal—or male-dominated—patriarchal. The strength of one can be due to financial security, decision-making capability, or overall life health.

The problems occur in this relationship if the anchor, or stable person, decides to leave or is separated by death. Then, when the second person loses their base of support, they often crash and burn.

Dependent Relationships in Action: Two Couple's Stories

Alex and June have raised a family together. It's a patriarchal relationship where the stability of the two is derived from Alex's income alone. In this case, June has established her role as a mother, home-maker, and community socialite. After years of marriage, Alex and June decide to separate. In this case, Alex is the stable, upright individual and June is dependent on him for financial support. If he leaves, June could fall down and have to find a way to rebuild her life.

Or let's look at an older couple, Robert and Hannah, who are in the first decade of Robert's retirement years. Robert has spent a majority of their relationship as the income earner and Hannah has taken care of the homestead. Now that Robert has given up his 9 to 5, he finds himself at Hannah's mercy. She is the one who feels comfortable with the daily routine at home. Hannah cooks the meals, plans their trips, and coordinates the household budget. Robert feels dependent on his wife to keep life in order. If she passed away, or ever decided to leave the relationship, Robert would have a challenging time starting over.

Relationship Type 2: Co-dependent

Co-Dependent

In a co-dependent relationship, both Person 1 and Person 2 are leaning back-to-back for support. They both rely on each other equally to get through the relationship and through life. There is an equal distribution of power.

If either person in the relationship decided to leave, or passed away, the other person might fall down. This can be very common in complementary relationships, where one person control the finances and the other cares for domestic responsibilities. Because both are so good at what they do individually, they don't take the time to teach the other person. Therefore, when the relationship ends, both can be unprepared to confidently move forward in life.

Relationship Type 3: Interdependent

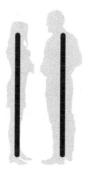

Interdependent

When a relationship is interdependent in nature, both Person 1 and Person 2 have a strong individual sense of themselves. Each person is aware of their likes and dislikes. They have a high sense of self-worth and expect the best to happen for them in life.

When two independent people come together, their lives are enriched by the relationship. They like themselves and they accept the other, regardless of strengths or weaknesses. There is a lot of love in an interdependent relationship.

In fact, interdependent couples form the strongest of the first three relationship types and are most likely to survive with long-term happiness. Person 1 takes the time to see life from the perspective of their partner and vice versa. Person 2 also works in cooperation with the other to joyfully maintain the relationship. They often discuss information openly, know each other's verbal and non-verbal cues, and are willing to learn important life lessons with their partner.

If this type of relationship were to end, then each person would have an easier time moving forward with life due to their own personal confidence, their independent life skills, and their flexible perspective on the world as a whole.

Relationship Type 4: Soul Mates

Soulmates

While it is commonly believed that people are drawn together for cosmic reasons, a soul connection with another does not always lead to an intimate relationship. This can happen due to timing, nature of the relationship, and geographical location. Soul mates often feel a natural attraction for one another, but it doesn't always indicate that an intimate relationship will ensue.

Yet, when it does, the fourth type of relationship is generated. It looks similar to an interdependent relationship in the fact that both Person 1 and Person 2 are independent. They know who they are and respect the other for their wide array of attributes. This soul mate energy has one more component—the divine bond connecting them together.

It is our belief that there is a divine purpose behind all events in life. The other three types of relationships offer important life lessons for each individual, and should they choose to learn from such experiences, they will be better off in the long run.

The divine guidance behind soul mate relationships is often miraculous in nature. Love is the glue that holds these two people effortlessly together. They share frequent thoughts, often without having to speak a word. Intuition, trust, and understanding connect soul mates at the deepest level of their beings.

Soul Mate Relationship in Action: Meredith and William's Story

Steve had an employee, Meredith, who worked with him for years in his interior design business. She was a designer and her husband, William, was an accountant. They both idolized each other and the love they had for one another was palpable. He was short and stocky. She was tall and lean. Despite their outward differences, they spoke highly of each other and seldom had any fights. Their household, with two growing children, was orderly and full of vibrant health.

Even though they came from different religious backgrounds, they had a strong faith in something bigger than themselves. William and Meredith felt destined to be together. Because of their spiritual connection, they had a broader perspective that helped them sort through life's challenges. In essence, their union celebrated the higher power that guided them through life.

Making any Relationship Successful

Whether two people come together because of similarities or respected differences, there are simple techniques to integrate into the relationship to make it last over a long period of time. Likewise, a co-dependent, dependent, or interdependent relationship can be improved through simple and easy techniques.

Similar Relationships naturally come together over commonalities. While it's easy to become bored or complacent over time, Similar Relationships need more spark to keep going. There are enough shared interests that the relationship has a strong foundation and both people can be free to pursue new endeavors.

Complementary Relationships are initiated by respected differences between two people. Now, over time, the relationship can get into grooves where one person might no longer need or want what the other has to offer. If he likes football and she likes opera, then it takes a bit more work in a Complementary Relationships to find common ground.

6 Common Sense Solutions for any Relationship Type

These activities are powerful ways to reconnect two people in meaningful ways. Some variations within each exercise can specifically target similar or complementary relationships.

Create a pictorial collage

Have both people make a collage about their unique interests, travel ideas, and personal inspirations. You can cut pictures out of magazines or print pictures from the internet. Combine those images on an 18" x 24" poster board in a creative way. Then, share your pictorial ideas with your partner. This work can be very powerful because it involves the visual, auditory, and kinesthetic senses to create harmony in the relationship.

If you are in a similar relationship, notice unique interests within your collages and begin to incorporate those new concepts into your lives.

If you are in a complementary relationship, notice parallel ideas in your collages and focus on those. If you both like warm weather, find a mutual place you can travel. Perhaps you can find new foods to try together, people to meet, or activities that can enhance a common bond.

Some collage ideas include:

- What you have in common, which focuses on unity
- Ways that each person is different, which establish independence and flexibility
- What you want your future to look like
- Things you love about the other person
- Goals and dreams

Write a Top 50 list

Have each individual make a list of their top 50 favorite things in life and share your ideas with your partner.

For similar relationships, highlight your differences. Focus on one item at a time and add the interest or activity into your lives for adventure.

For complementary relationships, focus on similarities that both of you enjoy. While you may not have the exact same items, places, or people listed, there are commonalities within categories. Then use those connections to create activities and goals for the future. Remember, compromise is essential here.

For example, if she loves to dance and he likes to play golf, the conscious decision by both people to take an interest in the other's passions can enhance their relationship. Perhaps he decides to take dance lessons to get an idea of why she likes ballroom. She might even take some beginning golf lessons and buy a set of used clubs to join her man in the game. While she may never match his enthusiasm or ability in the sport, her effort alone boosts the relationship. He might never become America's top dancer, but his determination to become competent on the dance floor shows her an incredible amount of respect. The relationship blossoms from the mutual bonding that takes place between both people.

Date night once a week

Date nights are one of the most fun and exciting aspects of a budding relationship. Now, the same spark can be used to keep the love alive. Take turns planning date nights for each other. One week she plans the activity and the next week he plans it. Scheduling the date night on a regular basis can be helpful, like every Thursday. They research or plan around what the other likes, which also sparks the interest to keep up with each changing fad, desire, or idea.

Plan something special

Part of the excitement of joining as a couple involves the anticipation that lies in the unknown. Generate unique experiences once a month that recreate this experience. This could include a weekend hideaway, anywhere from simple to luxurious in scope. It might be a game night with friends or day hike with a picnic. Choose something that is larger than a date night activity and adds excitement, enthusiasm, and romance into the equation.

Anniversary Collages

On an anniversary, make a collage about what's important to you and then share them with the other person. They can also do a collage of what they appreciate in you. This helps you stay in touch with one another as you grow in life. Collages can focus on what about the past year was special to you or what you would like to see happen in the year to come.

Yearly Binder

Use a one-inch binder to hold all of the memories for each year as a couple. This binder can hold cards, movie stubs, travel memorabilia, photos and other special memories for each year. The binder allows you to reflect on the good times you've shared together when times get difficult. With a way to remember shared memories, it keeps you focused on the positive aspects of the relationship.

Male and Female Triangles

In order to initiate and sustain a harmonious relationship, there are a few components that need to be addressed. Males and females each have certain needs to facilitate a strong bond. Both the male and female components can best be understood when placed in the shape of a triangle.

The Male Triangle

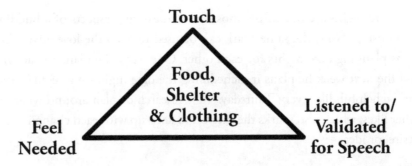

For males to feel content and supported in a relationship, their following needs must be recognized:

Touch

At the top of the male triangle is the need for physical touch. While the initial assumption linked to touch is sexual intercourse, touch includes hugs, hand holding, rubbing shoulders, and even massages.

Listened to and validated for Speech

On the right corner of the triangle is the need for males to be listened to and validated for what they say. While females might not agree with what the male has to say, it is important for them to address the fact that they hear what is being said. This falls in line with listening skills, where the listener repeats what was said in order to create understanding. When females hear what the male has to say, repeats it back to him, and then listens to the male's response, it allows the male to feel understood.

For example, if a man talks about taking a fishing trip with his friends for a week, the woman has several ways she can respond that let him know he's been heard. She can say, "Honey, what I hear you saying is that you want to go to Montana next week for a fishing excursion. Is that correct?"

She might know all the while that her mom is having surgery, which is going to take a lot of her time away from the family to care for her parent. By taking the time to repeat his request, she is validating his speech and letting him know she has heard what he said.

After he responds and clarifies his request, she can then explain the reasons why she disagrees with the decision to leave town. It offers the couple a chance to communicate in a clear, decisive way and boost a component of the male triangle.

Feel Needed

The left corner of the male triangle is the desire to feel needed. This means that men need to be appreciated often and recognized for their worth. Not only does it help boost their self-esteem and feed the male ego, it supplements a man's natural drive for production.

Males are hardwired to provide for their partner or family and their self-worth is intrinsically tied to those actions. When a man feels needed, he feels like he's doing his job. He feels better and his outcome-driven tendencies are appreciated.

The Male Core: Food, Shelter, Clothing

The center of the male triangle is comprised of the basic needs for food, clothing and shelter. Many jokes are derived from the notion that males are Neanderthals. Yet, there is a grain of truth in such jokes. When they have a roof over their head, clothes on their back, and food on their tables, males are generally content. In fact, they may be entirely oblivious to other problems in a relationship when these basic needs are met. They are happy to relax and enjoy their lives when their core is fulfilled.

The Female Triangle

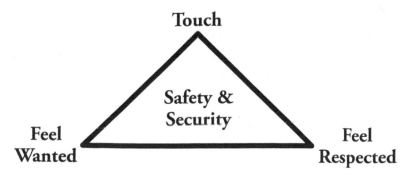

The female needs are entirely different from their male counterparts in an intimate relationship. For a woman to be satisfied in a relationship, the following needs must be acknowledged:

Touch

Just like male's, the top of the female's triangle is the need to be touched on a regular basis. This physical contact includes holding hands, hugging, and kissing as well as all forms of sexual interaction that are mutually agreed upon and enjoyed.

Feel Respected

When a woman feels the respect of her mate, it means that she knows her man thinks highly of her. Whether she is admired for her ability to have a career, manage money, creatively solve problems, effectively run a household, or how she helps the community, a woman likes to know she is revered by her partner.

Signs of respect are much different than expectations in the relationship. If a man assumes it's a woman's role to buy the groceries and it's his job to manage the finances, then she can often feel as though she's not trusted. Likewise, if her partner talks negatively behind her back, word traveling back to her via the grapevine can undermine any respect that's been built in the past.

It helps build a woman's respect when she is included in making important decisions. When a man gives her choices, requests her opinion, or allows her to feel like an equal partner in the relationship, her self-esteem gets boosted.

Feel Wanted

Women want to know that they are the number one priority in their partner's life. She wants to know that out of all the women in the world, she's at the top of his list. He can make her feel wanted just by the look in his eyes, a gift of flowers, or a love note. It's all of the romantic gestures that win her over in the first place that let her know he wants her more than anything else.

The Female Core: Security

The core of the female triangle is safety and security. As opposed to men, this center refers to more than food, clothing, and shelter. It means that women need to know that they're safe, protected, and will always be secure. Part of this necessity for protection evolves from the maternal care-taking instinct, even if no physical children are present.

This core of the female can relate to a sense of financial security, but it's not limited to that. Women want to feel secure in all aspects of her life, including relationships. If the core needs are not perceived to be met, a woman's primary search will be to find it, whether it be from someone or something else.

Fulfill the Male and Female Triangles

Both the male and female triangles rely on perception to be successful. If you recall, perception is the unique view we hold about the world around us. Therefore, males need to perceive physical touch, feel that they are listened to, and sense that they are needed by their woman.

Likewise, women need to perceive that they are touched often, respected, and wanted by their partner.

When there is an imbalance in either triangle, it makes harmony in a relationship more challenging. For example, if a man has forgotten to show respect for his woman for a long period of time, she will perceive that he doesn't value her good qualities. If a female has taken the independence reins for so long that she's fully self-sufficient, her male counterpart can feel that his skills are no longer necessary.

While there may be a broken or damaged portion of a triangle in any given relationship, on the male or female side, there are simple techniques that can help rebuild the relationship. One of the best ways to boost the perception of each partner is through improved communication. In fact, assertive speaking and skillful listening play a large role in bringing couples back into harmony.

Rebuilding the Male Triangle

Enhance Physical Touch

Communication between all individuals is best experienced in the direct positive quadrant communication. This is no different when addressing men in an intimate relationship.

One of the best ways to enhance physical touch with males is to utilize the power of questions to find out exactly what types of contact he likes best. Women, ask your man the following questions:

- What kinds of touch do you like most?

- Are you okay if we hold hands or walk arm in arm down the street?

- Are you comfortable with getting a kiss in public?

- Is it okay if I give you hugs? Are hugs appropriate in public as well as private?

- What kind of hugs do you like best?

- Do you like your feet rubbed?

- Can I give you a massage?

The goal to increase the physical touch is to talk about what kinds of contact is appropriate and desired by him. Instead of guessing, make your communication clear and open. When you know what he likes, you can support this component of his triangle. If he finds some affectionate displays uncomfortable, then find other ways to lovingly touch him.

Instead of nagging him about his poor hygiene habits, you can also offer to assist in keeping him looking his best. If you notice his toenails are getting long, you can offer to trim them for him after his shower. Perhaps he has long eyebrows or noticeable nose hair. You can buy him a nice pair of trimmers or offer to help keep those hairs tidy.

There are lots of simple ways to show you care. Be creative and sensitive, using questions and open dialogue, to enhance his need for physical touch.

Make him feel listened to and validated for his opinion

Women have the opportunity to enhance their listening skills while boosting men's triangles. It is important for males to perceive that they have been heard by their partner. The easiest way to do this is via the 3 R's exercise from Chapter 4.

When a man is sharing his opinion, sharing about his day, or telling a story, it is helpful to respond by:

- Repeating what you heard him say.

- Then follow your summary with a heart-felt question like, "Is there something you would like me to do about that? Or do you just want me to listen?"

Now, males don't expect their partner to agree with them all of the time. In fact, disagreements or misunderstandings are bound to occur when you have two or more perspectives given the same amount of information.

When a female disagrees, she can still validate his speech by repeating what she heard him say and then ask the following questions:

- "Is that what I heard you say?" or "Can you give me more information to clarify your point?

If she's given more clarification and she still disagrees, she can respond,

- "I think we'll have to agree to disagree on this subject. Is that okay with you?"

Simply by asking questions, she acknowledges his opinions and lets him know he's been heard.

Another way a female can confirm she received his messages is to request that he write down his ideas. This is especially helpful if she's busy with another task and can't give her partner the attention he deserves at that moment. Then, when both people have more time to talk, she can revisit his request with more attentiveness.

Make Him feel Needed

The simplest way to make a man feel needed is to thank him for all of the ways he contributes to the relationship. You can thank him for contributing financially and for his hard work. You can express your gratitude for his actions of taking out the trash, mowing the lawn, keeping the car serviced, fixing the plumbing, or putting his socks in the hamper.

Questions that express your need of him are always a great way to honor his skills. It's as simple as saying:

- "Honey, can you open this tomato jar? It's on so tight!"
- "Can you please get _____ from the garage, closet, or other room?"
- "I can't reach the top shelf. Would you please get that down for me?"

When he offers to do something on his own, like stop at the store to pick up some milk, or drop off the clothes at the cleaners, it's especially important to show your appreciation. The more you can bestow an attitude of gratitude for his help, the more his perception of feeling needed is enhanced.

There are also times when a man wants to show off his accomplishments.

The Male Triangle in Action: Steve's Story

Steve took a lot of time to fix the boat prior to putting it away for the winter. He provided Kym with an itemized list of his achievements numerous times. He was clearly proud of his hard work. While Kym could have been annoyed at the repetition, Kym met Steve's needs by responding to him with praise and thankfulness.

The bottom line: remind him that he's wonderful in a sincere and frequent way! The more you notice his deeds and appreciate his help, the more fulfilled he becomes within the relationship.

Rebuilding the Female Triangle

Enhance Her Physical Touch

While women need to take responsibility to ask the male what he would like for physical touch, she also needs to take the lead in telling her partner how she would like to be touched. Most males are not going to initiate this conversation, so it's her role to instruct him about what she prefers.

The Female Triangle in Action: Kym's Story

Kym was recently visiting two friends, Tim and Laura, who had started dating a few years prior. Laura was lying across the couch with her feet in Tim's lap and Kym sat across from them in an overstuffed chair. As they were all watching TV, Kym noticed how cozy Laura looked.

And, since Kym is a huge fan of foot rubs, she jokingly asked Tim, "Why don't you offer Laura a foot massage?"

Tim looked over at Laura. "Babe, do you want a foot rub?"

Laura smiled at the brilliant idea. While her eyes thanked Kym, she responded, "Well, yeah! That would be great!"

Kym giggled inwardly as she watched Tim awkwardly stroke Laura's feet. She couldn't help but send out a silent blessing for her Steve who gives the most thorough and comforting foot massages.

Again, it's the woman's responsibility to teach her man how she wants and needs to be touched. She can express her desire to hold hands, hug, kiss, have sex, give massages, get a backrub, or cuddle together. Because contact can be intimate, it's important to discuss that touch is wanted without always leading to sex. Touch can be fun foreplay, but it can also offer comfort and appreciation without the expectation to always lead to intercourse.

Make her feel Respected

Just as a female can teach her partner how to share wanted physical contact, she can also show him how to respect her. He might, in fact, already respect her for numerous reasons, but she can take the guesswork out of the process by openly discussing what's important.

There are many ways a man can respect a woman in an intimate relationship. Any one of these ways is effective:

- Hold the car door open for her
- Tell her she looks nice
- Notice if she's gone out of her way to clean the house, do things for the family, or support your business.
- Say "thank you" often and sincerely
- Ask her opinion about an upcoming decision
- Ask her about the books she's reading
- Show interest in her political views
- Listen, listen, listen

The Female Triangle in Action: Blake and Theresa's Story

Blake and Theresa have been married for five years. One evening, Blake had come home from work late in the evening feeling rather stressed about how much preparation he had for tomorrow's high school art lesson. Teresa, who wanted to help him out, stayed up late into the night cutting out paper shapes.

After an extremely late night and minimal sleep, their busy morning schedules kicked into gear. But, instead of thanking Theresa for her help, Blake left for work without acknowledging what had happened the night before.

In order to show his respect for Theresa, Blake could have left a thank you note where she'd see it before leaving for her job. He could have also called on his break to say "thank you" or even taken her to dinner to demonstrate his appreciation.

Make her Feel Wanted

There are numerous things a man can do to make his woman feel wanted. While birthdays and other holidays are easy reminders to show affection, random loving acts are often more powerful and recognized ways to boost her triangle. Ways to have her feel like your number one:

- Sending her flowers

- Sending a card

- Writing an unexpected love note

- Telling her how nice she looks

- Expressing endearments

- Winking at her across the room

- Creating secret love signals that only the two of you know. Then, you can share those signs across a dinner table or during a large party without using words. Steve and Kym use a light touch of their hand over their heart to share this message when around others and unable to speak.

By enhancing all components of the male and female triangles, a couple can remain in harmony and rapport. The goal is to have the male sense physical touch, feel listened to and validated for his speech, and appreciated for his skills. The goal in an intimate relationship is to have females experience physical contact, feel respected, and know that they're number one in their partner's life.

> The male and female triangles are easy illustrations to increase the understanding of complicated issues in intimate relationships.
>
> They can be used to identify major areas of stress as well as offer easy solutions to restore love and harmony.

Creating an awareness of the two triangles helps prevent miscommunications from occurring. With practice, both men and women can become proficient in meeting the needs of their partner.

The Common Sense Recipe for Conflict Resolution

Conflicts arise when the triangles are not fulfilled in relationships, false expectations aren't being realized, or miscommunications have occurred. Sometimes, the negative emotions in such conflicts cause rapport to be broken. (Revisit Chapter 4 for breaking rapport details.)

While communication may cease for a time, it's often necessary to resolve the situation as quickly and easily as possible.

Here are five easy steps to create a quick and confident resolution.

Step 1: Arrange a meeting with all parties involved in the conflict

The goal is to have a level playing field when meeting for conflict resolution. If you're arguing with your spouse, set a time when both of you can meet without any distractions. In an office environment, getting together with everyone present can prevent behind-the-scenes gossip and misunderstandings.

An emotionally-neutral setting is best.

Before meeting with others to discuss the issue, it's best to get yourself into a balanced, whole-brain state. You can do this by taking some deep breaths or sitting in a brain integration posture.

If you are leading the meeting, you can request that everyone involved write down their view of the problem, as well as practical solutions in a short, outline format, before they even enter the meeting.

For example, it's best to list complaints and solutions in bullet points, instead of lengthy paragraphs. Ideas can be paraphrased as follows:

- Problem: He's never on time. Solution: Call if he's going to be late.
- Problem: She takes a long time getting ready before we go out. Solution: Plan ahead for the evening and begin preparing earlier so we can leave on time.
- Problem: Bill over-talks everyone at the office. Solution: Plan meetings without Bill.

Just kidding, but you get the point. A real solution could be to give everyone two minutes to talk and use a timer. This makes it fair for everyone.

Step 2: Acknowledge the conflict

While some might want to avoid the problem entirely, it's necessary for all parties to agree on the nature of the conflict.

This includes being an assertive speaker and taking responsibility for whatever actions, ideas, or behaviors you might have contributed to the problem. Using "I" statements keep you accountable for your portion only.

Step 3: Ask direct questions about the conflict

Here, your skills as a listener come in extremely handy. The goal is to create clarity about the situation by repeating what you hear others say, asking questions when you need more information, and paying close attention when others are sharing their ideas.

Step 4: Discuss the desired outcome

We all want harmony. It's the goal of conflict resolution to get to an answer that benefits everyone as directly as possible. Focus on similarities here! The power of questions can be used to get others to dialogue in the direct positive quadrant of communication where solutions are created.

Acknowledge the problem-solving capability of everyone involved to help bring the issue to an agreement.

Step 5: Create a resolution

Whether or not you come to an agreement, you can at least agree to work toward a resolution that benefits everyone. Sometimes harmony can be created in one meeting. Other times, you need to schedule a follow-up gathering.

10 Common Sense Tips for Conflict Resolution

While the steps for conflict resolution are very effective for restoring harmony between people, there are ten simple tips to support the entire process.

1.   Choose your timing wisely

There are obviously more appropriate times than others to resolve a conflict. It's best to decide on a time that works for both you and the other person, if possible. This way, you can both be prepared and balanced before even beginning.

Some of the inappropriate times to initiate a discussion would be late at night, during the other person's favorite TV show, after several alcoholic drinks, or just before the other person leaves for work.

Common-sense solutions for unresolved issues are best discussed at a time when both people are able to respond equally.

2.   Stick to the issue

At the core of a conflict is a specific issue in question. For example, there might not be enough money to pay the bills for the month or the way one parent gets angry at the children upsets the other. Thus, to resolve the problem, it is necessary to handle one issue at a time. If this problem is linked to past miscommunications, then it's best to focus on the present issue and work to create solutions for the future.

This can be done without digging into the past. In fact, when you try to list as many problems that you can remember, you only put the other person on defense. A similar tactic to this is cross-complaining. This is where each person responds to one complaint with one of their own. Before you know it, the miscommunication has only escalated without any solution in mind.

Sticking to the issue can be accomplished by writing down your specific frustrations, as well as solutions to problem, in an outline format. That way, when you're meeting with the other person, you can both move forward to create a resolution.

3.   Be specific

Eliminate over generalizing a situation by using words like "always" or "never". Although, no doubt you've had or witnessed arguments where phrases like "you're always late" or "you never help out" have been spoken. Instead, it's best to be specific about what actions or behaviors are the source of the problem. By using direct dialogue, you and your partner can create solutions that benefit everyone involved.

4.   Minimize complaining

Instead of refuting one complaint with another, it's best to respond with a direct positive question that begins to add clarity to the situation and has a solution in mind. When someone argues that "When you leave the cupboard doors open in the kitchen, I've hit my head numerous times unexpectedly."

Rather than refute this domestic complaint with one of your own, like "well, you left the toilet seat up again today," you could say, "I can tell my forgetfulness is making you upset. Is there a way you can help remind me to close those cabinet doors?"

This helps bring the person into a solution-focused mindset.

5. Accept personal responsibility

Complaints are often accompanied by the finger of blame that points out faults in any given situation. By placing guilt entirely on the other person, they usually become defensive or entirely dismiss the accusation.

To bring a conflict to a resolution, it's best to take personal responsibility for your own actions, feelings, and opinions. This is true when being an assertive speaker in general, and is especially true when verbally in a disagreement. By discussing openly what can be done to improve the situation in the future, both people can alter their perception or actions for the better.

6. Utilize your listening skills

Numerous tactics, like talking when your partner is talking, pretending to read, or being engaged in another distraction, are all dirty fighting techniques that promote conflict.

With the various Common Sense Tools from Chapter 4, and the relationship-specific ideas presented in this chapter, you have the ability to respect the other person with your listening skills. You can practice listening twice as much as you talk in a conversation. You can repeat what you heard the other person say to gain clarity. You can also ask direct positive questions to look for solutions.

Then, if you're unable to maintain your boundaries while listening, you can break rapport.

7. Focus on the present moment

This means sticking to the current situation. This also means staying physically present. It can be easy to walk out of the room or leave the house entirely when you are upset. Remaining present honors the other person with your focus and with your ability to stay composed. If you notice you're becoming too upset to continue the discussion, let the other person know that you'd like to take a break and continue this conversation later. The sooner you reconvene, the sooner the conflict can be resolved.

8. Use direct-positive language

There are several tactics used in fights to tear the other person down. You can label a person as "immature, neurotic, paranoid, or alcoholic", but these direct negative phrases only increase the division between two people. Similarly, sarcasm is an indirect negative way to cover up any vulnerability.

While you may be able to concoct a seemingly positive phrase like "you're smart," it can be easy to change your tone, imply the other person is quite the opposite, and still deny that you said anything negative at the same time.

By moving into direct positive language, often by asking questions, you can move to the heart of the issue quickly, as well as keep everyone's self-image intact.

9. Discover a win-win solution

If you view the conflict as a competition, with only one winner, then you've already lost before the fight has even started. Having a one-winner philosophy creates a limited perspective in which many possible solutions get overlooked.

10. Remain consistent

This is similar to the "saying what you mean and meaning what you say" component of being an assertive speaker. In conflicts, it's easy to say one thing and do another in order to keep the other person entirely off balance.

However, returning to your values and having those principles infuse your character, even in difficult times, can prove to be one of the best tools for resolution.

Putting it all Together

Relationships can be an enjoyable and uplifting aspect of life. We are, in fact, social beings. But the energy underlying each encounter can determine whether a relationship adds or detracts from your overall life energy. By taking the time to build up your energy bank reserve, and using awareness to assess which action is best in a situation, you can experience balance and compassion with others. This harmony can exist within all types of relationships, from casual acquaintances to soul mates.

New Common Sense Tools to Generate Harmony in your Relationships:

- **Feel, Felt, Found:** The Feel, Felt, Found template helps you recognize the feelings of others. It also develops trust and offers helpful guidance or direction in a situation.

- **WAWAHs:** Who Asks Who And How is a Common Sense Tool that is used to create clarity of when and how it is appropriate to hug others. Numerous studies show the benefits of human contact. As a non-verbal gesture in the right context, hugging can be an excellent way to share compassion with others.

- **Male and Female Triangles:** The simple shape of a triangle explains how men and women can best uplift each other in an intimate relationship. By creating balance in all points of the triangle, and fulfilling core needs, men and women can improve communication and closeness.

- **Recipe for Conflict Resolution:** Using the ten tips for conflict resolution within this recipe, you'll be able to solve problems with clarity and confidence for all involved.

Chapter 6

Chapter 6

Make Decisions with Confidence

"When you come to a fork in the road, take it." — *Yogi Berra*

In this Chapter

- Make decisions easily and purposefully

- Overcome fear

- Assess a situation and resolve it

- Eliminate indecision and worry

- Create a clear path to help you reach your goals

Life is an ongoing string of choices. We're presented with endless options in any given 24-hour period. What do I want to eat for breakfast? Will I call my family today? What's the fastest route to work today? Should I hold my tongue or tell my boss what I really think about this project?

The list goes on and on.

The variety we experience in life is part of the joy and adventure in the journey. We, as humans, celebrate our many senses that interpret our surroundings, acknowledge our beliefs that help us perceive the situation, and take pride in the ability to weigh out the many options presented to us on a daily basis.

The decision-making process can be quite easy when we know what we want and we go for it. Sometimes, it can be very challenging, causing us to vacillate back and forth between options. And other times, we're so overtaken by fear, that we're unable to make a decision at all.

Yet, it's the decisions we make, based on the abundance of choices in front of us, which influence and direct our lives for the future.

Common Sense Tip: As a confident decision-maker, you take charge of your own life.

You're focused and able to accomplish your goals, despite external distractions that may arise. With this certainty, you're able to see the bigger picture, recognize risk when it pops up, and have a clear perspective on which actions will best benefit you and your surroundings. Other people often notice such confidence and begin looking to you as a leader. They will seek out your opinion and ask for advice based on your certainty, values, and outlook.

When you utilize common sense in everyday life, feelings of chaos and confusion are diminished. By removing these, and other negative emotions, your ability to make decisions with confidence increases.

This chapter also eliminates the myth that stepping into a passionate and purposeful life requires drastic and risky behavior. By learning to identify and mitigate risk, you can psychologically manage unknown factors that might cause feelings of fear or indecision. When you have managed your levels of risk, you have the confidence to step forward and take those necessary risks required to reach your goals.

Then, with confident decision-making capabilities, you can fully enjoy your free will to reach your goals, improve your relationships, and enhance your overall life Energy Bank Account.

Know your Destination

In order to make purposeful, clear, and effective decisions in life, it's essential to know where you want to go in the first place. This way, you know what it's like when you reach your destination and you can set a clear path to get there. Setting clear goals and having a meaningful intention behind your actions helps to make the everyday decision-making process a bit easier.

If you recall back to the introduction, we suggested that all of life can be broken down into three circles—the Personal, Business, and Spiritual Spheres. While these areas may seem independent, they're actually interwoven, working together to help your life run smoothly. When one area is out of balance, the others suffer. When all are working in harmony, supported by your strong foundation of values, then life becomes more harmonious.

Before we delve into powerful and practical ways to enhance the everyday decision-making processes, let's have you create goals for each area of your life.

Common Sense Goal Quiz

Below are a series of questions that help you create goals in the Personal, Business, and Spiritual Spheres.

Directions:

Step 1: Read each question.

Step 2: Use a separate sheet of paper to answer the questions honestly and fully.

Step 3: Mark the appropriate life sphere, or spheres, that relate to each goal.

Note: Some questions might elicit answers that fit solely into one category, while other answers might cause goals to spread across all three domains.

Ideas for Goals in Life	Personal Sphere	Business Sphere	Spiritual Sphere
Self-Image:			
• What values would I like to use to describe my character?	O	O	O
• What perspective of my body, mind, and spirit would I like to create/maintain?	O	O	O
Home:			
• What is my ideal living environment?	O	O	O
• What colors bring me joy?	O	O	O
• What part of the country/world would best suit my natural preferences?	O	O	O
• What aspects of my current home make me feel good?	O	O	O

Ideas for Goals in Life	Personal Sphere	Business Sphere	Spiritual Sphere
Health:			
• What is my definition of health?	O	O	O
• What areas of my health would I like to improve?	O	O	O
• What simple steps can I do to enhance my health?	O	O	O
• How does health relate to all aspects of my being (physically, socially, emotionally, intellectually, spiritually)?	O	O	O
Relationships:			
• What types of relationships do I want to create (intimate, friends, and associates)?	O	O	O
• What attributes do I look for in my companions?	O	O	O
• What role do I typically play in my relationships?	O	O	O
• What role would I like to play in my family, community, or social group?	O	O	O
Work:			
• What is my ideal profession or vocation?	O	O	O
• What natural gifts and talents do I have to offer others?	O	O	O
• Am I passionate about what I do? If not, how can I improve that in any way?	O	O	O
Personal Pursuits:			
• What would I like to learn about?	O	O	O
• Where would I like to travel?	O	O	O
• Are there any new books I would enjoy reading?	O	O	O
• What activities, people, or ideas peak my interest?	O	O	O

Ideas for Goals in Life	Personal Sphere	Business Sphere	Spiritual Sphere
Community:			
• What types of people would I like to surround me in a community?	O	O	O
• What types of environments makes me feel comfortable?	O	O	O
• How does my current community match my overall life goals?	O	O	O
Tangibles:			
• What material things are meaningful to me?	O	O	O
• How can the material things I already possess add to the quality of my life?	O	O	O
• How can I use my possessions to create well-being for myself, my family, and my community?	O	O	O
Life Purpose:			
• What do I want to accomplish before I die?	O	O	O
• What kind of legacy would I like to leave after my death?	O	O	O
• What would I like to contribute to others, the community, or the world as a whole?	O	O	O
• How much meaning infuses my daily actions?	O	O	O
Totals:	_____	_____	_____

Now, count how many times each sphere related to your goals and place the total at the bottom of each column. Your personal sphere might have a high score—meaning you have many goals in that area—while your business sphere might not. In order to help create more balance in your life, it's important to look at those areas that might be lacking goals and create direction there first.

The specific answers to your questions help define where you want to go next. With a new direction, or goal in mind, write one of the most important goals in each Sphere of Life below:

Personal Goal:

_____

_____

Business Goal:

_____

_____

Spiritual Goal:

_____

_____

Great! Now that you have a specific, detailed concept of where you'd like to direct your life, it will be much easier to understand how to make confident decisions to help you reach those goals.

The Roadblock of Fear

In order to purposefully and confidently make decisions toward your dreams, fear must be eliminated. Fear might be evident as a lack of self-assurance, internal confusion, or any other negative emotion hindering your ability to move forward.

There are two very appropriate acronyms, and definitions, for the feeling of fear. The first one is:

FEAR = False Expectations Appearing Real

Every choice at your fingertips is assessed through your beliefs about the world. These beliefs can be limitless, or supporting of your overall life goals, or they can be limited, causing a hindrance as you try to move forward.

When fear dominates your perception, it's like looking at the world with the glass-is-half-empty viewpoint. The limited beliefs you hold form a negative expectation about your future. The catch is that these predictions are really an illusion.

Fear in Action: Matthew's Story

Matthew thought he would overcome his fear of flying and purchased a plane ticket home to visit his family for Thanksgiving. When the day of his trip arrived, he drove to the airport, checked his luggage, and proceeded through airport security. Despite feelings of nervousness, Matthew seemed alright.

When passengers started boarding the plane, Matthew noticed his heart began to race. His palms started sweating and his breath rate shortened. He was gripped by fear—fear that the plane would crash and he might die. Considering very few airplanes actually crash relative to the amount of global air travel daily, this was a false expectation appearing very real to Matthew.

This fear prevented him from boarding the plane. He called his family and sadly let them know he wouldn't be home for the holidays after all.

The second acronym for fear is:

FEAR= Forgetting Everything's All Right

This definition of fear also builds on the concept that negative emotions have become the filter through which you see life. While the other acronym focuses on false expectations about the future appearing real, fear can also cause the view of the present moment to be tainted.

When we experience discontent, or a desire to change our experience, we are resisting the present moment. When we fight what is, we clash with our internal power to make positive changes.

Instead, it serves us to release fear, remove our pair of negativity glasses, and replaces our perspective with acceptance, love, and understanding—all of which can help us to powerfully take control of our lives, make purposeful decisions, and reach our goals.

When you forget everything is all right or believe that your false expectations about the future are real, your body and mind can experience the following negative effects:

- Unclear thinking
- Feelings of powerlessness
- Negative internal dialogue
- Stress-related hormones released in the body
- Muscle tightness or tension
- Shortness of breath
- Physical illness
- Defensive attitudes or postures
- Inability to move forward in life

Eliminate Fear

While fear can stop you from being who you want to be or accomplishing your goals, fear can be transformed into a positive emotion to propel your personal growth. We mentioned that fear is the strongest negative emotion that can be experienced, and the strongest restraint keeping you from making a decision.

However, fear can manifest itself in other forms, such as frustration, anger, insecurity, limitation, and discouragement.

The good news is that fear is not an inborn trait, but rather it's a learned characteristic. While it was easy for your youthful innocence to be trained in worry, anxiety, and tension, your adult self is just as capable to retrain your mind and body in the other direction. Common Sense Tools can be used to transform any form of a negative emotion—which has its roots in fear—into a supportive belief system that promotes personal power, confidence, and trust.

The first step to eliminating fear is to recognize which negative emotion you are currently experiencing. If you feel frustrated, you can honestly say, "I am frustrated." If you are angry, you can acknowledge that anger for what it is in the moment. Then, from that point of understanding, you can choose to change your focus. This is where a new, positive emotion has the power to transform your thoughts, words, and actions into deposits in your life Energy Bank Account.

Frustration becomes Acceptance

There are many things that happen in the world today that would seem to cause frustration. Perhaps it's your neighbor who tosses their trash into the street or the varying opinions you have with the current political regime, whether it be local or federal. Frustration leads to a feeling of helplessness, where you're unable to make a difference in what's going on around you.

While acceptance does not mean that you condone the activity, action or viewpoint, acceptance embraces the idea that there is a purpose, bigger than you can currently see, for the way things are at the moment. It returns your energy bank back to neutral, so the situation no longer drains your life energy. From this neutral point of acceptance, you can choose to move forward and take positive actions that are purposeful and energy-enhancing.

Let's take a look at how feelings of frustration of unwanted trash in the environment can be transformed into feelings of acceptance.

Frustration to Acceptance in Action: Kym's Story

When Kym was traveling in Brazil, she encountered numerous, beautiful isolated beaches. In fact, that was one of the most exciting parts of seeing the country in its unspoiled, uncrowded, and undeveloped nature.

Many of the beaches, although miles from civilization, had candy wrappers and empty water bottles lining their shores. Now, at first, Kym felt frustrated at the situation. She felt that many people disrespected the sacred ocean that she spent so much time in as a surfer.

Instead of focusing on the frustration and feeling powerless to change how people discarded of their trash, she decided to make beach cleanups a part of her ocean-going experience. She accepted that she couldn't change everyone's behaviors and by neutralizing that energy within herself, she could decide to step into an empowering posture to take action. From that point forward when Kym found a deserted surf spot, she would set her gear down and walk along the beach collecting discarded or washed-up garbage before even taking to the waves. She then allowed the feelings of acceptance to support her trips up and down the Brazilian coast.

Anger becomes Forgiveness

Anger is a powerful negative emotion that can keep you from moving forward into the future. For example, you might have a family member who is making choices that seem irresponsible. You find yourself angry at their decisions, and when you've brought your concerns to their attention, they're not willing to compromise or help out in any way.

When it comes time for family gatherings, your internal anger causes you to feel stressed about these events. It affects you so much that you almost don't even want to go for holiday get-togethers, but you know mom would be really disappointed if you didn't make it. When you do go to the party, you're tense and you try to avoid your family member the entire time.

Instead of living with the anger, or letting that negative emotion drive your actions, you can embrace forgiveness. You might use some Common Sense Tools of communication to write down your thoughts and concerns in a clear, direct positive way. You can also set up a meeting—either in person or on the phone—to discuss the issue at hand.

Once you have your feelings out in the open, and have forgiven another for past behavior, you are able to move forward with confidence. **Remember, forgiveness does not mean you ignore the bad behavior of the other**

person or persons. You just stop drinking the poison of anger in hopes that they will get sick.

Even if the maddening behavior continues on your family member's part, you have the power to make different choices for your life. You might spend time with your parents elsewhere. Or, you could even be able to see that particular family member and know that they're doing the best they can from their perspective. By forgiving others, and yourself, you can release anger from your situation and move toward your goals.

Blame becomes Self-Responsibility

Blame, is like a pointed finger pushing into your chest, which puts you in a defensive and powerless position. It can make you feel like a victim to your surroundings. Blame takes your individual sense of control and relinquishes it to other people, circumstances, and events.

Blame in Action: Amanda's Story

Amanda, a young saleswoman, was one of three people in her company competing for a management position. While Amanda deeply desired this new position, she was insecure about her talents and abilities to step up to the new demands. She began downplaying her anticipation of the job. She talked to co-workers about how the increased workload might take away from her family. She told her friends about the close relationship between the other individuals and the company owner.

When the position was given to one of the other salesman, Amanda was crushed. Yet, she blamed the company for favoring certain employees and having a bias towards women. She used her own internal excuses to hold herself back from reaching her goals.

Instead, Amanda could have taken self-responsibility for her actions. She could have realized she was doing her very best at the moment. She could find areas to improve her own skills in sales and communication. She could prove her dependability and confidence to her company. Or, she might have the realization that she's ready to move on to another company or position elsewhere.

"Three characteristics of the noble man's life: being virtuous, he is free from care; possessing knowledge, he is free from doubts; being courageous, he is free from fear." –Confucius

By taking time to recognize her own strengths and weaknesses, Amanda can make this hurtful experience a learning opportunity.

With self-responsibility, we can express our own wants with confidence, respect others, and enhance our own well-being by making clear, purposeful decisions.

Insecurity becomes Confidence

Imagine this scenario for a moment. You are in a pitch black room and barefooted. Your only aim in this room is to find the door and get yourself out of the darkness. While there is no furniture in the room, the floor is covered in mousetraps.

Each step is tentative at best.

When you get whacked by the first mousetrap, you pull it off your foot and rub your toes to ease the pain. You take a few deep breaths, but notice how timid you are when it's time to move again.

But, you know you have to get out of the dark, so you take another nervous step.

This could take hours for you to find an exit and with every whack of the foot; your insecurity grows, further exacerbating the problem of getting out.

Insecurity in making decisions often feels like this.

Instead of moving through life unsure and hesitant, the goal is to move into confidence. Confidence gives you night-vision goggles to see your way effectively through the maze of mouse-traps.

When you see your path clearly, you can take sure-footed steps to reach your goals, whether it is to improve your communication, attain the relationship you want, or passionately follow the career of your dreams.

Limited becomes Limitless

Fear puts on blinders to what is actually possible for your life. Instead of being able to think clearly and see numerous options available to you in any given moment, you feel restricted in how you can take action. It's like the blinders that are put on horses in races so that they focus on the racetrack toward the finish line. Yet, instead of the finish line being a goal you want to achieve, fear puts only those things that you don't want in your line of sight. It's as though you can only see the things that can go wrong with a choice or the negative aspects of any given option. Fear provides only a narrow scope of what's possible.

The goal is to take the blinders of fear off, so that you can see unlimited options. You can then use creativity, inspiration, or innovation to create a new future, where you're not stuck with just one or two options, but where you have numerous, feasible ones.

Discouragement becomes Hope

This limited perspective can lead to a discouraged attitude because no option seems to fulfill your passion, ideals, or values. It's as though each decision you're faced with offers no way to win.

Yet, we have a saying that goes, "When you come to the edge of all that you know, and you're about to step into the darkness of the unknown, faith is knowing that one of two things will happen: You will find something solid to stand on or you'll be given wings to fly."

This is what hope is. It's an optimism that is founded in trust and excited anticipation of what's to come. Hope takes your disheartened, dejected viewpoint and transforms your perspective into one of faith and possibility for what is and what's to come.

Common Sense Tip: The most effective way to transform fear—frustration, anger, insecurity, limitation, and discouragement—into powerful, positive emotions is through focus in the present moment.

It goes back to the saying, "The past is a cancelled check, and the future is a promissory note. So therefore it's best to live in the present, which is your gift right now."

Yes, the past is the past. Negative emotions can be tied to memories or previous experiences. It's only when we use those circumstances to cloud our future with false expectations that we block ourselves from our true power to make changes. The future is, in fact, very fluid. It's the unknown and unwritten. But we do have the power of choice in this present moment to transform limitations of the past into possibilities for the future.

Letting go of Fear Activity

This activity is best done with a partner. Find someone who knows your goals, matches your values, and supports your decision to move forward. Carefully read all of the steps involved in this activity before taking action.

Directions:

Step 1: The first step to eliminating fear is creating an awareness of that fear itself. This requires total self-honesty about what is going on. Once you recognize what you are afraid of, write it down. "I am afraid of _____". Explain this fear briefly to your partner.

Step 2: Put your fear in front of you. Imagine yourself watching a movie of your worst fears coming true. That picture screen is right in front of you, playing out your worst thoughts. Visualize that screen, holding your fear, as a solid object.

Step 3: Notice your breathing. Take a deep breath in and out. Imagine all of the air exhaling from your lungs and soften the tongue in your mouth. Take another deep breath in and hold it.

Step 4: Have your partner pull you through the screen of fear to love on the other side.

Step 5: Exhale deeply and notice any sensations of being free of the fear.

Step 6: With this new awareness, talk to your partner about what positive actions you can take to move towards your goal. Keep it simple at first, trying one new idea at a time, so that you can savor your small successes.

Letting Go of Fear in Action: Amanda's Story Revisited

Amanda, the young saleswoman who previously missed the first job promotion, was offered another position within her company to motivate other sales personnel. The new job involved speaking in front of a large crowd every Monday. But Amanda was terrified to speak in public. Every time she even thought about talking in front of others, she recalled her embarrassing experience in junior high where she had to give a speech to the entire class and she messed up the presentation horribly.

Amanda decided to take the position, despite the concerns of being in front of a group on a weekly basis. Once she learned the letting go of fear exercise above, she imagined the fear of speaking as a screen in front of her seat. Then, when Amanda was introduced as the speaker, she stood up out of her chair, walked through the screen of fear, and walked confidently to the podium. Soon, her poise and confidence became the habit and she no longer was confined by fear of speaking. As an additional bonus, her salary tripled that year. She not only let go of fear but also increased her sense of self-respect, value, and capability of success.

Life on the Flying Trapeze

Imagine that life is like a series of trapeze swings with no safety net below. We're either swinging on one trapeze bar, with a confident grip, or for a few moments in time, we're hurtling in space before grabbing on to another one.

Most of the time, we spend life hanging on for dear life to the trapeze bar of the moment. We are comfortable with the steady rate of the swing and have the feeling of being in control of life. It feels like we even know most of the answers to life's questions that are going to be thrown our way.

There are other times where we're hanging on to the trapeze bar of the moment, terrified of where we are, but even more scared of letting go.

Whether enjoying our current trapeze bar or not, there are transition points in life when we can see another trapeze bar swinging our direction. It's empty and it has our name written all over it. This bar is our next step on the path towards personal growth or the realization of our dreams.

Sometimes we hope, other times we pray, that we don't have to grab the new trapeze bar. But we know in our heart of hearts, that in order to take this leap of faith, we have to release our grip on the present, well-known bar, and move into the unknown.

Just before releasing our grip, a myriad of emotions—including some fear—can take over. It doesn't matter how many times we've done this before. We can tell ourselves it's just a simple process of releasing and grabbing again. Sometimes, out of the dark places in the mind, we fear that we'll miss the next bar and tumble into the bottomless chasm between bars. Once we let go, there are no guarantees, no nets, and no insurance policies.

Once we muster up the courage to let go, we are in transition.

We are in the instant of eternity that can last a microsecond or a thousand lifetimes. We're in that sacred space where the past is gone and the future is not quite here. And it's the only place where real change can occur.

This sense of flying can be looked upon as a scary, confusing, disorienting space that needs to be passed as quickly and as unconsciously as possible.

However, this can be an exciting time, full of adrenaline, where you are intensely focused. With confidence, clarity, and awareness, we can enjoy the richness of the transition. We can honor these special times, even savor them. And even with the wide range of emotions that can accompany these transitions, they can be the most alive, passionate, and expansive moments of our lives.

In fact, the transformation of fear may have nothing to do with making our fear disappear entirely. But rather, it's the ability to give ourselves permission to "hang out" in the transitions between trapeze bars. By transforming our natural tendency to grab at the new bar quickly, we allow ourselves to dwell in the place where change really happens. It can be terrifying, and as mentioned before, it can be enlightening.

Common Sense Tip: *In those transitions where we hurtle through the void, we may just learn to fly.*

6 Common Sense Questions to help you Manage Risk

Oftentimes, we think that letting go of the current trapeze bar requires a blind faith, where we have no idea of what the next bar will hold for us. In fact, quite the opposite is true. By learning how to mentally and emotionally manage the risks involved with change, while you keep your end destination in mind, flying into the transitional space becomes natural. It's as though you know what that shift will feel like and you look forward to the excitement that awaits you.

When it comes to risk, we often weigh out the pros and cons of a situation before making a decision. By asking the following risk-related questions, you can psychologically adjust your perspective so the risk itself doesn't seem overwhelming. By checking in with the various aspects of risk itself, you can make decisions confidently as you move passionately into your future.

Before confidently making a decision, consider the answers to the following questions:

- Will I love it?
- Will I be good at it?
- Is there a real chance for me to succeed?
- Once I make the commitment, will I be better off?
- Once I make this decision, how much time will I give it to work in my favor before moving on to another choice? This is called creating a timeline sequence.
- Will my decision have any negative effects on others?

Each of these questions can be answered to help moderate the risk involved with letting go of your present situation and taking the next step. Through reflection, and some necessary research, you can understand what dangers lie ahead and calculate if any areas of your life—the Three Spheres—will be in jeopardy. The last question asks you to consider your family, friends, community, and any other people that could be negatively affected by your choice.

Let's look at two examples to see how the six questions for risk assessment can be applied to almost any life situation.

Risk-Assessment in Action: JoAnne's Story

First, let's look at JoAnne, who has been in a relationship with Sam for three years now. There has been some talk of marriage, although there is no question that each is fully committed to the relationship. After a year of Sam being unemployed, there are strains between the couple. JoAnne realizes that she is feeling trapped, uninspired, and doubting her future with Sam. When she is at this junction, of whether to stay in this situation, where she is noticing more and more of her happiness slipping away, or start over on her own, she could ask herself the six questions when assessing the risks involved with leaving.

JoAnne asks herself, "Will I love it?"

This question speaks directly to the amount of passion involved in the decision she wants to make. JoAnne's lived alone before and enjoyed the freedom of coming and going as she pleased. She has lots of friends who make her laugh and offer support, and she knows that being single gives her the control of when to have companionship. The thought of coming home to a quiet space makes her feel excited and free.

JoAnne asks herself, "Will I be good at it?"

Again, JoAnne was able to find a place of her own for the past ten years. In that time, she cooked, cleaned, went on dates, started new relationships, organized her life between work and play, and was good at it. Being single was easy enough and getting along with others, or starting new relationships, are also personal strengths.

Since there will be times of sadness, does JoAnne have the tools to make herself feel better when she's missing Sam? Yes, she's confident in calling a friend, watching a comedy, or taking a bubble bath when she notices sadness. JoAnne is also good at managing her emotions, and knows she can handle challenging times just like the positive ones.

JoAnne asks herself "Is there a real chance for me to succeed?"

JoAnne already knows that she is capable of handling herself as a single woman, but there are logistical concerns that need to be taken into account. For example, on her own salary, can she find a place of her own in the area that will fit into her budget? Can she find such a place in a three-month timeline? Are there places on the market in her budget? Does she have a friend she can stay with, if necessary, while she searches for a new home? If this is possible, it helps JoAnne know that chances of her success are high.

JoAnne asks herself, "Once I make this decision, will I be better off?"

In this case, JoAnne has already weighed out the pros and cons of staying with Sam against the pros and cons of separating. At this point, the answer is yes.

JoAnne asks herself, "Once I make this decision, how much time do I give it to work in my favor before moving on to another choice?"

This is where setting a timeline comes in handy. JoAnne decides to set a goal of finding a new place within three months and living on her own for another three. This six-month window provides plenty of time to explore her options as a single woman, get used to making her own decisions, building confidence on her own, and notice what life is like without Sam.

At the end of that six month period, she can then reassess the situation and know what to do then. If she is miserable without him, they could choose to meet then and discuss the possibility of rekindling their relationship. If she feels settled with herself and knows that she is better off, she can continue down this road of freedom or independence.

JoAnne asks herself, "Will my decision have any negative effects on others?"

Although Sam might also be sad at their separation, JoAnne has taken his feelings into consideration. However, she knows that she needs to take care of herself first in this situation.

Risk-Assessment in Action: Joe's Story

Joe hates his current occupation and is looking for a new job. Right now, he's in the accounting industry. The daily grind drains his energy. Yet, the company has been in his family lineage for years, and he feels obligated to follow in the footsteps of those before him.

When Joe realized how unhappy he was after so many years, he knew a switch would be in order. He's done some freelance writing in the past and wants to shift his focus to a writing career. By asking the six risk assessment questions, Joe can create a better understanding of what a switch in jobs will entail.

Joe asks himself, "Will I love it?"

Joe loves writing. He knows that he will be happier with more freedom in his scheduling, time at nights with his family, and the use of his creative side in whatever new endeavor he pursues. All of the benefits of writing as a career and the lifestyle values that he holds, makes this a passionate switch for Joe.

Joe asks himself, "Will I be good at it?"

With a background in accounting, Joe is good with numbers. He also is a detailed writer who has had success in the past. If he decides to go out on his own, he knows that his creative ability and strong logical sense will help him succeed.

Joe asks himself, "Is there a real chance for me to succeed?"

This question involves looking at the surrounding economic climate. Is there an appropriate market for his skills? If he wants to be a writer, where can he offer his services? Perhaps many companies are downsizing. It might seem more challenging to find a new career that he's good at. He can do research here to see which industries are on the rise, and what new niche markets can match his skills.

If business is slow in the transition period, will he have enough money in savings to support him through the process? If not, will he find a temporary position or work part-time in accounting while he transitions into a career that aligns with his passions?

Joe asks himself, "Once I make the commitment, will I be better off?"

Without a doubt, Joe would say he's ready to live with more joy, passion, and excitement in his life. By leaving the accounting world, he can see himself smiling during the day, drinking less at night to cover the frustration, and even taking time off to travel with his kids.

Joe asks himself, "Once I make this decision, how much time do I give it to work in my favor before moving on to another choice?"

Joe decides to set a timeline of one year. In this period, he decides to cut back his hours to part time in the accounting world and begins making contacts in the writing one. Through research and persistence, Joe will know at the end of the timeline what his prospects are moving into his new career. He can assess his progress at that time and make a new decision, if needed, when the time arises.

Joe asks himself, "Will my decision have any negative effects on others?"

If Joe did all of this without telling his family, it could have negative repercussions. But because Joe discussed his ideas with his wife and family before making any changes, they were aware of his passion and had time to adjust. He also held family meetings once a month to discuss his progress throughout the transition time.

Risk is often inevitable, but we want to know as much as we can about the results of our decision before taking action. The purpose of asking the six risk-related questions is to break down risk into separate, manageable parts.

Then, by tackling each aspect of risk independently, and educating ourselves about those areas, we can confidently decide to move into the transitional phase of our lives. We can confidently let go of what is with a joyful expectation of what is to come. Risk can now be used as a force to help us move forward with more clarity, purpose, and knowing.

The trapeze bar that is coming towards us can be grabbed with determination, awareness, and success. Remember to remain flexible in the outcome. Oftentimes, in this process, an even better opportunity becomes apparent.

Common Sense Risk Assessment Activity

Choose one of your goals, that you formulated during the beginning of the chapter, which appears to have the most risk involved. Write down five to ten unanswered questions that are preventing you from moving forward. Now, use any of your Common Sense Tools to help find answers to these questions. Perhaps you need to talk to others and get outside input. You might need to check in with your internal beliefs and see why you're avoiding certain actions. You could even do some research to help clear up any ambiguity.

This activity begins to move you in the direction of your dreams by managing the level of psychological risk you appear to be taking.

Common Sense Tip: By breaking the risk down, and looking for solutions, you will increase your confidence to take action.

Eliminate Indecision

Indecision can be one of the worst effects of a fear-dominated perspective on life. It can cause feelings of sluggishness, prevent the possibility of reaching your goals, and can spark negative habitual patterns. When you don't know how to move forward, but you don't like where you are right now, it's easy to procrastinate. In those times of indecision, actions that help you disassociate from the current experience are common.

One of the easiest ways to delay making a decision is to sidetrack yourself. We call that disassociation. It starts out by simply wasting time, like taking a trip to the refrigerator even when you're not hungry, checking your phone continually in hopes of a new message, or even a meaningless, multiple hour internet searches without a purpose. Sidetracking is just a fancy way of saying you're wasting time, or buying time, before you're forced to take action. Addictions are an extreme example of sidetracking, where substances—such as alcohol or marijuana—or behaviors—like watching pornography—help you disassociate from the uncomfortable current situation.

Whether you encounter indecisiveness regularly, or only once in a while, it's important to get yourself out of chaos. It's essential to release feelings of unhappiness, frustration, or uncertainty.

And one of the best common sense ways to do this is through the following exercise.

Get out of the River Activity

You're probably familiar with the phrase "go with the flow". It's often an indicator that life can be easier when you take it easy, don't sweat the small stuff, and let time take care of unnecessary worry.

When life is easy and we're happy, creative, and loving, it's like flowing down the river of life in a motor-powered boat. We have control of the situation and feel comfortable on our journey.

However, sometimes challenging circumstances in life can throw us out of the boat. The water can be cold and the current swift. Within a short amount of time, our body temperature drops, and we get tired from the constant effort to keep our head above water. We know that if we don't get to shore soon, we're going to drown.

This example of being in the river without a lifeboat represents the times in our lives where we experience indecision. The surrounding chaos drains our energy quickly, and we often struggle to decipher what to do next. The shoreline on each side of the river represents the options we have to return to safety.

The goal is to get out of the river of indecision as quickly as possible by finding a solution that serves you and your overall goals.

When you notice yourself in indecision, take the following steps to help you make a decision confidently to move forward into certainty. This activity works especially well when you have two choices in front of you and you're unsure of which one to decide on.

Directions:

Step 1: Determine your options. Oftentimes you know what choices you have available at the moment, but you just can't decide which one will be more beneficial.

Take out a sheet of paper and list the pros and cons of each option.

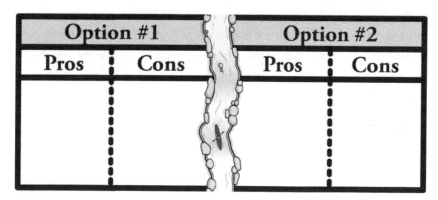

Option #1		Option #2	
Pros	Cons	Pros	Cons

Step 2: Listen to your gut. Often we make decisions based on what our thinking mind alone believes to be the best solution. Yet, the subconscious mind, which communicates with every cell in the body continuously, can have very powerful input as you make your decision.

Take out a coin. **Option #1 will take the head's side** of the coin and **Option #2 now becomes the tail's side** of the coin. Make a commitment to follow whatever option the coin decides.

Then, close your eyes and flip the coin. Open your eyes and see which side lands face up.

Close your eyes again and take a deep breath. Notice if you are elated or disappointed with the result of your coin toss.

If you are experiencing joy, relief, or acceptance, you're headed in the right direction. Your gut instinct believes this is the best path for you to take. If, on the other hand, you feel upset, discouraged, or unsatisfied, move immediately to the other option.

This might seem like you've been tricked. The important point is to let your heart and gut help decide your actions. Now, you're tuning into feelings associated with the actions, instead of just logical thoughts about the solution.

The point is that you have free choice to make your own decision. You're not bound to take action based on the ruling of the coin. However, your emotions have now become part of the guidance system, which often is the heart's desire. Trust the process and begin to move forward.

Step 3: You're now committed to your decision, and it is necessary to place your focus on taking steps to make you successful on that path. To provide a safety net for yourself, create a timeline to move forward.

By setting certain time limits on your decision, you give yourself some flexibility in the outcome. If we look back at JoAnne's break-up with Sam, she gave herself six months to give her new single lifestyle a try. Joe did the same thing with his new business endeavor; only he gave himself a year to start over.

Then, after your prescribed set of time, you can reassess your decision. If you feel confident where you are with the decision you've made, great—celebrate!

If you're plans don't work out as expected, you will have new decisions to make. Repeat the process, including flipping the coin, and start over. Since time has passed and the current situation has changed, you have a whole new set of options at your fingertips.

Remember, you are now able to stay out of the cold, tiresome river of indecision. Your feet are already set firmly on the ground. From this standpoint, you can have a broader perspective of what to do and where to go next in order to reach your goals.

Remove Worry

While indecision is the inability to decide between current options available, worry is simply a feeling that accompanies fear, even if no decision needs to be made at the time. We are the only species that can fret about the past and agonize about the future. This sense of worry can be so overwhelming that it prevents you from enjoying life. It can also affect your ability to see clearly and take decisive action when it's necessary.

Just like fear, worry is a learned trait. Kids aren't naturally anxious on their own. Instead, they pick up feelings of worry from their surroundings. They might hear their parents fighting over how the bills with be paid for the month. They pick up the negative energy in the house and associate those sensations with the content of the conversations they hear. Young girls might see their mothers standing on the scale in the bathroom and notice the feelings of frustration that emanate from their concern about weight. This can cause even youthful girls to begin worrying about their weight, when there is no problem in their physical body whatsoever.

Worry, at whatever age, detracts from our life Energy Bank Account. Negative thoughts not only distract us from what's truly important in our lives, but they are also continually deducting from our total life energy. The amazing thing about negative thoughts, which take energy away from accomplishing our goals, is that most of what we worry about in the first place never comes to fruition. Our worries lead to naught. Life seems to work itself out and the extra energy we put in the worry direction didn't help us out in any way, nor did it help solve the problem, which was often too big for us to handle on our own, anyway.

> "People wish to be settled. Only as far as they are unsettled is there any hope for them."
> –Ralph Waldo Emerson

Worry In Action: May's Story

A perfect example of this is Gregory's mother, May, who is always concerned about every aspect of his life. When Gregory and his wife were taking a trip up to their family cabin for Thanksgiving, May worried terribly about their trip. She was scared that the recent snowstorm would cause the roads to be slippery and icy. She was anxious that the driveway wouldn't be plowed and that heat in the house wouldn't work properly.

Yet, all of May's nervous energy was for nothing. Gregory, having lived in the mountains years before, is a confident and safe driver in the snow. The drive to the cabin was slow going, but easy. The driveway to the cabin wasn't plowed, but the garage was still accessible. And, everything in the house, including the heat and water, worked wonderfully.

When May received the phone call that Gregory was okay, she felt entirely relieved. Half of her day, however, had been consumed with negative thoughts and their effects on the physical body. If May had realized that this situation was out of her control, and trusted the wisdom of her son to take actions that would best suit him and his wife, she could have relaxed and enjoyed her Sunday afternoon.

And that's our goal—to **take decisive action when we have control and release worry when we don't.** One of the best ways to reduce the amount of worry in life is through "The Box" activity below.

The Common Sense Box Activity

Materials: For this activity, you'll need a small box (the size of a shoe box or smaller), some pieces of paper, and a pen.

This activity begins to take the negative, unwanted thoughts from your mind and put them out of sight.

Directions:

Step 1: When you notice a worry arise, write down the concern and the date on a strip of paper.

In May's case, she's an excessive worrier and would have numerous sheets just for Gregory's trip to the cabin. Instead of listing every little detail separately—like being nervous about road conditions or concerned about the house working properly—May could have just written Gregory at the cabin.

For example, at the end of your day, you might be worried about next week's presentation or concerned about losing your job entirely. You could be worried that your son or daughter will be injured in sports or that the neighbor will complain about your dog barking too loudly.

Step 2: At the end of week one, open up your box. Pull out each piece of paper, one at a time, and notice what has happened with the thought.

If the worry has worked itself out, or is no longer a concern for you, throw the piece of paper away. Perhaps you already talked to your neighbor about your dog and you worked out a solution.

If the worry still exists, place it back in the box. You might still be hearing gossip around the office that company layoffs are just around the corner and you're still worried about your job security. It's okay if the worry still exists, just place the sheet of paper back in the box.

Step 3: Repeat steps 1 and 2 for one month.

Step 4: Take out the box after one month and notice which worries have been there for four weeks. At this point, you'll probably notice that many negative thoughts have already worked themselves out. Yet, there are times when a situation is ongoing, and it can still have the potential to drain energy from your life Energy Bank Account.

If the concern is still present, it's time to take decisive action.

For example, if you are concerned about not having money at the end of the month consistently, it's time to find a common-sense solution. Either you work on cutting excess spending or find a way to generate more income.

Common Sense Tip: If you know you need to take action, but you're unsure of what to do specifically, get help!

Contact other people that you respect—in the business, personal, and spiritual spheres—and get input on what action to take. Sometimes researching solutions to the problem can be done on your own. Other times, we need someone with an outside perspective to provide support.

By using the box activity, you transfer negative, unwanted worry from the space in your mind to space in a box out of sight. Within a few weeks, you gain a new perspective on what worries actually matter and which ones naturally worked themselves out.

By eliminating excess worry, you can focus your attention and energy on productive, life affirming activities. Then, when you notice a concern still draining your Energy Bank Account, you know that a decision is necessary and you can confidently take action.

Common Sense Decision-making Decrees

Eliminating fear, indecision, and worry can make it much easier to make decisions with clarity. Here are a few other recommendations to create common-sense solutions in your own life:

Make a List

This is probably one of the most common goal-setting tools used to create a destination and plan of action to get there. Problems can occur where there is an inability to separate what is important from what is urgent.

Take your to-do list to the next level by prioritizing each activity in the following way:

- Place an "A" by the activities that have the highest priority. These are things that are urgent.

- Place a "B" next to the activities that have a medium priority. These are things that are important but don't necessarily need to get done right away.

- Place a "C" next to low priority items.

Now, rewrite a list with only the "A" items. This is your new guide on how to take action to make the biggest difference in your life first.

Once you have accomplished those items, revisit your "B" and "C" activities. Often the "C" items resolve themselves without any effort on your part. Or, they eventually move up to the "A" or "B" positions over time. It just makes common sense to accomplish the highest priority tasks first.

Buy Some Time

Feeling rushed or hurried can lead to poor decision-making. Before taking action, buy yourself some time. This can be one of the most valuable tools to provide confidence that you're moving in the right direction.

The best way to buy time is to ask questions. If you recall, asking questions is a direct positive way to take control of a conversation.

Let's say you have the habit of always answering your cell phone when it rings. Only, this time you take the call, it's your good friend inviting you to a last-minute lunch. Since you've scheduled this time for yourself today, you feel torn about what to do.

By responding to your friend's request by saying, *"I need a few minutes to make my decision. Can I call you right back?"* you alleviate the pressure to make an immediate decision. You can then weigh out the pros and cons before calling them back. An even better solution might be not to answer your phone until you have time. Then, listen to your message at your convenience, and take action.

While the choices posed in such quick moments may be more substantial—instead of going to lunch your boss wants you to work late—buying yourself time allows you to prioritize your schedule. It allows you to check in with your values, your time constraints, your family, and any other considerations before responding.

Take 24 Hours

Sometimes a big decision needs more than a few minutes to create clarity. In this case, we recommend taking 24 hours—one whole day—to create a new perspective on the situation and make a confident decision.

24 Hours in Action: Kym's Story

Kym had this experience on a trip to Colorado a few years ago. She loves Native American jewelry and found a spectacular jade necklace that she really wanted to buy. When she saw the price tag, it was a bit out of her current budget.

She really wanted the necklace and knew from past experience that these pieces were hard to find. Her logical side told her that she should keep an eye on her spending and buy the necklace another time. Her creative side liked the necklace enough to dip into savings and make up the difference later.

Kym waited 24 hours to make her decision. In that time, she left the store, had dinner with her sister, and got a restful night's sleep. The next morning, she had an entirely new perspective on life. In the end, she decided not to get the necklace.

Time worked to Kym's benefit and provided the time to reflect on her core values before taking action.

Ironically, a year later when Kym was in Florida, she found a similar version of the necklace she admired in Colorado. Only this time, it was made of opals instead of jade, and she had the budget to support her purchase.

Little did she know that honoring her principles and following the 24 hour rule in Colorado would come around to be a pleasant surprise a year later when the time came again to make a new decision. But, she made each one with confidence and purpose.

Get Support

Just as Chapter 2 encourages you to create a vision team, or support team, to help you reach your goals, the same people can often be used to help offer direction along the way when indecision arises. Utilize an outside perspective that offers logical guidance, emotional support, and validation of your values before taking action.

Utilize Common Sense Communication Skills

Honoring your voice by sharing your concerns with others can be an effective way to reduce worry. Let's use May as an example again. If she was anxious about Gregory's trip to the cabin, she can say to him, "Son, I'm nervous about your trip to the cabin. Please drive safely and check out the cabin when you arrive to make sure everything is working properly. Will you please call me and give me an update when you get there?"

Then, once May has shared her concerns vocally, she can let her stress go.

By ending her request with a direct positive question, May allows her son the opportunity to be part of the solution that decreases her worry. Gregory can then add energy to his own Energy Bank Account by listening to his mom, repeating her request, and following through when he gets to the mountains safely.

Putting it all Together

Choices are offered in an unlimited abundance throughout life, some of them smaller in scale and some of them drastically life-changing. When a strong foundation of values is present, and a clear destination is in mind, decisions can be made with assurance and ease. But, sometimes, there are still specific tools that need to be utilized in order to reduce fear, manage psychological risk, and eliminate worry as you move forward towards your goals.

New Common Sense Tools to Make Decisions with Confidence:

- **Letting Go of Fear:** Fear is often a compilation of false expectations about a person or situation that appear to be a reality. By placing fear in front of you, the power of visualization can help you walk past fear and on with your life.

- **Get out of the River:** Indecision can be a river in which you lose your energy, your vision, and potentially your life. By understanding what options are available on each shoreline, and using your instincts as guide through the use of a coin, you can move to a decision with clarity, safety, and purpose.

- **The Box:** Worry is a feeling that accompanies fear and inhibits your ability to take action confidently. Placing negative, draining thoughts out of sight and out of mind can free up extra energy to be used elsewhere, and it can sort out which alarming thoughts really need action taken to create a resolution.

Chapter 7

WHEREVER DAD GOES ON CONFERENCE, HE BRINGS ME BACK A SWIZZLE STICK FOR MY COLLECTION.

Form Meaningful Rituals

"It is good to have an end to journey toward; but it is the journey that matters in the end." —*Ursula K LeGuin*

In this Chapter

- Discover the components of meaningful rituals
- Enjoy the power of laughter
- Share the joy of giving
- Become centered and grounded
- Integrate tools from other chapters into meaningful rituals

After the other six chapters provide Common Sense Tools to increase your values, enhance your communication skills, and strengthen your choice-making capability, this section infuses those concepts with meaning, regularity, and purpose through meaningful rituals.

Most of our daily actions are driven by common routines. Think about how you arise every morning and take the steps necessary to get ready for the day. You probably brush your teeth in the same fashion or scrub yourself in the shower with some sort of subconscious pattern.

Thanks to the millions of previously-stored programs in your mind, you're able to do those common tasks without re-learning the motor skills and coordination to perform such functions. Now, you're able to go through those daily motions with your conscious mind focusing on other thoughts of the day, including your relationships or whatever other important ideas are painting the canvas of your focus.

There are many differences, however, between a habitual routine and a meaningful ritual.

Meaningful rituals are actions taken with conscious awareness and a goal in mind. Each task undertaken has importance in your overall life and a mindful approach is utilized to bring significance to the practice, action, or event. Meaningful rituals can be done alone, or they can include other people. They can be done daily, weekly, monthly, or annually.

The goal is to take repeated, focused action to enhance your well-being. Would you consider going for two weeks without taking a shower, changing your clothes, brushing your teeth and still go out in public?

The answer is most likely not.

However, if you chose not to do regular physical hygiene for a couple of weeks, the consequences on a large scale are rather minimal. You might have some social repercussions, but your physical health wouldn't be greatly diminished.

We are creating meaningful rituals that liken to emotional hygiene.

Common Sense Tip: By regularly setting time aside to check in with your internal balance and use tools to keep your life Energy Bank Account high, all components of your well-being benefit.

If you ignore emotional hygiene, your stress levels increase, your physical body experiences negative ramifications, and your relationships can feel strained. Lack of emotional hygiene has far greater consequences than ignoring physical hygiene over the course of a lifetime.

During meaningful rituals, the self-conscious mind gets entirely absorbed in the present moment. Thoughts of the future and past can subside altogether. Hours can pass quickly, as if only minutes have gone by or minutes can slow to feel like hours. Because of this, time has little relevance in the grand scheme of things.

Our goal for you is to utilize the power of your focus to infuse your actions with meaning. By placing a dedicated attention on certain daily activities, you lay the foundation for lasting personal changes. It's common knowledge that ongoing, long-term transformation takes place when there is a perceived sense of value tied to your behavior. This also includes a sense of freedom and expansion in the time you are taking for those events.

By creating significant rituals in your life, you infuse your day with purpose, meaning, and direction. It's the time set aside to clear out the old psychological patterns and form new ones. It's a conscious choice made, with careful awareness that helps keep us tuned up mentally and emotionally. It's the way we stay connected to something larger than ourselves, and keeps all of the daily chores, activities, and interactions in perspective.

Common Sense Tip: Meaningful rituals add energy to your life Energy Bank Account.

By taking action with creativity and care, you lift your vibration. You're able to feel more passion, connection, and spirit in all that you do. These energy deposits become ongoing, adding reserves to your account and supporting you through the ups and downs of life.

By moving from rote routine into meaningful rituals, you'll be able to:

- Add energy deposits to your bank account

- Stay on track with your goals

- Increase inspiration

- Spark creativity

- Remain emotionally balanced

- Enhance your connection to God and others

- Reduce stress

Each of us is beautifully unique, which is why the one-size-fits-all approach is inappropriate. In fact, this chapter outlines five foundational components that all meaningful rituals have in common. Then, we provide numerous ideas on how to combine those concepts into actions that make you feel good.

Not every one of us is fulfilled by the same activity. And, in fact, we go through so many personal transitions in a lifetime that not all activities provide the same satisfaction for ourselves over the years. Find a ritual that works for you—an action, or activity, that you'll feel excited about and willing to continue on a regular basis.

It may take some experimenting at first, but we'll provide many ideas that can help you get started right away.

Have fun with this process. Tune into a childlike nature that explores the internal world just as you would the external one. And enjoy the process of creating meaningful rituals that enhance all areas of your life.

5 Common Sense Components of Meaningful Rituals

While there are numerous activities that qualify as meaningful rituals, they all have commonalities that give them their powerful role in our lives. The five components that we recognize to be essential in meaningful rituals are:

- Set time aside

- Identify a specific goal

- Create a sacred space

- Follow a consistent process

- Enhance love

Let's take a close look at these attributes of meaningful rituals in detail.

Set time aside

In the time-bound world we share on earth, with 1,440 minutes in a day, every moment seems to become more valuable, especially as the pace of life speeds up. With many waking hours devoted to our work spheres, our free time is sacred. We want to make the most of the time we have with our family, and friends, and even more importantly the time for ourselves.

Thus, **one of the most important components of a meaningful ritual lies in setting time aside to spend alone.** It's the time for us to hit the re-set button for our day, week, or year ahead. It's true that there are significant practices we enjoy sharing with others, like attending a church service or a meditation group. However, it's the action of setting time aside for your personal ritual that's important.

The amount of time needed for an activity depends on the nature of the ritual itself. Sometimes 15 minutes of sitting quiet in the morning offers an exponential energy boost to the rest of your day. Maybe once a week you schedule a date with yourself to reflect on your Business, Personal, and Spiritual Spheres. In this valuable time, you're able to connect with your values and organize for the days to come with undivided focus.

Meaningful rituals might require less time than you think. Even 15 minutes a day can make a huge difference in your overall life Energy Bank Account and your feelings of internal balance. Once you get used to setting the time aside, you might want to increase that amount because you find the ritual so enjoyable.

Identify a specific goal

To become a powerful creator in your life, it's essential to have an idea of where you're going, what you'd like to experience, and what kind of relationships you want to have along the way. This concept of setting an intention, from the creative process in Chapter 2 (see page 67) and organizing a direction for your life in Chapter 6 (see page 175) can be used on a smaller scale with meaningful rituals.

When you decide to set time apart for yourself to boost your energy, satisfy your reserves, or connect with your spiritual self, it makes your time more productive and purposeful when you have a specific goal.

Your direction for this time can include any of the following ideas:

- Relax or unwind
- Reduce stress
- Gain inspiration
- Reflect on an experience, a relationship, or any aspect of your life
- Set new goals for any given area of your life
- Connect with God or any higher power greater than yourself
- Change your perspective

Create a sacred space

As an energetic being, you're constantly sending and receiving messages from your environment. Your senses—seeing, hearing, smelling, feeling, and tasting—all contribute to the quality of your experience in every given moment.

Thus, when creating a sacred ritual, you want your surroundings to align with the purpose for your time alone. If your goal is to focus on reflection, it's helpful to be somewhere quiet, perhaps with soft music playing or even outdoors with birds chirping or water rushing by in a stream.

If your purpose for your specific practice is to receive inspiration, perhaps you play tunes with uplifting lyrics as you write in your journal. Or, you might recognize your religious sanctuary as a reverent place where you connect with God.

But, it doesn't necessarily have to be formal.

Sacred Space in Action: Kym and Steve's Story

Kym gets up early in the morning and makes her way to the living room. In this comfortable setting, with the lights low and the entire house quiet, she writes in her journal and prepares for the day ahead.

Steve, on the other hand, has created a meaningful and ritual of meditating in his office before starting the workday. He dims the lights, sits in his comfortable chair, and turns off all of the phones so that he's entirely detached from interruption.

There is no one setting that is more appropriate than another in which a ritual can take place. It is important, however, that your surroundings appeal to your senses and support your overall goal for your sacred time.

Follow a consistent process

You've probably heard the saying, "practice makes perfect" or Vince Lombardi's famous quote, "perfect practice makes perfect" when talking about mastering a skill. In essence, you're becoming proficient in taking time for yourself and adding energy to your bank account on a regular basis.

While meaningful rituals don't rely on precision, they do rely on a continued practice for long-term success. Just as learning to ride a bike takes lots of concentration and conscious focus, after the movements become hard-wired into the subconscious mind, riding a bicycle become effortless.

It's the same for a meaningful ritual. A ceremonial process simply means that you are following the same steps over and over again until they are ingrained into the subconscious mind. It's taking awareness into those steps that make it different than a habitual routine.

Let's go back to Kym's morning quiet time for a moment. She follows specific steps to get herself ready and alert for her writing. She makes some hot tea, brings a blanket and her notebook to the couch, and sits in her favorite corner to begin her journaling. After she's poured out her thoughts onto paper, she sits quietly for 10 or 15 minutes. This silence allows inspiration for the day to arrive or creates a centered position from which to tackle all of the daily tasks ahead.

Again, there are numerous kinds of meaningful rituals that you can create to fulfill your ever-changing needs. Whether your practice is daily journaling, meditating, praying, or reflecting, your subconscious mind memorizes those patterns for the future. Every cell in your body becomes energized by the time you've set aside and anticipates the benefits to come. You're using the tradition of a given specific process to make lasting changes in your mind, body, and spirit.

> "The real juice of life, whether it be sweet or bitter, is to be found not nearly so much in the products of our efforts as in the process of living itself.
> —Mr. George Leonard

What Materials support your Process?

It's important to note here that varying processes require different materials to be successful. If you're writing, a journal or notebook is necessary. If you're meditating, then a comfortable seat or cushion can make or break your time alone. Even if you choose morning walks as a time of reflection, it's important to think about appropriate shoes and clothing.

When choosing your meaningful ritual, consider the process it takes to prepare, spend your time, and what materials you'll need to make the most of your sacred practice.

Enhance Love

Love is what separates meaningful rituals from satanic or sadistic ceremonies. While the Ku Klux Klan has rituals that involve time, a specific process, a purpose, and a sacred space, they are basing their premise on judgment and supremacy.

This is why having a foundation of love—the value and emotion that's enhanced during the activity and resulting from it—is so important.

You've probably heard the phrase, "my cup runneth over". This image of having a spirit so abundant in love and energy that it naturally spills over into all other areas of life is what we're aiming for here. In a common-sense way, we want your meaningful rituals to nurture, support, and inspire the deepest aspects of you. And, these activities create a greater expression of love for yourself and others.

Find Your Center

Taking purposeful action in all areas of life begins with the quiet moments utilized in meaningful rituals. It is in this reflective time where internal balance, or centeredness, can be restored.

In the introduction of this book, we talked about the analogy of a personal boat anchored in a lake by a line of values. By creating a strong line from your vessel to the water's floor, you can remain centered and balanced, regardless of the situations around you.

While a boat's concerns are weather-based, you are surrounded daily by people, places, and things that have signals of their own. Some situations make you feel good, enhance your life energy, and further increase your sense of personal balance. Other people or circumstances do quite the opposite—they leave you feeling worse, decrease your life energy, and create a sense of imbalance.

Common Sense Tip: The goal of finding your center, or creating internal balance, is to control your own life energy exchanges with the world around you, therefore having more power over your entire life Energy Bank Account.

It is creating a centeredness that increases your personal power. It increases the harmony between ourselves and the world around us. And it promotes well-being in the body, mind, and spirit.

With centeredness, you're focused in the present moment. You're undistracted by past or future, although perhaps aware of those in the timeline continuum.

Get Grounded

There are many ways to become grounded—stable in your foundation and purpose—which is another way of enhancing your internal balance. We want to feel confident, secure, and stable in all of our life experiences. By doing this, you are less vulnerable to other people, situations, and negative energy perceived in your environment.

For the following activity, invite your inner child to participate. While this may sound odd, take on a child-like perspective for a moment. Kids like to play games. They pick up new concepts quickly, and having fun in the present moment is something that makes every activity more meaningful to them.

With an open-minded curiosity and fun-filled spirit, a child-like attitude makes learning how to feel grounded much easier.

Common Sense "Get Grounded" Activity

The goal of this exercise is to learn how to remain grounded as much as possible. This keeps you at a higher state of awareness and centeredness. It also increases internal balance and life energy.

Directions: Find a partner for this exercise. Take turns playing the role of the participant and as the helpful partner.

Stand face-to-face with your partner, with a distance of about three feet between you. This exercise can also be done seated, with the same amount of space between both people.

Part 1: Create a Grounded Feeling

As the participant, close your eyes and sense both of your feet touching the ground beneath you. Picture your favorite-colored rope—strong, long, and sturdy—and tie it snugly around your waist.

Once your line is secure, shift your attention to the center of the earth. Imagine that there is a large graviton ball at the earth's core with giant, iron loops on its surface.

Envision casting your bright-colored rope down between your legs and tie the other end to one of the hooks on the graviton ball. Cinch the rope so there is no slack between you and the center of the earth. Pull the length of the rope so tight that you feel the soles of your feet even more strongly connected to the floor beneath you. It can almost be so tight that your feet are sinking into the ground.

When you feel the rope is secure between you and the earth's core, open your eyes and look at your partner.

Your partner now comes over and pushes on your shoulders, as if to push you backwards, with a medium-strength push. Notice how strong you are. Observe how easy it is to remain upright and balanced. This provides the feeling of being grounded.

Part 2: Discover an Ungrounded State

Stay in the same role as you were in Part 1.

As the participant, close your eyes again and sense both of your feet touching the ground beneath you.

At this moment, you still have your rope tied from your waist to the graviton ball at the center of the earth.

It's time to undo that connection. Unhook the line from around your waist and set it aside on the floor next to you.

When you feel that line is entirely disconnected, open your eyes and look at your partner.

Have your partner step forward once again and push on your shoulders with the same strength. This doesn't have to be a hard shove, as you will most likely be a bit unbalanced and unsturdy. This provides the feeling of being ungrounded.

Notice the differences you felt between Part 1 and Part 2 of this activity. There is often a significant difference between the grounded and ungrounded feelings.

Part 3: Return to your Grounded Nature

Repeat Part 1 so that the participant feels grounded and secure once again. Observe any changes or sensations that arise from this exercise. Share them with your partner. Then switch roles, allowing the partner to become the participant, and start the entire activity over.

Common Sense Tip: Remaining grounded creates a higher state of awareness and centeredness.

Grow a Monkey Tail

Now, growing a monkey tail is another form of remaining grounded and centered on a regular basis. And it encourages the child within to participate.

It is a shortcut to the previous rope exercise, and we think it's a lot more fun. This activity also utilizes the power of a graviton ball at the center of the earth. Instead of shooting a colored rope from your waist to the earth's core, imagine that a cord is always connected from the graviton ball to an invisible loop on the surface of the earth just below your feet.

When you want to instantly create a grounded state, you imagine growing a monkey tail from your backside—at your tailbone—and hook the end of your tail on that invisible loop. Then just tighten your tail. You will automatically feel a sense of connection with the ground beneath you, sturdiness in your posture, and clear perspective of the world around you.

You don't need anyone to push on your shoulders, because you know that you're centered. From this grounded state, you'll be able to recognize when imbalances arise in your life and then know how to use common-sense tools to regain your stability. To top it off, you'll be able to maximize your own energy to be used in the most joyful and productive ways possible, starting with your meaningful rituals and expanding to all other areas of your life.

Meditation

Meditation is one of the most powerful meaningful rituals that can be included into daily living to enhance life energy, boost self-esteem, and create personal clarity. Recent studies have shown that meditation:

- Improves quality of life
- Increases creativity
- Develops intuition
- Enhances productivity
- Decreases stress
- Alleviates pain
- Reduces depression
- Minimizes sleep disturbances
- And much, much more

For Kym, the concept of meditation first conjured up a vision of some cave-bound ancient yogi, draped solely in a loin cloth, chanting the mantra "Om" ceaselessly.

Little did she know, meditation was far from her premature notions.

In fact, meditation is an activity that can be done in numerous forms, with many different techniques. There's not always a need to sit still, nor does there need to be chanting involved, although there can be.

> "Meditation is a way of clearing away the mental clutter that surrounds the subconscious. And when our minds are clear, we can see and experience the joy of our own soul." —Gurmukh

For the purposes of Common Sense Living, we define meditation as: any activity set aside to create present-moment awareness and joy. Regardless of the type of meditation that gets you there, the practices share three basic similarities:

- **Focused Attention**

First, meditating involves focusing on one thing at a time, or generating a sense of uninterrupted concentration. Focus can be created by placing attention on one single thing at a time, such as the breath, an aspect of a project, or even a specific body movement.

- **Heightened Awareness**

Second, the mind is a thought-generating organism that communicates constantly with every cell of the body. Meditation enhances a sense of awareness of such thoughts, which naturally wander from the focal point, and guides the mind back to the original place of concentration.

- **A Sense of Detachment**

Finally, while there is a heightened awareness of thoughts and body sensations, a sense of detachment is created. The mind is aware of thoughts, emotions, and feelings, but as the practitioner, we realize that we are not those thoughts, emotions, or feelings. They are simply one aspect of our being.

And, because we are not attached to those ideas as our identity, there is no need for judgment when they arise. For example, if you are focusing on your breath during meditation, and you notice a thought arise about what you need to do for the day, you don't get mad at yourself for losing focus. Instead, you get to celebrate your awareness of the mind's content, and get to powerfully choose to return back to observing your inhales and exhales.

This third component of meditation detaches our identity from thoughts, feelings, and sensations, without judgment, which opens the possibility for us to connect to an eternal aspect of our beings. It's an opportunity to connect with our souls—the loving, unchanging, and non-physical aspects—that help guide us through life's circumstances with a broader perspective. Through the process of staying focused, and open-minded, we invite a much larger aspect of ourselves to give us direction as we move through the daily activities of life.

There are so many ways to meditate. In order to simplify this meaningful ritual, we divided meditation into three basic categories—passive, active, and creative. They all offer the same benefits, but can be interchanged based on your mood, level of energy, and personal preferences during changing stages of life.

Passive Meditation

This type of meditation is probably the most common when first picturing the practice. Passive meditation involves sitting passively while the subconscious mind processes thoughts, emotions, and sensations. It's as though the subconscious is the deep waters of a lake, and bubbles, or thoughts rise up from the storage of the mind to the surface, or the conscious mind, where you're aware of those thoughts, emotions, and sensations.

A common misconception is that the goal of meditating is to empty the mind.

Passive Meditation in Action: Kym's Story

As Kym can attest to after ten days of a silent meditation retreat, creating a perfectly still mind is not possible for any length of time. That's right! Kym voluntarily signed herself up for a retreat in Brazil where no speech, eye contact, or any form of interaction with others was permitted. For a week and a half, she was dedicated solely to learning the process of meditation.

It only took two days for her to plan an escape route. Option 1: Find Tarzan in this wild jungle by blatantly making animal calls at nightfall. Option 2: Pay off one of the (hopefully) English-speaking cooks on site for a ride back to civilization. Or, Option 3: Stick it out no matter how painfully real those endless thoughts and emotions were that bombarded her during the time of silence.

Option 3 inevitably won and Kym survived the intense meditation practice. In fact, by the end of ten days, she appreciated silence in a way she never imagined possible.

She learned, just like we're sharing with you, that thoughts might continually arise from new stimuli, old memories, or whims of inspiration from beyond.

However, the goal of meditation is to realize you are not defined by those thoughts, emotions, or perceptions. It's the ability to be detached from them, to watch them as though on a movie screen, that allows you to move forward freely.

It's true, meditation at times can create the possibility of feeling in the zone, entirely connected with all that is around you, and there can be silence in the mind.

With practice, this can become easier. And, if it takes a long time, that's okay. Meditation is all about the journey. It is about sitting still despite what is surrounding you. There are tough situations that arise. Difficult or challenging people may cross your path.

Passive meditation develops the skill of being still. In this state, you can observe outside situations instead of attaching to them. This provides a broader perspective about solutions for current problems you might be facing. It also offers insights to life lessons you may be learning.

That being said, passive meditation often requires some point of focus. In the type of meditation Kym learned in Brazil, the focus was on body sensations that arose on the skin. For hours, she would sit and observe tingling on the skin, or her T-shirt meeting her arm, or the air brushing across her face. At times, the sensations all merged into one, creating a euphoric feeling. Then she would return to scanning the body from head to toe for sensations.

Other types of meditation train the mind to focus by placing the attention on breathing. There are endless inhales and exhales that flow in and out, like waves crashing onto the ocean's shore. Watching or observing the breath becomes the focal point when you notice thoughts arising, memories replaying, or any other distraction taking your focus away from the breath.

Gazing at a candle is another way to hold your attention. Repeating a mantra—short saying—helps the mind stay centered on one thought. Meditation can also contemplate or reflect on a concept. You can choose an attribute or value, such as love or integrity.

Another goal of meditation is to heighten the ability to focus in a given situation and elevate the senses. This can then be taken from the seat of meditation to relationships, the workplace, the sporting realm, and any circumstance.

Passive Meditation in Action: Cathy's Story

Cathy was a mother of three, with all children under the age of six. Her mornings were busy, starting early as her kids arose before dawn and her husband was out the door for work before 8:00a.m. She wanted to increase her centeredness before starting her day with the kids. Cathy would have her husband watch the kids in the morning for 15 minutes, while she sat in the bathroom to focus on her breathing. This small, unusual space took on sacred meaning. It was a short amount of time that started to make a big difference in her day. She was more present with her kids, aware of her surroundings, and capable of responding to each child without taking on any emotional stress or frustration when things would go wrong.

As the kids grew, so could her meditation practice. Cathy eventually set up a small corner of their bedroom and extended her time to 30 minutes. But, she still laughs about the meaningful ritual that started years ago with the toilet as her seat.

We can make anything significant when we attribute meaning to it. Cathy's passive meditation incorporated all of the components of a meaningful ritual. She:

- Set 15 minutes of time aside each day
- Had the purpose of focusing on her breath and practicing detachment from thoughts
- Used the small space of her bathroom to create a sacred place for herself
- Followed the specific process of sitting, taking ten deep breaths to bring her into focus
- Wanted more love to infuse her relationships as a result of her practice

Passive meditation opens up a channel for creative insights and thoughts. It can generate feelings of peace, freedom, and relaxation. Sitting passively also allows you to tap into the creative essence of all that is, whether you call it God, the Universe, the void, or the vortex. This connection with an all-knowing aliveness can even be accompanied by angels or guides to help you on your life journey.

Passive Meditation Activity

Find a comfortable, seated position where your spine is upright. If you recline, it's easier to fall asleep. Start to become aware of your breathing, without changing it in any way.

Once you observe the natural rhythm of your inhales and exhales, relax your jaw, soften your eyes, and drop your shoulders down away from your ears.

Now, on your next inhale, silently think of the number one.

As you exhale, repeat number one.

The goal is to count up to 15, without losing focus. If you notice your mind begin to wander, start over at number one and begin counting again.

When you are able to sit and focus your breathing all the way to 15, then increase your number to 20.

This simple practice begins to hone in your skill of maintaining attention in the present moment through the simple use of numbers.

Active Meditation

Active meditations involve physical movements of the body while focusing the mind. There are numerous ways to harness excess energy to empower the mind and inner spirit.

Walking meditation is a common practice of the mind connecting with the body in action. It's often easier to be more intensely aware of the body in motion, as opposed to trying to find subtle sensations of the body while seated. The goal is to become mindful of the act of walking itself—how the arms are moving in conjunction with the legs, what surface is below the feet, where the sense of balance is distributed through the whole body, how you're breathing throughout the entire process.

You can take walking meditations into the transitions of your day, such as walking from your car into the office or supermarket. You can take ten minutes on your lunch break and use a nearby park or open space to help facilitate your focus. It's easier to begin in less crowded spaces, but with practice, you can use mindfulness on the sidewalks of New York City.

Walking a labyrinth is also a form of moving meditation, although this activity now takes walking into a one-directional path. A labyrinth is different from a maze in that there is one way in and one way out, free of blind alleys and confusing turns.

This walk from the outside of the circle to the inside is spiritual in nature. It represents the symbol of walking into the deeper aspects of ourselves, to the soul within, that which is beyond the ego. Then, when you walk back out, you have a greater understanding of yourself and the broader world to which you are re-entering. Often, in large cities, you can find a labyrinth to walk or you can research how to build one for a creative activity.

Various forms of movement exercises qualify as active meditations. Tai Chi, for example, is a series of graceful and continuous movements of the body through various postures. This provides bodily benefits, such as increased flexibility and endurance, and is done in a non-competitive environment. It also focuses the mind on the graceful flow of energy through each posture.

Similarly, Qigong (pronounced "chee gong") is the art of balancing the breath and the energy in the body through physical movements. Slow body movements are combined with concentration and relaxed breathing to enhance balance, vitality, and mental focus.

Perhaps the most commonly recognized form of active meditation in the west today is Hatha yoga. Hatha yoga incorporates physical postures, or asanas through the facilitation of the breath to cleanse the body and mind. Just like Tai Chi and Qigong have various styles of practice, Hatha yoga can be found in many forms around the world. Power yoga, Astanga yoga, Bikram yoga, and Anusara yoga are some practices that have formed from various lineages under the umbrella of Hatha yoga. Despite their initial differences, they all use the breath as a point of focus as the body moves through simple or challenging physical movements.

Active Meditation Activity

This activity stimulates the frontal lobe of the brain. It requires a focused attention and patience. The goal is to start small. By doing this activity, you improve your short-term memory, create a whole brain state, enhance information recall, and spark creativity that is within you already.

Materials needed: A deck of cards

Directions: Before you begin, take a deck of cards and shuffle them. Place the deck face down in the middle of table in front of you.

Step 1: Start with your left hand, take the top card off of the deck, look at it and try to memorize the card (like king of hearts), then place it face down on the table to the right side of the deck.

Step 2: Now, take your right hand, take the top card off of the deck, look at it and memorize it (two of spades), and place it face down on the table to the left side of the deck.

Step 3: Repeat the above process one more time, with the left hand and then the right.

Pause with the cards face down and see if you can name all four cards, such as king of hearts or two of spades that are still face down on the table.

If you are unsuccessful at remembering the cards, gather them up off of the table and place them *face up* on the bottom of the card deck.

If you are successful at remembering all four cards, gather them up off of the table and place them off to the side.

Now, continue through the deck, four cards at a time. You can count your success by looking at the number of cards to the side of the deck.

After you have gone through the entire deck with no errors, you complete the same exercise by taking three cards with your left hand and three with your right, thus memorizing six cards at a time. When you have gone through the deck completely without errors then add four cards to each side.

In the beginning, this can seem challenging and only 15 minutes of the activity will suffice. Ideally, 15 to 30 minutes of this activity a day significantly enhances memory, creativity, and focus.

Creative Meditation

The intention or purpose behind the meditation is really what makes the ritual special. With creative meditation, the goal is to invoke your inner artist or imagination to get your body and mind in a focused, harmonious space.

We have had clients attest to getting in a focused space by making jewelry, losing themselves for hours when working with their hands. Others use sewing, collage making, or painting as forms of creative meditation.

What sets these activities apart from just a task is their purpose for the activity in the first place. They are following the guidelines of a meaningful ritual. They:

- Set time aside for themselves

- Have a goal to reduce stress, be alone, or allow their inspiration to flow

- Create a specific, consistent environment for the activity to take place

- Follow a consistent process to get their materials out, have their favorite music playing, or take dependable steps to start, perform, and clean up the activity

- Enhance love through the activity. They enjoy what they're doing and know that the outcome of their activity shares that positive emotion with others, either as a by-product of the artwork or their attitude

Using purposeful action can create a spontaneous joy or sense of calm within the mind and body alike.

Creative Meditation in Action: Erika's Story

In fact, Erika was a woman who really enjoyed the art of scrapbooking. She decided to create the ritual of making travel scrapbooks, based on her love of travel. Erika blossomed in her creative time alone. Within weeks, she wanted to share her experience with others. She invited two close friends, who also enjoyed scrapbooking, to join her in this weekly endeavor.

They were so pleased with their travel books that the three women decided to share their work. Out of love, they donated the scrapbooks of Egypt, England, South Africa, and many other global destinations to senior citizen centers. The residents could reminisce about their own travels, and many, who had never been abroad, were able to see the world through a new perspective.

Creative Meditation Activity

Take any joyful activity that enhances your creativity and dedicate one hour of your time with mindful purpose. Activities can include: writing poetry, creating a collage, or designing jewelry, building furniture, playing an instrument, or arranging flowers. Add your personal favorites to this list.

"What is YOUR creative activity?" Say it aloud or write it here:_____

The goal is to be so focused on the activity that you lose yourself in the creativity and feel nurtured when you're done.

The Power of Laughter

Laughter is part of our natural and inborn gifts as human beings. Infants begin smiling within the first few weeks of life and begin to laugh out loud within a few months. Even if your household didn't support much humor and laugher growing up, it's never too late to incorporate this joyful and beneficial action into daily life.

Laughter in Action: Kym's Story

Kym didn't always have the boisterous laugh that she does now. In fact, she had to work on it at first. When Kym was 13 years old, her father passed away. For the next few years, she took life too seriously and intensely. She noticed that her younger sister had quite the unique laugh and many commented on her sister's joyfulness.

Kym realized that she wanted that same happiness. Slowly, Kym started to look for the humor in life. She forced laughter at times, with the "fake it 'til you make it" idea. Soon enough, laughing came more easily, and this laughter was genuine. Now, when you walk into a room and hear a contagious laugh, it's probably Kym. It's noticeable and infectious.

Laughter has so many wonderful benefits. It's one of the quickest ways to bring the body and mind back into balance. Laughter is a powerful antidote to stress, pain, and conflict. The body can relax, the function of the heart improves efficiency, and a boost to the immune system all result from laughter. When laughter is shared, it brings people together and can increase intimacy.

Other benefits of laughter include:

- Enhanced teamwork
- Improved mood
- Attraction of others
- Increased coping capabilities and resilience
- Eased anxiety and fear
- Broader perspective of life as a whole

Because laughter has the ability to heal and renew, it's one of the best Common Sense Tools to use on a regular basis. It is also one of the most effective concepts that can be interwoven into a meaningful ritual for exponential and lasting energy in your Energy Bank Account.

Here are some ideas to incorporate humor and laughter into life as meaningful rituals.

Bring humor into your conversations

While many daily conversations talk about superficial or mundane aspects of life, spice up your dialogue by asking people humor-related questions like,

- *"What was the funniest thing that happened to you today? Or this week?*
- *"What was the funniest thing you've seen or heard today? Or this week?*

Schedule a date with a playful person

We all know someone who laughs easily or has a contagious laugh. It could be a friend or an intimate partner. These people often find themselves humorous and look to the lighter side of life for enjoyment. Their playful and positive perspective results in high energy can easily rub off on you and increase your own life Energy Bank Account.

Host a game night with friends

Bring the humor into your own home by hosting a game night at your home. This can range anywhere from a casual evening of board games to a more elaborate night of a murder mystery game where everyone comes in costume. These fun times of shared laughter can create a meaningful ritual for you and those you interact with on a regular basis.

Watch a funny movie or T.V. show

Many T.V. shows or movies focus on crime, death, illness, and deceit, which drain your Energy Bank Account. Yet, comedies provide a way to naturally and positively release energy. Not only are you able to relax your body, you're able to temporarily escape the hassles or frustrations of the real world. This can be done to purposefully shift your focus to what's funny in life. Even replay your favorite scenes over and over or tell them to a friend. This makes the good feelings last much longer than their initial moment of experience. [see Appendix for movie ideas]

Enjoy belly laughs

Shared laughter is one of the best ways to add excitement and freshness to relationships. It's a way of strengthening bonds and uniting differences. Boost your energy through a belly laugh. With a partner, have one person lie on the floor (or a comfortable bed) and have the other person lay their head on the first person's belly.

Then, turn on a comedian or listen to jokes and notice what happens when you both begin laughing. The belly laugh, and the vibration that results, add to the energetic boost of the laughter itself. Switch positions and notice what happens from the other person's perspective.

Take a laughter yoga class

That's right. Yoga shifts your attention away from specific postures to humor and laughter in these classes.

Here are some other ideas:

- Go to a comedy club
- Browse the humorous card section at the grocery store, drug store, carwash, or post office.
- Play with a pet
- Check out the humor section of your local bookstore
- Watch children interacting on a playground
- Go to the latest kids' movie being released and enjoy their laughter
- Read the funny pages

The goal is to have fun and increase the amount of laughter in your life. By creating a time, space, and process to your laughter, where love can be increased, you take the habit of laughing and transform it into a meaningful ritual that enhances your entire life.

The Common Sense Power of Laughter Activity

This activity is a three-step process that can be done within any time range—a week, three weeks, or a month. The exercise can go on indefinitely, if you enjoy talking to people and laughing freely. There is no right or wrong way to do this. If you like it, continue on for as long as you'd like. If you find other activities bring you more joy, stick with those.

Directions:

Step 1: Choose a comedy that you would like to see or that you know you already enjoy. Watch this movie without an agenda and just have fun.

Step 2: Then watch this movie a second time through and find out why you laughed at certain points of the film. Find out what was so funny. Ask yourself, *"What about this made me laugh."*

Step 3: Make a point to tell someone about the funny movie you watched and share what parts of the film you found hilarious. Then, ask them about a comedy they enjoy. Find out why they like that movie and then make a point to watch that movie on your own. This allows you to find new avenues of humor and create a list of comedies for yourself.

The Joy of Giving

Giving is an act of openly sharing with others without expecting anything in return. When you give of your soul energy, it's a beautiful exchange of energy that increases the life force bank accounts of all involved with deposits.

Getting an energy boost, however, is not the reason for giving in the first place.

It's like an automatic deposit. By authentically sharing from your heart, your energy levels increase. Your spirit is nurtured and the intrinsic values of generosity and love are effortlessly enhanced.

The joy of giving can also become a meaningful ritual. When we think of giving, it can be in four main categories.

It's what the Church of Religious Science calls the Four T's: Time, Talent, Treasure, and Tithe.

> "Your willingness to receive blessings is directly related to your ability to give them."
> —Lao-Tzu

Time

With the fast-paced lifestyle many of us live today, time is a valued commodity. In fact, this can be one of the most generous gifts to share with others.

Time can be used as a meaningful ritual by:

- Helping at a food kitchen
- Reading to senior citizens
- Being a Big Brother or Big Sister
- Babysitting for friends who need a date night

Ask yourself the following question: Do I have time in my life that I can give to others?

Talent

Each of us has natural skills and abilities that can be used to benefit others. By giving of your talent, you share your natural gifts with others. For example, if you are a capable plumber and your unemployed neighbor's sink gets clogged, you might offer your services free of charge. This is a charitable contribution of your talent to get their system up and running again.

Or you might have the skill of growing incredible vegetables in your garden and you share your crop with friends and family. You could even offer to teach friends how to grow a garden of their own.

Ask yourself the following question: What talents do I possess that can be shared with those around me?

Treasure

A treasure is a material good that holds great value to us. It can be something we've had for a long time or that was even passed down to us by a loved one. It could be a favorite guitar, photograph, or pocketknife.

One of our treasures need not hold a great monetary value, although it might. The perfect example of this is a rock that Steve had polished by hand and held for many years. Being a collector of beautiful rocks, he became accustomed to one in particular that he deemed his healing stone. The rock stayed in his pocket through 15 years of counseling sessions, workshops, and travels.

Giving a Treasure in Action: Steve's Story

During one trip to Crestone Colorado, Steve took a hiking tour up in the hills to discover the Buddhist stupa. When he passed the wall where prayers were said, he learned of the Buddhist tradition to leave a gift with the blessing. Earrings, notes, trinkets and other miscellaneous items were placed between the rocks as a token of love.

The tour continued on, but Steve stayed behind. He was led to say a prayer for a sick friend, but realized he didn't have much to give. Suddenly, the rock in his pocket came to mind. For a moment, many of the special memories associated with the stone came to mind. Was he ready to give it up? Is this what was to be given with his prayer to send the message forward?

It was a clear message for his heart that leaving his healing rock on the stupa was truly the act of giving a treasure.

The item had meaning. It was a symbol of love. And the gift had purpose.

Ask yourself the following questions: What do I have materially that has significant meaning? Will I pass this on as a legacy? Is there something I own that can be given to someone else for a specific, giving purpose?

Tithe

Tithing, in most cultures, refers to a monetary gift. If this is an important and accessible way for you to give, money can be donated to your favorite charity, cause, or institution.

Ask yourself the following question: Is there a particular cause that I would like to help financially?

Common Sense Tip: Giving with any of the Four T's—time, talent, treasure, and tithe—is based in love and freedom.

Yet, giving with the intention of receiving an award, recognition, or control counteracts any benefits that might result from the ritual of giving.

We've seen many donate money to a charitable cause, but then want a say in how the money is spent.

This is why genuine giving is not attached to expectations.

The ritual of giving is centered in the heart-space, full of love and hope that all of mankind received an energy boost from the actions of sharing your time, talent, treasure, or tithes.

Your life is constantly changing. Sometimes you have time to give, other times you have a talent. Perhaps the opportunity arises to share a treasure or to monetarily donate to those in need.

If and when you decide to use giving as a meaningful ritual, notice which of the 4 T's matches your heartfelt inspiration to share.

And have fun doing it!

Expand the Purpose of Everyday Encounters

While several meaningful rituals have been discussed in detail, there is endless potential to expand the purpose of everyday events into purposeful practices.

Blessing a Meal

It's a tradition in many cultures to bless the food as it arrives on the table before being consumed. This meaningful action involves people recognizing the reverence of the mealtime, combining their effort and energy and love through holding hands, and following a specific process of verbally or silently blessing the foods about to be eaten.

Just as Thanksgiving in America is accompanied by an attitude of gratitude, for the company and the food, this tradition can be expanded to evening family meals or dining with friends to regularly add deposits to your Energy Bank Account.

Celebrate your Birthday or the New Year

Your birthday comes around once a year, as does January 1st. These monumental days can be used to reflect on the past and powerfully create new goals and visions for the future.

Celebration Activity

Consider the following activity to boost your energy in celebration.

Step 1: Schedule at least an hour of uninterrupted time alone.

Step 2: Review the previous year's goals, which can be saved as a word document on your computer or in an old journal. Notice which goals came to pass and which ones did not. Reflect on how those aspirations affected your life. If you did not set any previous goals, reflect on your previous year as a whole. You can use the daily support questions as guidelines for reflecting on your year. (see page 62)

Step 3: Think carefully about the year ahead. Set ten new intentions or goals that you have for yourself in all areas of your life. Think about the Business, Personal, and Spiritual spheres, or use questions from Chapter 6 for ideas. (see page 175)

Step 4: Finish the ritual by writing a letter to yourself, acknowledging how you have grown as an individual and how you have positively affected the lives of others around you.

Once you finish your birthday or New Year ritual, it helps to keep your intentions in a place you see them regularly. You might want to keep the list on your refrigerator, in your daily journal, or by your desk at work. Placing these items at the top of your list means that you are willing to dedicate time and energy to their manifestation.

Gather with Others

You might feel compelled to share your meaningful ritual with others. Just as Erin opened her scrapbooking time to close friends, you might enjoy fellowship with others while adding mindful deposits to your Energy Bank Account. This includes starting a group of your own or joining one already in progress.

Meaningful rituals are done regularly. They're not just one-time actions. Here are some examples of ongoing significant practices shared with others:

- A weekly meditation group
- Gathering to pray or send blessings
- Going to church on Sunday
- Weekly dinner with friends
- Weekly meeting with the spouse to reflect on 3 spheres of life
- Have an inspirational movie night

The goal is that your meaningful ritual adds to your life Energy Bank Account and that activity nurtures you.

Common Sense Tools become Meaningful Rituals

This book contains numerous tools that can help bolster values, enhance communication, and support relationships. While they are effective when done independently, their power can be increased by consistently using them in daily living.

Below is a summary of many Common Sense Tools, their purpose, and a suggested way of using them for a balanced and successful life.

Chapter	Common Sense Tool	Purpose	Meaningful Ritual
Intro	Three Spheres	Create awareness of how life energy is used	Take one hour a week and reflect on how much energy is going to your business, personal, and spiritual activities. Create new goals for the upcoming week if necessary.
1	Value Wheel	Provide meaning and purpose behind actions	Choose one value each morning from Appendix A to support your decisions.
1	4-Way Test	Increase integrity internally and with your community	Chose one question from the 4-way test and ask yourself that question with each decision you make today.
2	The Hand Model of Wellness	Check your internal state of well-being and create personal goals	Take the hand model of wellness quiz once a week. Journal about your balances and imbalances. Create one new goal for the upcoming week.
2	The Daily Support Questions	Instantly transform your perspective from limited to limitless	Keep a journal of the daily support questions. For one month, write your responses daily.

2	I AM	Become a powerful creator in your life	Choose a birthday, anniversary, or New Year's celebration to write down ten new intentions or aspirations. Post these where you will see them over the next 12 months.
2	Vision Team	Provide support when making important decisions in life or need guidance on which steps to take next	Create a vision team of three people and schedule meetings with them once a month for ongoing support.
3	21-Day Plan	Rewrite self-defeating language or regrets into positive statements that support your goals	Get a journal and commit to rewriting three limiting beliefs for 21 days. Then, reflect on how your life and perspective has changed after those three weeks.
3	Direct Positive Dialogue	Increase your skills as an assertive communicator	Set aside 30 minutes once a month and treat yourself to your favorite coffee shop. Take a journal. Then, when seated, listen to how other people communicate. Notice who is using direct positive dialogue and how their conversations flow. Reflect on this experience.
3	Develop Rapport	Create harmony in your conversations with verbal and non-verbal cues	Set aside 30 minutes once a month and treat yourself to your favorite coffee shop. Take a journal. Then, when seated, watch how other people communicate with their non-verbal cues. What body actions increase harmony and which ones break rapport. Reflect on this experience.

3	Balance on the Self-Responsibility Spectrum	Become an assertive speaker	Take the assertive communication quiz once a week when you are alone and free of interruptions. Notice where you can improve your communication skills and focus on that for the upcoming week.
4	Ask Questions	Ensure that you as a listener understand the content and meaning of the speaker's message	While we talk on the phone regularly, practice asking questions before starting a conversation. Choose one day a week to begin all of your phone calls by asking the other person, "is this a good time to talk?" Notice how this instantly builds rapport in the relationship.
4	Expanding Balloon	Remain centered and neutral when communicating with a challenging individual	Take time once a month to catch up with a good friend. Practice envisioning a balloon between you, collecting energy that is sent from your counterpart. Practicing this technique in a comfortable environment helps you get used to using it when your emotions are involved.
4	Master the Art of Listening	Improve your ability to hear what other people are saying and create harmony in your relationships	Set aside 30 minutes of uninterrupted time once a week. Take the listening quiz and observe where personal improvements can still be made. Focus on creating goals around those skills for the next week.

5	WAWAH	Amplify your personal energy through the physical act of hugging	Schedule one day a week where you are open and honest about hugging with others. Set a goal of giving or receiving ten hugs for the day. Reflect on your experience.
5	The Male and Female Triangles	Meet men's and women's needs in a relationship	Set aside time once a week with your spouse or partner and discuss the status of your triangles. Notice where you have boosted the other's triangle and where you can make improvements over the next week.
5	Steps to Conflict Resolution	Quickly solve a relationship problem with clear communication	Select this process when a conflict arises. Take a journal and go through the five steps of conflict resolution as if you were with all people involved. Imagine the situation going as smoothly as possible. Journal any insights you have during the process.
6	Know your Destination	Setting personal goals using the three spheres of life	This activity can be done daily, weekly, monthly, or annually to check in with where you want to go in life and how you're doing along the way. It is best to set aside regular time intervals to check in with such goals.

6	Mitigating Risk	Six questions to help decrease doubt or confusion as you make daily decisions	Set aside time once a week to look at your upcoming goals. List ten questions, which if you already knew the answer, would decrease fear to move forward. Then decide how to answer those questions, either through research, other people, or any means necessary. Notice how you feel as clarity comes into the process of moving forward.
6	The Box	Decrease and eliminate worry	Add to your worry box daily. Check the box weekly and throw out any worries that have resolved or dissipated. At the end of the month, take action on those worries still present.
7	Meditate	A practice to stay focused in the present moment and detached from thoughts, emotions, or sensations.	Set aside five to fifteen minutes in the morning to sit in silence and focus on your breathing.
7	The Joy of Giving	Create a meaningful ritual of sharing from the heart	Set one goal each week to give using one of the Four T's
7	The Power of Laughter	Experience joy and love through laughing	Create a comedy night for yourself or with a friend. You can rent a movie or go to a comedy club. Laugh freely and often. Write down your insights and feelings when you finish the evening.

As you get used to meaningful rituals in your life, some of the most fun activities you create are those rituals of your own. Use your creativity. Allow your innovation and unique style to form meaningful practices for your lifestyle.

Putting it all Together

Meaningful rituals, which can vary in content and purpose, offer us opportunities to infuse life with meaning. Regardless of their nature, they all share similar components. Rituals involve time set aside for their practice, they have a specific purpose, they occur in a sacred space, they follow a detailed process, and they are based in the emotion of love. Using your infinitely creative mind can help you form meaningful rituals into daily life to increase your overall life energy.

New Common Sense Tools to Form Meaningful Rituals:

- **Grow a Monkey Tail:** This child-like visualization involves all human senses to increase the feeling of groundedness and balance.

- **Meditation:** Whether active, passive, or creative, focusing on the present moment adds clarity, purpose, and limitless perspectives to all of life's events.

- **The Power of Laughter:** Spontaneous, joyful laughter can be some of life's best medicine. Lightening up life through the use of humor can be a long-lasting ritual with far-reaching effects.

Afterword

Afterword

"New is something old that has long been forgotten." —*Russian Proverb*

Just by reading this book, you have changed your viewpoint of the world around you. You're aware of ways to increase your internal balance, to create harmony in your relationships, and to establish meaningful rituals that support all aspects of your life. By taking a common sense approach to improving your inner world, your outer one will inevitably change.

Wouldn't you agree that all of the Common Sense Tools create common sense solutions?

- Adding deposits to your life Energy Bank Account increases your energy
- Knowing your values offers direction and purpose on your life path
- Being open-minded provides freedom and flexibility
- Changing internal beliefs can create new options
- Speaking clearly enhances self-esteem and credibility
- Listening to others can improve communication
- Setting clear boundaries prevents feelings of victimization
- Understanding emotions in relationships can add clarity to interactions
- Releasing fear allows you to move forward with confidence

- Setting time aside for yourself keeps you centered

- And much, much more!

Perhaps the most common question is: "Where do I go from here?"

The easiest way to start creating success with the lessons taught in this book is to take one step at a time. Reflect on your notes and insights from each chapter and list the top 3 areas of your life that need support. With your new priorities, observe which chapters and Common Sense Tools will make the biggest improvements.

Now, the awareness you have about Common Sense Living can infuse your daily activities. Your everyday conversations and interactions provide a playground to practice your new Common Sense Tools.

Then, at the end of each week, evaluate what you have done. Notice any personal changes and continue to improve your skills until you feel the lessons becoming natural and effortless. At this point, you can move on to a new Common Sense Tool and follow the same process. With this new knowledge and application in your everyday life, you increase your personal power and create a new, positive reality in which you exist.

As you make your way towards your goals and dreams, there are a few final words we'd like to share with you on your journey.

Live lightly

Just like inviting spontaneous laughter can become a meaningful ritual, it is best not to take life too seriously. Smile often. Have fun and enjoy the journey.

Focus on your improvements

When you face a challenge or perceive a failure, step back into your personal power by shifting your perspective from limited to limitless. Celebrate that you recognized your current mindset and use your set of Common Sense Tools to move forward.

Get to know your Self

While various life circumstances change and your preferences ebb and flow, there is a part of you that is unchanging. You are more than just your physical body. You're more than the thoughts roaming around in your mind.

Tuning into the qualities of the heart, such as love, joy, and creativity begin to reconnect you with your true Self.

Bolstering your values is a way to enhance the relationship with the deepest part of your being. Meditating also allows you to put aside daily distractions and tune into a broader perspective of your current experiences. Whatever Common Sense Tool you utilize on your journey is rooted in the fact that you have the answers within yourself to solve problems, confidently make decisions, and take personal responsibility for your actions.

Share your journey with others

While much of the implementation of Common Sense Living begins within yourself, it's essential to include others in the process. Talk to your friends about the Common Sense Tool you're currently utilizing. Allow others to provide outside feedback and create the playing field for improving communication skills. A support team can also be helpful to keep you on track towards your goals. Maximize your social interactions to support your values, your improvements, and your life purpose.

Celebrate often

Celebrate the fact that you no longer need to be in the passenger seat of your own life. You get to be the driver and that deserves a round of applause!

The lessons and principles in this book are a life-long practice and everyday you make the choice to move forward. We are still learning this! Even through this writing endeavor, we encountered miscommunications and varying opinions. Yet, through it all, our love and ability to share love has been enhanced.

We would like you to thank yourself for taking a positive, attentive focus to enhance all aspects of your being.

And, more importantly, thank you for including us on your journey.

www.ItJustMakesSense.com

As you finish this book, we invite you to visit

www.ItJustMakesSense.com

to further enhance your personal development.

Download your FREE Common Sense Living Toolkit, which includes:

- Recipe cards for conflict resolution

- Interviews with the authors

- Positive beliefs to eliminate fear

- Printable reading guides for book groups/clubs

- And much more

The website also offers information about upcoming workshops and events, where you can learn more tools to change beliefs, improve relationships, reach your goals, and enhance your spirituality.

Appendix Contents

Value Words

Abundance
Acceptance
Accessibility
Accomplishment
Accuracy
Achievement
Acknowledgement
Activeness
Adaptability
Adoration
Adroitness
Adventure
Affection
Affluence
Aggressiveness
Agility
Alertness
Altruism
Ambition
Amusement
Anticipation
Appreciation
Approachability
Articulacy
Assertiveness
Assurance
Attentiveness
Attractiveness
Audacity

Availability
Awareness
Awe
Balance
Beauty
Being the best
Belonging
Benevolence
Bliss
Boldness
Bravery
Brilliance
Buoyancy
Calmness
Camaraderie
Candor
Capability
Care
Carefulness
Celebrity
Certainty
Challenge
Charity
Charm
Chastity
Cheerfulness
Clarity
Cleanliness
Clear-mindedness

Cleverness
Closeness
Comfort
Commitment
Compassion
Completion
Composure
Concentration
Confidence
Conformity
Congruency
Connection
Consciousness
Consistency
Contentment
Continuity
Contribution
Control
Conviction
Conviviality
Coolness
Cooperation
Cordiality
Correctness
Courage
Courtesy
Craftiness
Creativity
Credibility

Cunning	Enthusiasm	Gratitude
Curiosity	Excellence	Gregariousness
Daring	Excitement	Growth
Decisiveness	Exhilaration	Guidance
Decorum	Expectancy	Happiness
Deference	Expediency	Harmony
Delight	Experience	Health
Dependability	Expertise	Heart
Depth	Exploration	Helpfulness
Desire	Expressiveness	Heroism
Determination	Extravagance	Holiness
Devotion	Extroversion	Honesty
Devoutness	Exuberance	Honor
Dexterity	Fairness	Hopefulness
Dignity	Faith	Hospitality
Diligence	Fame	Humility
Direction	Family	Humor
Directness	Fascination	Hygiene
Discipline	Fashion	Imagination
Discovery	Fearlessness	Impact
Discretion	Ferocity	Impartiality
Diversity	Fidelity	Independence
Dominance	Fierceness	Industry
Dreaming	Financial independence	Ingenuity
Drive	Firmness	Inquisitiveness
Duty	Fitness	Insightfulness
Dynamism	Flexibility	Inspiration
Eagerness	Flow	Integrity
Economy	Fluency	Intelligence
Ecstasy	Focus	Intensity
Education	Fortitude	Intimacy
Effectiveness	Frankness	Intrepidness
Efficiency	Freedom	Introversion
Elation	Friendliness	Intuition
Elegance	Frugality	Intuitiveness
Empathy	Fun	Inventiveness
Encouragement	Gallantry	Investing
Endurance	Generosity	Joy
Energy	Gentility	Judiciousness
Enjoyment	Giving	Justice
Entertainment	Grace	Keenness

Kindness
Knowledge
Leadership
Learning
Liberation
Liberty
Liveliness
Logic
Longevity
Love
Loyalty
Majesty
Making a difference
Mastery
Maturity
Meekness
Mellowness
Meticulousness
Mindfulness
Modesty
Motivation
Mysteriousness
Neatness
Nerve
Obedience
Open-mindedness
Openness
Optimism
Order
Organization
Originality
Outlandishness
Outrageousness
Passion
Peace
Perceptiveness
Perfection
Perkiness
Perseverance
Persistence
Persuasiveness

Philanthropy
Piety
Playfulness
Pleasantness
Pleasure
Poise
Polish
Popularity
Potency
Power
Practicality
Pragmatism
Precision
Preparedness
Presence
Privacy
Pro-activity
Professionalism
Prosperity
Prudence
Punctuality
Purity
Realism
Reason
Reasonableness
Recognition
Recreation
Refinement
Reflection
Relaxation
Reliability
Religiousness
Resilience
Resolution
Resolve
Resourcefulness
Respect
Rest
Restraint
Reverence
Richness

Rigor
Sacredness
Sacrifice
Sagacity
Saintliness
Sanguinity
Satisfaction
Security
Self-control
Selflessness
Self-reliance
Sensitivity
Sensuality
Serenity
Service
Sexuality
Sharing
Shrewdness
Significance
Silence
Silliness
Simplicity
Sincerity
Skillfulness
Solidarity
Solitude
Soundness
Speed
Spirit
Spirituality
Spontaneity
Spunk
Stability
Stealth
Stillness
Strength
Structure
Success
Support
Supremacy
Surprise

Sympathy	Trustworthiness	Vitality
Synergy	Truth	Vivacity
Teamwork	Understanding	Warmth
Temperance	Unflappability	Watchfulness
Thankfulness	Uniqueness	Wealth
Thoroughness	Unit	Willfulness
Thoughtfulness	Usefulness	Willingness
Thrift	Utility	Winning
Tidiness	Valor	Wisdom
Timeliness	Variety	Wittiness
Traditionalism	Victory	Wonder
Tranquility	Vigor	Youthfulness
Transcendence	Virtue	Zeal
Trust	Vision	

Humorous Movie List

These funny movies span the decades and offer enjoyment in many realms. Keep in mind that what some people find funny, others find offensive. Here are some movies that we have found to be helpful when sharing with clients or friends. If you choose a movie for a family gathering, please check the rating and make sure the movie has values you want to instill for your group.

A League of their Own
Arthur
Bad News Bears
Beethoven
Best Little Whorehouse
Big
Butch Cassidy and the Sundance Kid
Coming to America
Continental Divide
Crazy People
Crocodile Dundee
Cross my Heart
Curly Sue
Danny Kaye Movies
Dave
Doc Hollywood
Does this mean we're Married

Don't Tell Her It's Me
Duchess and Dirtwater Fox
Dutch
Face the Music
Father Goose
Father of the Bride (series)
Fish Called Wanda
Frankie and Johnny
Fun with Dick and Jane
Funny about Love
Funny Girl
Green Card
Groundhog Day
Hanky Panky
He Said, She Said
Her Alibi
Home Alone, I or II
Hot Shots

House Calls
Housesitter
Just You and Me Kid
King Ralph
L.A. Story
Leap of Faith
Let it Ride
Life Stinks
Life with Mikey
Little Miss Marker
Loose Cannons
Lost in Yonkers
Love Sick
Mad Dog and Glory
Mad Mad Mad World
Made in America
Major League
Marx Brothers Movies
Maverick
Mel Brooks Movies
Men at Work
Mr. Baseball
Mr. North
My Cousin Vinny
Naked Gun, Naked Gun 2 ½, Naked Gun 33 1/3
Necessary Roughness
Night at the Museum, I and II
Night Shift
North to Alaska
Nuns on the Run
Only the Lonely
Operation Petticoat
Opportunity Knocks
Other People's Money
Outrageous Money
Overboard
Paper Moon
Parenthood
Partners
Pink Panther (series)
Planes, Trains, and Automobiles
Protocol
Pure Luck

Risky Business
Robin Hood, Men in Tights
Ruthless People
Scrooge
See no Evil, Hear no Evil
Semi-Tough
Short Circuit, I and II
Shot in the Dark
Silver Streak
So I Married an Axe Murderer
Stake Out
Stir Crazy
Straight Talk
Summer School
Support your Local Gunfighter
Support your Local Sheriff
Switch
Taking Care of Business
Ten
The Freshman
The Gods must be Crazy
The Quiet Man
The Toy
Three Fugitives
Three Stooges
Throw Mama from the Train
Tootsie
Turner and Hooch
Uncle Buck
Unfaithfully Yours
Victor Borge
Victor, Victoria
Waiting for the Light
Who's Harry Crumb?
Wildcats
Working Girl

Additional Resources

Here are additional resources that can provide more information on the various topics covered in this book.

Introduction

Books:

- *Anatomy of the Spirit* by Caroline Myss (New York: Harmony Books, 1996)

- *Molecules of Emotion* by Candace B. Pert, PhD (New York: Touchstone, 1997)

- *The Subtle Body* by Cyndi Dale (Korea: Sounds True, 2009)

- *Vibrational Medicine* by Richard Gerber (United States of America: Bear and Company, 2001)

- *Why Zebra's Don't Get Ulcers* by Robert M. Sapolsky (United States of America: Holt Paperbacks, 2004)

Chapter 1

Big Brothers Big Sisters of America

http://www.bbsa.org

For over 100 years, Big Brothers Big Sisters of America has provided one-to-one mentoring between adults and at risk youth. This is a great way to share your internal values with others.

Chapter 2

Books:

- *Ageless body, Timeless Mind* by Deepak Chopra, PhD (United States of America: Three Rivers Press, 1993)

- *The Biology of Belief* by Bruce Lipton, PhD (United States of America: Hay House, 2008)

- *The Missing Peace* by Robert Williams, MA (United States of America: Myrddin Publications, 2004)

- *Zero Limits* by Joe Vitale and Ihaleakala Hew Len, PhD (New Jersey: John Wiley and Sons, 2007)

Videos:

- *The Biology of Perception, the Psychology of Change: Piecing It All Together*

  http://www.spirit2000.com
  1-800-550-5571

- *The Tapping Solution*

  http://www.thetappingsolution.com
  1-800-507-1657

- *The Secret*

  http://www.thesecret.tv

Chapters 3, 4, and 5

Books:

- *The 5 Love Languages* by Gary Chapman (Illinois: Northfield Publishing, 1992)

- *The 7 Habits of Highly Effective People* by Stephen R Covey (New York: Free Press, 1989)

- *Date or Soul mate?* By Neil Clark Warren (United States of America: Thomas Nelson, Inc, 1999)

- *Men are from Mars, Women are from Venus* by John Gray (United States of America: HarperCollins Books, 1992)

- *The New Peoplemaking* by Virginia Satir (United States of America: Science and Behavior Books, 1988)

- *When Mars and Venus Collide* by John Gray (United States of America: HarperCollins Books, 2008)

Audio Recordings:

Voice Dialogue International
http://delos-inc.com
Hal Stone, PhD and Sidra Stone, PhD have used effective voice dialogue techniques to enhance self-understanding and facilitate personal growth over the past 35 years.

Chapter 6

- *The Feeling Good Handbook* by David D. Burns, MD (United States of America: William Morrow and Company, Inc., 1989)

- *The Leap* by Rick Smith (United States of America: the Penguin Group, 2009)

Chapter 7

Books:

- *The Artist's Way* by Julia Cameron (United States of America: Tarcher/Putnam Books, 1992)

- *Journey to the Heart* by Melody Beattie (United States of America: HarperCollins Books, 1996)

- *The Presence Process* by Michael Brown (United States of America: Namaste Publishing, 2005)

- *Relax and Renew* by Judith Lasater, PhD (China: Rodmell Press, 1995)

- *The Right to Write* by Julia Cameron (United States of America: Tarcher/Putnam Books, 1998)

- *Wherever you go, There you are* by Jon Kabat-Zinn, PhD (United States of America: Hyperion Books, 1994)

Meditation-Related Resources:

- **Vipassana Meditation**
  http://www.dhamma.org

- **Transcendental meditation**
  http://www.tm.org

- **Integrative Restoration (iRest)**
  http://www.irest.us

Relaxing Music/Meditations:

- 2002—"Land of Forever"
- Adiemus—"The Journey: Best of Adiemus"
- Deepak Chopra—"The Soul of Healing Meditations"
- Drala—"Drala"
- Vidhano—"Secret Lake"

Magazines:

Yoga Journal
http://www.YogaJournal.com
1-877-364-2935

Acknowledgments

Collective Acknowledgements:

We want to thank Imbue Press and Morgan James Publishing, whose support and encouragement made this book a reality. Kristen Moeller believed in us and our message. Margo Toulouse answered our numerous questions and made this publishing process easy. We would also like to thank David Hancock for his wisdom, Rick Frishman for his publicity support, and Bethany Marshall for her marketing magic.

The unique vision of this material was refined through the fabulous help of our editors, Maryellen Smith (www.reinventionqueen.com) and Sue Golson. We are grateful for their flexibility and quickness in completing this project.

Paul Lowe is the wonderful cartoonist who brought our common sense principles to life. He patiently worked with us from overseas to create scenes that truly reflected our sense of humor. A special thanks also to Adele Lawson, who coordinated our contact with Paul Lowe via Cartoon Stock, Ltd (www.cartoonstock.com). Ryan Fiscus, from LRT Graphics, brilliantly crafted our signature stick figure and in-text diagrams (www.lrtgraphics. com). His numerous revisions are deeply appreciated. We also recognize the natural talent of Diane Clifford, who set up numerous photo shoots to get individual and couples pictures we enjoyed.

We also want to thank Scott Roberts, Lanita Trehern, and Lance Wirtanen, who dedicated their time to read and revise our manuscript. Their sincere comments and critiques offered clarify to our message.

Kym's Acknowledgements:

Common Sense Living has touched all aspects of my life, and thus everyone in it has inevitably contributed to its creation.

I want to thank my mom, Colleen Coco, for her unending love and confidence. Her hard work, dedication, and love for life are such an inspiration. Special thanks to my sister, Jennifer Coco, who hosted me for many weekends of writing and yoga in Santa Cruz. Lisa and Travis Coco, my other two siblings, kept me laughing when I wanted to take this project too seriously. Their persistence in school also reminded me to celebrate the fact that I am pursuing a career I love. My dearest Nana, who passed away in 2010, has been an ongoing inspiration from the spiritual realm.

Most importantly, my deepest appreciation goes to my husband, soul mate, and co-author of this book, Stephen Thompson. You are my greatest teacher. I love you!

Steve's Acknowledgements:

It is with humble reverence that I acknowledge the friends that have encouraged me over the years and helped make this book possible. Their confidence and trust has inspired me beyond words. I'd like to thank Beth Holstein, a fellow teacher, who has demonstrated what it looks like to live from the heart. Lance Wirtanen, business advisor and friend, has always looked out for my best interest and enthusiastically supported each of my new endeavors. Gordon Little has recently become a most trusted confidant. He sets the example of what it's like to live a life of integrity. Marc Hiscox, formerly a student, has become a teacher in his own right, often enhancing some of my own work with his own ingenuity and creative mind. I'd also like to thank my parents, who have provided unwavering support through the ups and downs in my life.

I'd like to give special thanks to the teachers in my life who have influenced who I am today: Reverend Wendal Pew, my Pastor, and the most compassionate man I know; Bruce Lipton, author of Biology of Belief, who is scientifically supporting my heartfelt knowledge (www.brucelipton. com); Rob Williams, founder of PSYCH-K®, who offered me the chance to teach his wonderful life-changing modality for the past 20 years (www.psych-k.com); Jim Self, a metaphysical master, who taught me the ability to stand in my own truth, even when others did not understand me (www.masteringalchemy.com); Lynn Edwards, who was a consummate hypno-anesthesiologist, trained me for four years in all forms of hypnotherapy and neuro-linguistic programming.

Lastly, my wife, Kym Coco, has had the faith to take all of my teachings and put them into written word. Together, we are the perfect couple and this project has only strengthened our love. Thank you, yogii.

About the Authors

Kym Coco, MA is the founder of Solution-Oriented Therapy, located in Chico, California and specializes in emotional kinesiology. While having been a student of life for almost thirty years, she has specifically focused her training in the mind-body realm for the past six. Coco combines her dynamic teaching style and compassionate heart to share powerful stress-reducing techniques with her private clients, workshop participants, and college students at California State University, Chico.

When she met Stephen Thompson three years ago, the perfect blend of youthful spark with seasoned wisdom was created. Through their unique gifts, Thompson and Coco create and facilitate healing workshops nationwide.

Stephen Thompson has been a teacher for over 30 years in the areas of philosophy, psychology, sociology, and plain, common-sense living. After a motorcycle accident in the early 1990s, it took 28 reconstructive surgeries and six years to fully heal. During his recovery process, Thompson was introduced to alternative healing modalities. His rapid recovery through such powerful mind-body techniques prompted several years of study with psychological kinesiology and Intuitive training. His personal transformation, as well as the accident-inspired ability to read auras, led to the opening of The Personal Search and Growth Center in 1992.

Thompson is a humorist who combines passion and joy with life lessons in the workshops he facilitates around the country. His success is founded on the principle that education without implementation is void. Therefore, he joins his authentic knowledge with practical tools for change that allow people to truly accept and apply the information they receive when learning with him.

Index

BUY A SHARE OF THE FUTURE IN YOUR COMMUNITY

These certificates make great holiday, graduation and birthday gifts that can be personalized with the recipient's name. The cost of one S.H.A.R.E. or one square foot is $54.17. The personalized certificate is suitable for framing and will state the number of shares purchased and the amount of each share, as well as the recipient's name. The home that you participate in "building" will last for many years and will continue to grow in value.

THIS CERTIFIES THAT

YOUR NAME HERE

HAS INVESTED IN A HOME FOR A DESERVING FAMILY

1985-2010

TWENTY-FIVE YEARS OF BUILDING FUTURES
IN OUR COMMUNITY ONE HOME AT A TIME

1200 SQUARE FOOT HOUSE @ $65,000 = $54.17 PER SQUARE FOOT
This certificate represents a tax deductible donation. It has no cash value.

Here is a sample SHARE certificate:

YES, I WOULD LIKE TO HELP!

*I support the work that Habitat for Humanity does and I want to be part of the excitement! As a donor, I will receive periodic updates on your construction activities but, more importantly, I know my gift will help a family in our community realize the dream of homeownership. **I would like to SHARE in your efforts against substandard housing in my community!*** (Please print below)

PLEASE SEND ME _____ SHARES at $54.17 EACH = $ $_____

In Honor Of: _____

Occasion: (Circle One)   *HOLIDAY*   *BIRTHDAY*   *ANNIVERSARY*

     OTHER: _____

Address of Recipient: _____

Gift From: _____ *Donor Address:* _____

Donor Email: _____

I AM ENCLOSING A CHECK FOR $ $_____ PAYABLE TO HABITAT FOR HUMANITY OR PLEASE CHARGE MY VISA OR MASTERCARD (*CIRCLE ONE*)

Card Number _____ Expiration Date: _____

Name as it appears on Credit Card _____ Charge Amount $ _____

Signature _____

Billing Address _____

Telephone # Day _____ Eve _____

PLEASE NOTE: Your contribution is tax-deductible to the fullest extent allowed by law.
Habitat for Humanity • P.O. Box 1443 • Newport News, VA 23601 • 757-596-5553
www.HelpHabitatforHumanity.org

Printed in the USA
CPSIA information can be obtained
at www.ICGtesting.com
JSHW052015140824
68134JS00027B/2483